The Reason of Metaphor

The Reason of Metaphor

a study in politics

DONALD F MILLER

Sage Publications
New Delhi   Newbury Park   London

**TO JAN, MADELINE AND HARRIET
WITH MY LOVE**

Copyright © Donald F Miller, 1992

All rights reserved. No part of this book may be reproduced or utilised in any form or by any means, electronic or mechanical, including photocopying, recording or by any information storage or retrieval system, without permission in writing from the publisher.

First published in 1992 by
    Sage Publications India Pvt Ltd
    M-32 Greater Kailash Market-I
    New Delhi 110 048

  Sage Publications Inc **Sage Publications Ltd**
  2455 Teller Road   6 Bonhill Street
  Newbury Park, California 91320 London EC2A 4PU

Published by Tejeshwar Singh for Sage Publications India Pvt Ltd; phototypeset by Jayigee Enterprises, Madras; and printed at Chaman Enterprises, Delhi.

Library of Congress Cataloging-in-Publication Data

Miller, Donald F., 1930-
  The reason of metaphor : a study in politics/Donald
  F. Miller.
    p. cm.
  Includes bibliographical references and index.
  1. Political science. 2. Metaphor—Political aspects. 3. Rationalism—Political aspects. 4. Religion and politics—India. I. Title.
  JA74.M48 1992 320′.01—dc20 91–35791

ISBN 81–7036–264–4 (India)
    0–8039–9410–9 (U.S.)

'Reason in the late seventeenth and early eighteenth centuries was referred to in adoring tones. It was eulogized, apostrophized, invoked and venerated; it was the means by which men could solve their problems, could understand their world, and eventually attain their salvation they all pretended to hold dear, if they did not seem to hold it dear by their lives and activities. Yet amidst all this debate and discussion, in which the word 'reason' was never omitted and rarely defined, there were few who questioned its nature, or wondered why so many men, all applying reason to the same problems, found so many different answers.'

John Redwood 1976

'Whenever humanity seems condemned to heaviness, I think I should fly like Perseus into a different space. I don't mean escaping into dreams or into the irrational. I mean that I have to change my approach, look at the world from a different perspective, with a different logic and with fresh methods of cognition and verification. ... In the boundless universe of literature there are always new avenues to be explored, both very recent and very ancient, styles and forms that can change our image of the world.'

Italo Calvino 1988

'... I cannot help thinking....
Jacques Derrida 1973
from **Etienne B.de Condillac 1746**

Contents

Foreword by **Ashis Nandy**	9
Acknowledgements	13
A Precaution	16

I Politics as a Location — 19

1. The Necessity of Euphemism — 21
2. Boundaries and Proper Places — 31
3. The Metaphoric Modes — 56
4. A Question of Language — 69

II The West and Modern Times — 95

5. Social Policy and its Rationality — 97
6. The Reiteration of Modernity or Do I Repeat Myself — 119
7. Omnipotence and its Enemies — 142

III India and Occidental Accidence — 157

8. Religion, Politics and its Sacred State — 159
9. 'I am Thou' — 181
10. A Maha-raga or a Lesson in the West — 204

IV Here and There — 223

11. The Politics of Irresolution — 225

Bibliography	260
Index	265

Foreword

Ashis Nandy

AT ONE place in this book, the author uses a telling quotation from Bankimchandra Chattopadhyay, an early proponent of virile nationalism in India. Around the middle of the nineteenth century, this intrepid novelist said about the medieval poet Jayadeva's work: 'From the beginning to the end, it does not contain a single expression of manly feelings—of womanly feelings there is a great deal—or a single elevated sentiment. I do not deny its high poetical merits—but that does not make him less the poet of an effeminate and sensual race.' Don Miller makes no attempt to hide where his sympathies lie, with the nationalist novelist or with the mystic poet. For he believes that the more challenging forms of creativity can lie only at the borderlines of cultures, self-definitions, politics and genders. To him, the play of liminalities always retains the capacity, not merely to decompose a sterile world by decomposing its central metaphors, but also to generate new sets of metaphors that hold the promise of defining a new world.

Such an approach to scholarship cannot remain content with the thematic structure of worldviews, with what is literally said or not said and with what is actually done or not done. It has to be concerned with the processes of world-making and self-construction that mediate between systems of knowledge and systems of power.

It invariably has to be open to tentativeness and incompleteness. Parts of this book can be read as a vibrant protest against the hard-eyed, masculine, analytic frame of politics in which concepts are well defined, the fundamental truths are known, and only the realities of behaviour and policies remain to be worked out. Such theories of politics, Miller believes, are ultimately based on literality, a literality which 'breeds a certain rigidity to thoughts, often an intolerance and dogma.' Such literality to him is an index, as it was for the late Gregory Bateson, of schizophrenia. Schizophrenics cannot read metaphorically; they can only read literally.

Does all this have anything to do with the fate of the present cultural order in the world or with the predicament of the culture that dominates that order? Perhaps a partial answer to the question lies in the social psychiatry of cultures. More than a generation ago, a number of psychoanalysts suggested, with varying degrees of confidence, that schizophrenia was the ultimate disease of modern civilization both because the disease was the 'preferred' mode of failure in facing the typical problems of modernity and because the inner crisis the schizophrenic faced was *the* unrecognized public crisis of our times. Some of the more didactic clinicians among these psychoanalysts even went so far as to offer the diagnosis that large sections of the modern world were suffering from an identifiable, persistent, but not full-blown, form of schizophrenia. Parts of this book may be read as an attempt to provide, perhaps unwittingly, an epidemiology of this pathology. It is an attempted epidemiology of the collapse of metaphors and metaphoric skills and the spread of uncritical literality.

As Miller walks through the ruins of some well known epistemologies, he celebrates the breakdown of literalities that the ruins signify. In the process, he seeks to restore the dignity of metaphors both as the heart of all political discourse and as the primary tool of political analysis and demystification. The recognition of this double-edged nature of metaphor is the point of departure of his work.

Not that metaphors have not been previously used in political and social analysis. For, after all, our world of language and communication is built on metaphors. But they have been used previously with diffidence, without a full awareness of how their illusory nature—their metaphoricity—ensures the plurality of political discourse. Miller revalorizes not merely metaphors but also their transience as the very heart of plural politics.

Foreword

This methodological dissent is part of a larger enterprise. It should be pretty clear at the end of the twentieth century that no knowledge of politics is complete without an adequate awareness of the politics of that knowledge. It is possible to sharpen this aphorism and adapt it to cover the concerns of this book. Not only is the understanding of metaphors vital for an understanding of politics, this understanding in turn has to be informed with an understanding of the politics of metaphors. Interpretations can not merely demystify; they can also problematize, politicize and re-empower.

This awareness contextualizes Miller's dissent from the discourse of mainstream political science. He wants to build plurality into the very heart of the analytic apparatus used by the students of public life. By increasing the reliability and validity of its measures, mainstream political science hopes to capture within its frame, and thus control, the hard realities of politics. In such an exercise, the aim is to reduce the range of interpretations and, thus, increase the area of certitude. In metaphoric analysis of the kind Miller undertakes, the aim is not to contribute to the growing mass of certitudes but to expand the range of interpretations and, thus, widen the range of options in an open-ended human future. Somewhere in the book, Miller says that Hinduism—the Hinduism that scaffolds the Indian way of life, not the various versions of *Hindutva* available a dime a dozen these days in urban, westernized India—has this odd tendency to produce more Hinduisms. Something very similar can be said about his work on the metaphors of politics and the politics of metaphors. It, in turn, should produce a myriad political metaphors and plant the seeds of a myriad politics.

Predictably, such a frame of analysis cannot end up by being only a critique of conventional political wisdom; it also willy nilly becomes a critique of the dominant public consciousness in the West—massified, with its metaphors frozen. Such a frame must seek to reconnect the interpretation of politics to important aspects of the western intellectual tradition, hitherto ignored or underplayed in the dominant culture of the West. Following Nietzsche, Miller believes that truth is 'a mobile army of metaphors, metonymies, anthropomorphisms' that have become fixed, anaemic, and binding after long usage; 'truths are illusions of which one has forgotten that they *are* illusions.' If Nietzsche is right, the primary responsibility of every generation of intellectuals is to demystify the given or inherited truths of its time into their constituent illusions.

Miller tries to share this responsibility by drawing upon forms of consciousness in South Asia which are in alliance with and endorse the lost or subjugated aspects of western consciousness. These are the aspects which have not been deprived of their heuristic usefulness through long usage within the dominant public consciousness of their times. Being marginal, they have not turned, as yet, collaborationist. They retain the capacity to revaluate aspects of the West's secret self and to serve as allies of those who, in their struggle for cultural survival, constitute the Other of the West's dominant self. What Miller says about Freud can be said about many other western thinkers he deals with in this book—they deserve greater appreciation than the West has offered them. One suspects that the southern world has often held, by default, important aspects of the West in trusteeship and protected them from the murderous amnesia to which a dominant culture is particularly prone. That which is a disowned self in the West often becomes a manifest, if not a celebrated, aspect of the public self in the dominated world.

The reader must judge for himself if Miller has succeeded in the tasks he sets for himself. I can merely affirm that his concerns, however academic and reified they may at first sight seem, are bound to become more salient over the coming decades in the intellectual agenda of those to whom the knowledge of politics cannot afford to remain innocent of the politics of knowledge.

25 March 1991

Acknowledgements

- I would like to thank the Committee on Research and Graduate Studies of the University of Melbourne for its financial assistance towards the publication of this book.
- I owe a lot to my many students over the years; they have been my own 'visible college' of good friends and critical supporters. In particular I want to extend my warmest thanks to Nikos Papastergiadis, John Hutnyk, Scott McQuire and Michael Healy.
- Jan Souter, Rita Corelli and Wendy Geekie remained patient, efficient and constantly helpful in the typing and retyping of my work. Thank you.
- Certain of the chapters of this book initially appeared in a different form in other publications. I would like to thank the following publishers for their permission to reproduce this material in either modified or radically different form: *Etc.: A Review* of *General Semantics* (USA), *Knowledge* (USA), *Diogenes* (France), *Economic and Political Weekly* (India), *Chai* (Australia), *Meanjin* (Australia), and *Third Text* (England).

Many publishers/authors have kindly permitted me to quote extensively from their works. I thank them all:
Six Memos for the Next Millennium, by Italo Calvino. Reprinted with the permission of Harvard University Press. Copyright © 1988.

The Rule of Metaphor, by Paul Ricoeur. Reprinted with the permission of University of Toronto Press. Copyright © 1977.
Tales of Love, Sex and Danger, by Sudhir Kakar and J Ross. Reprinted with Sudhir Kakar's permission. Copyright © 1986.
Asceticism and Eroticism in the Mythology of Siva, by W.D. Doniger (O'Flaherty). Reprinted with the permission of W.D. Doniger (O'Flaherty). Copyright © 1973.
Contingency, Irony and Solidarity, by Richard Rorty. Reprinted with the permission of Cambridge University Press. Copyright © 1989.
The Virginia Statute for Religious Freedom, edited by M. Peterson and R. Vaughan. Reprinted with the permission of Cambridge University Press. Copyright © 1988.
History of Australia, Vol 4, by C.M.H. Clark. Reprinted with the permission of Melbourne University Press. Copyright © 1978.
Farewell to Reason, by Paul Feyerbend. Reprinted with the permission of Verso. Copyright © 1987.
Reason, Ridicule and Religion: The Age of Englightenment in England 1660–1750, by J. Redwood. Reprinted with the permission of Thames & Hudson Ltd. Copyright © 1976.
Thought and Language, by L.S. Vygotsky. Reprinted with the permission of M.I.T. Press. Copyright © 1962.
Philosophy of Science, by Stephen Toulmin. Reprinted with the permission of the Hutchinson University Library. Copyright © 1958.
Theory of Literature, by R. Wellek and A. Warren. Reprinted with the permission of Penguin. Copyright © 1973.
Death and the Labyrinth (Postscript 'An interview with Michel Foucault by C. Ruas), by Michel Foucault. Reprinted with the permission of Georges Borchardt, Inc. Copyright © 1963, by Editions Gallimard. Copyright © 1986 by Doubleday & Co., Inc. Postscript Copyright © 1986, by Charles Ruas.
'Is Nothing Sacred', by Salman Rushdie. Reprinted with the permission of Granta Editions. Copyright © 1990.
'Address', by Salman Rushdie. Reprinted with the permission of *Kunapipi*. Copyright © 1985.
I am Thou: Meditations on the Truth of India, by Ramchandra Gandhi. Reprinted with the permission of Indian Philosophical Society Publications. Copyright © 1984.
'Rascism's Last Word', by Jacques Derrida. Reprinted with the permission of *Critical Enquiry*. Copyright © 1985, by the University

Acknowledgements 15

of Chicago Press. 0093-1896/85/1201-0007$01.00. All rights reserved.

'Thugs and Terrorists: A Reply to Bernstein', by Richard Rorty. Reprinted with the permission of Sage Publications Inc., from Political Theory, Vol 15, No 4 (1987), p. 573. Copyright © Richard Rorty.

A Precaution

THE 'METAPHOR' of this book is, of course, a metaphor. It is used to signify the insightful but necessarily incomplete perspectives on things which we daily take and enact in our language, thoughts, behaviour and institutions. It is an insight on our insights. It tells something specific about the state of our knowledge, its unprivileged base, its inevitable omissions and its unavoidable consequences. The reason of metaphor. It reveals how we live our many metaphors, or rather, how metaphors shape our lives. The politics of metaphor.

A metaphor is Janus-faced. It conceals as it reveals, it represses as it liberates, it is not as it is. It feigns. It celebrates the improper, the bastard: 'similars among dissimilars—equating the unequal—relating the unrelated—the thisness of a that and the thatness of a this': all familiar descriptions of metaphor; but instead of simply highlighting its virtues, we demonstrate its vices as well. Not that we have an option; we cannot step beyond metaphor. It is our only means of relating, of connecting. Which means our connections will always be incomplete; will, in one way or other, miss. A non-dualism brings out its paradoxical both-andness or neither-norness. Conventional rational logic, literalisms, unequivocal boundaries and the exclusiveness of laws of contradiction—all the techniques by which our knowledge and our cultures are normally understood and judged—do not. They also misrepresent what we can and cannot do.

This particular appreciation of metaphor allows a novel and strategic entry into social theory and the cultural sciences. More particularly

A Precaution

it provides here a critique, a guide, a re-reading of certain familiar interpretations, of some of our common dispositions, of the many unquestioned elements of our commonsense. It suggests alternatives, at times unfamiliar 'perspectives by incongruity'. It is, therefore inevitably, also a critique of the West; one which, without any desire to condemn totally, reminds us of the price we have paid for our benefits. A use of metaphor is always also an abuse. The book challenges certain of our dominant assumptions; it deplores a common overbearing certitude; it regrets our many inherent blindspots.

Nothing we do or say is free from politics: both as an explanation of our 'choice' of action and language and as their consequence. We cannot step outside politics, just as we cannot step beyond philosophy, or metaphor. We can, however, manoeuvre. Through chance, necessity and deliberation, we make choices, even conceive new metaphors. And so with this book. It does not pretend to be neutral. It is overtly political. It selects, attacks, espouses.

It is selective for another reason as well. Attuned to the metaphoricity of culture and society, indeed to the many mixed-metaphors by which we live, it rejects any pretensions to a one homogeneous world, a global theory, any single coherent set of universal propositions. So, it does not seek one social theory; it does not attempt to advance a theory of metaphor. The book argues in terms of exemplary cases, not abstractions. What is discussed is, therefore, doubly partial.

Nor have I felt obliged to forge detailed chains between the many, apparently disparate parts of this work. I wished to illustrate certain compulsions, not exhaust some comprehensive coverage. There are connections, but the reader is encouraged to construct its own links, and, ideally, to imagine its own exemplars.

Western thought, however, is in one powerful way universalist. There is a dependent interaction between a dominant western mode of thinking on the one hand and 'non-western' reality and its interpretation on the other (for which, as is evident, we even have no independent name). India and things Indian constitute the illustration here. The impact of western thought (in which the very form of the metaphor is as important as its content) on the Indian situation is explored; the West is in turn re-read through an Indian discourse. Such dual waters are then muddied.

We positively propose no resolution. The ultimate and preferred metaphor of this book is a constant rephrasing, an ever new reconstitution of the self and the other; never a finality. Politics has no end.

I

Politics as a Location

The Necessity of Euphemism □ 1

EMILE BENVENISTE, the French linguist, begins an essay on 'Euphemisms Ancient and Modern' with a paradox about the early Greek definitions of euphemism.[1] 'To speak words which augur well' is one meaning given, but another is 'to maintain silence'. This initial contradiction is further compounded by yet a third expression, 'to shout in triumph'. How can a euphemism be a directive, at one and the same time, to be silent, to shout triumphantly and to speak auspiciously? How can anything be so self-contradictory? The dilemma is, however, easily dissolved. To speak words which augur well implies, for special occasions, an exhortation to shout triumphantly, 'to assent by an auspicious outcry'; it further implies, again depending on the circumstances, 'to avoid words which augur ill', hence, if necessary, to say nothing. As one definition explains *'avoid all unlucky words* during sacred rites; hence, as the surest mode of avoiding them, *keep a religious silence'* (original emphasis). Paradox terminates; we are merely dealing with 'a euphemism for a euphemism' taking an expression of Benveniste out of context.

---

[1] This essay by Benveniste appears in his *Problems of General Linguistics*, English translation by M.E. Meek, University of Miami Press, 1971. This chapter is based on a shorter article of the same name which appeared in *Diogenes, International Review of the Human Sciences*, Gallimard, Paris, No. 134, April–June 1986, pp. 137–44.

Euphemism would certainly be recognised by most people as one common application of metaphor; avoiding something potentially unpleasant by substituting one form of expression by another, by inserting a metaphor. The use of disguise; or more neutrally, taking advantage of the flexibility of language for specific purposes. The uses of language, or as certain faddists would have it, the abuses of language. It is satisfying to discover not merely ambiguity in the original Greek meaning of the word, but patently internal contradictions: to cry out and to be silent. Benveniste explains this away as the confusion of *langue* and *parole*— language as the abstract system and language as it is actually used: a coming and going between a 'purely linguistic value' and its use-value, which therefore varies with the context of use.

But we can go further. What is in common between speaking words which augur well and avoiding words which augur ill is an exhortation to use words to gain benefit in and of a situation: thus it contains a prohibition 'avoid', 'do not use', and an affirmation 'speak', 'do use'. But you cannot have one without the other: they are created simultaneously, they are the two different yet identical fusions of the same thing. We tend to forget that to do or say something is always, as well, *not* to do or to say something else. We should not have been surprised at the paradox—unless we had acquired some deep-seated suspicion or fear of contradictions as inauspicious, and so euphemistically avoid them, and speak only rationally, one side of the coin at a time: That augurs well for simplicity, augurs ill for comprehension. To gain benefit in the situation is necessarily open-ended; and here the Greek for euphemism illustrates the point with hyperbole: we may cry out triumphantly or we may maintain a religious silence or anything between these extremes. Euphemism extravagantly proclaims itself.

We further untangle the apparent contradiction by appreciating the interplay of means and ends. Silence, one extreme imperative, is the means to the end of avoiding inauspicious language; a triumphant cry, another extreme imperative, is the means to the end of expressing auspicious language. We naturally tend to equate means with ends, possibly because we constantly try to distinguish them. Each move is understandable. Yet each time we separate a means from an end, we realise the 'endness' of that means; each time we consider ends we see them for what they 'really' are, only other means. Each analysis forces a synthesis, the metonymic equation of the two, which somehow keeps reminding us of its components. A shout in triumph is the end as much as the means, we think of it and we treat it accordingly, sometimes. Other times, we disentangle the two, lest we conflate and confuse a silence for a shout, a mean end worth avoiding. Is a shout of silence only an oxymoron? Is it a mental confusion or are we being merely duped by words? Perhaps the cultural sciences can learn from the auspiciousness of Greek euphemism.

Silence itself has resonance. We are confronted with an apparently unequivocal absence, a nothing, a negative; yet Greek euphemism rightly saw it as a positive, as a real, tangible phenomenon, as much as any word or shout. It is an intentional gesture urged upon people as much as anything else could be. Once again, the cultural sciences are commonly deaf to such no things. Gaps apparently are not real, they don't exist; they are, if anything, only the temporal-spatial intermissions between the real, the 'features'. We have, however, been recently warned about such lacunae of interpretation. Gregory Bateson[2] reminds us that, for example, the letter we fail to send our aunt is as significant as one that we may have sent unexpectedly. That author insists that information, communication, knowledge itself, derive from a 'difference that makes a difference'[3] rather than from lumps of hard, material fact. Such an enriched reading of cultural phenomena is consonant with the perspective of Foucault, who is as alert to the anti-history, the non-history, the excluded from history as he is to the thoughts, words and actions that actually take place. That nothing occurs can be telling. A particular nothing! Likewise, those certain decisions never considered, never placed on the agenda; and those decisions *not* to do something. Non-decisions can make a difference. Just as their neglect by scholars can make a difference to our knowledge of persons, organisations and nations.

Euphemism displays an intercourse of words, ideas and actions in a variety of positions. Benveniste refers to two. 'One process', he says, 'consists in endowing an unpropitious notion with a propitious name'. 'But for other ideas', he continues, 'there is also a different process by which the expression considered bad is *desacralized* by substituting for it an equivalent which is remote or much weakened'

[2] Gregory Bateson, *Mind and Nature: A Necessary Unity*, E.P. Dutton, New York, 1979, pp. 46–47.

[3] *Ibid.*, pp. 98–100. See also his *Steps to an Ecology of Mind*, Paladin, St. Albans, 1973, esp. Parts 2 and 3.

(original emphasis). We can easily think of copious contemporary examples of both, not least in the arena of diplomatic vocabulary. Their application in domestic politics is just as constant, yet more readily condoned. We could describe national politics, in general, as the conflict between two forms of euphemism: the government of the day employing enhancing euphemisms for all situations no matter how unpropitious; the opposition employing demeaning euphemisms for all situations no matter how propitious (and note the two ways of reading election results; means by which each party always wins irrespective of the count). The battle is to persuade the public to believe one set of euphemisms rather than the other.

In all politics, the resort to extreme forms of euphemism is common. Silence, in particular. Certain politicians are noted for the infrequency of their press interviews; and most try religiously to avoid them during moments of government embarrassment. But too frequent a recourse to 'no comment' is heard as saying too much. And, of course, on auspicious occasions, the same statesmen shower us with their loquacity. Domestic partners are likewise attuned to comparable stratagems. We all know of the added value, when words fail, of the shout or scream or silence.

Silence and the shout, thanks to the Greeks, are apposite reminders of the limits of language; for, of course, both are beyond language. Euphemism, at large, is any human behaviour directed to improving a situation. In place of words we may smile auspiciously; or, depending on circumstance, refrain from smiling, equally auspiciously. And surely our collective actions and our sustained behaviours can likewise be re-read as euphemism. Do we not, for example, avoid situations which augur ill; as we encourage relations, practices and habits which augur well? Nor should we assume that the reward of such motivated behaviour need always be temporally contiguous to our euphemistic efforts. Here, as elsewhere, we frequently postpone our gratification. Is, perhaps, our overtly gratuitous behaviour intended to compensate for some prior inauspicious word or deed? Such gratuity may take many forms: posthumous military awards constituting surely the extreme deferment of euphemism.

The mental operation (conscious or unconscious) behind all euphemism is simple: the creation of compatible yet enhancing metaphors for the purpose of self-amelioration. To euphemise is to compensate, to counterbalance, to increase pleasure or to reduce pain. To achieve this one strives not for a consonance between the two or more elements (be they words, ideas, emotions or actions) as the redundancy created by such an equivalence would reinforce rather than alter the message or occasion. Nor does one aim for incongruous metaphors as these may create anxiety, confusion and doubt. Irony would therefore seem inappropriate for most euphemistic purposes. What is needed is a metaphoric coupling which qualifies, even challenges the subject of concern. Such a choice of words, behaviour or affect may distance the object, reappraise its connotation, even dare it to appear its opposite. Contradiction or negation is invariably conceivable—death, for example, may be deemed happy rather than sad; but hardly hilarious or trivial, both being incongruous. In all cases the choice aims to change the nature of the object to the better for one or all parties involved. How often, after some defeat, do we think of ourselves as the *moral* victor?

The strategy remains constant; particular solutions do not. Language changes for example. A nice reminder of this is provided by the 1964 edition of the *Concise Oxford Dictionary* still being printed in 1978. Its sole illustration of euphemism is the substitution of 'mad' by 'queer'. Predating, or failing to take into account both the anti-psychiatry movement and gay liberation, this word substitution seems a quaintly inappropriate illustration: 'queer' could be received as more offensive than 'mad' by the 1980s. Where simple and successful renaming (see Ten Little Nigger Boys) is not possible (see Little Black Sambo), mass circulation is strategically contracted (to create a euphemism by circumlocution).

Euphemisms may change value over time. At times, dramatically, drastically, historically, unwillingly. Apartheid, the official watchword 'for the separate development of each race in the geographic zone assigned to it' was proudly, if not arrogantly, announced to the world forty years ago by the government of South Africa. By 1983, when an international exhibition, 'Art Against Apartheid', was launched in Paris, the *word* was being denied by the same government, but kept alive by others as a symbol of the concept and deed of racism which were still very much alive. As Jacques Derrida[4] begins his contribution in the catalogue to the exhibition:

APARTHEID—may that remain the name from now on, the unique appellation for the ultimate racism in the world, the last of many.

[4] See 'Racism's Last Word', *Critical Inquiry*, vol. 12, Autumn 1985, pp. 291–92.

May it thus remain, but may a day come when it will only be for the memory of man.
A memory in advance...a rearview vision of a future for which *apartheid* will be the name of something finally abolished...the name will resonate all by itself, reduced to the state of a term in disuse. The thing it names today will no longer be.
But hasn't *apartheid* always been the archival record of the unnameable?

And Derrida makes a striking observation on the power and mystery of words.

No tongue has ever translated this name—as if all the languages of the world were defending themselves, shutting their mouths against a sinister incorporation of the thing by means of the word. ...

Greek euphemism recognised both the autonomy and power of language a long time ago. Not only does it possess remarkable flexibility and independence, its appropriate usage can dramatically alter, for good or bad, that which it accompanies. It pervades and qualifies its social context; it is very much a partner with the more tangible actions, emotions, ideas and circumstances it conjoins and helps shape. Quite profound implications follow, for example, the outcome of a current debate—struggle—to qualify certain terrorist organisations as either 'criminal' or 'political'. The choice of euphemism may determine future history as well as the writing of the past.
Partly in recognition of its power, euphemism is often seen as disguise, dishonesty and deception, of others, even of oneself. In some ways this is so. But we must realise that all language is in a sense deceptive. 'Language conceals as it reveals' are the often quoted words of Heidegger. Words are never innocent; they are carriers of some particular philosophy, of an entire metaphysics, which Derrida so persistently demonstrates. Nor transparent, as they carry traces of their forgotten history and of their relations with the entire language system. Their meanings are always sliding elsewhere; they are allusive and elusive. Further disguise may result, of course, from either conscious intention to mislead, or from an unconscious motivation to hide. Freud abundantly illustrates the complex operations of the latter.
But perhaps a danger, even error, exists in this emphasis on the

deceptions of euphemism. George Orwell's attack on Newspeak is the most well-known, modern-day critique on this subject. His name is conjured up, as patron, benchmark and copyright holder whenever some liberal commentator wishes to expose and condemn the propaganda-language of a government (especially when at war), the misleading lure of advertising copy, or the sociological-managerial jargon identified with some particular form of American expertise and scientise. It implies that a correction can be made; that we can, and often should, return to the literal. Distortion suggests some movement away from an accurate or true presentation to which one may return with the requisite degree of honesty, truth, objectivity, knowledge or self-awareness. The accusation implies some hidden or lost standard which can be found or formulated, which ought more often than not be aimed for, and which, with some application of rigour, intellectual or therapeutic, can be recovered. That there is somewhere, attainable, a *neutral* description of things; that words, ideas, emotions, circumstances can be fitted together with congruence, with an accurate identity of match, without one feature in any way qualifying the integrity of the other. Truth is mirroring, is redundancy, is description without elaboration. Perfect correspondence. Duplication. A window transparent. No artefact. No artifice.

But saying all that surely makes us realise the foolishness of the critics' demands. To insist that an accurate, true language be used to designate some deed assumes both the deed and the chosen words to be unequivocally single and simple; a dubious belief about word or deed. Take an illustration, like 'I shot my wife'. To be literal, and non-euphemistic, do we describe it as 'killed', 'murdered', 'shot fatally', 'executed', 'assassinated', 'put to death', 'got rid of', 'terminated the life', or something else? Which is the only possibly true word? We would respond, I imagine, by admitting that more information is first needed; for example, let us say that the wife was terminally ill, or about to leave her fortune to a lover, or had discovered my infidelity, et cetera. Would we know, and how would we know (again et cetera) when we had obtained sufficient contextual information to make a judgement about what language would be true and accurate?

Let us leave the problem of information and words (unresolved) to consider the deed; that also has to be indisputably one and only one thing. But how do we discuss the deed without representing it in words? And how do we know whether we are debating a matter of words or a matter of deeds? We cannot replay the deed as we can words; we cannot re-create variation's of the deed in order to choose the correct one. We are left, not so much wordless as deedless. Suppose we have resolved that problem and have settled on one deed and one set of words to describe it. How do we know they match or correspond with each other? How would we know if they do not correspond? Let us say they do not correspond, how do we know whether it is the deed or the word that is at fault? Does that remind us of something? of René Magritte's painting, 'This is not a pipe'? of the problem of translation? For example, we could say that the pipe (or the shooting) is a correct presentation but that the words are wrong. Alternatively, we could say that the words 'this is not a pipe' ('I terminated her life') are accurate but the drawing of the pipe (or the deed I did) is not truly presented. That sounds strange, but if there is a choice of deed, and there has to be because there is more than one way of shooting someone, then we have to consider the possibility that the deed may be wrong and not only the words. The two domains are related but independent of each other. Courts of law operate (on) such dilemmas.

Another, more demanding attribute is also called for by anti-euphemists, by our Orwellian tradition. In science, there is a constant concern that the piece of equipment being used, such as a microscope, does not interfere with the object being observed; it is essential that it leaves no mark, that what one observes is the object facilitated or made available by the particular equipment but not distorted, re-marked, added to by it. And so with language; literalists believe that if one uses the appropriate language to describe a deed accurately, that deed is left quite intact, in full plenitude, unblemished, neither improved nor reduced, unlike that which results from the use of euphemism. In that sense the literally correct language is transparent—one sees through it the untouched, virginal deed. One sees it in its truth, its essence; no modification occurs for which we feel obliged to make an adjustment in our judgement. The object, the deed, is now there before us, unhandled, unmanned.

But how can this be so? How can words, any words, carry no weight? Surely whatever language one uses to refer to some deed has, by its very utterance, added something to that deed. If one had done nothing more than pointed a finger and uttered the bland, contentless declaration 'This is it', one has added something; one has at the very least given it some prominence, more prominence than it had one moment before. Words alter the deed, in one way or another. So, if the intention is to ensure that the deed remains as it is, unadorned by any further, extraneous impingements, then there is no option, it would seem, other than express no comment at all. Only the deed left entirely untouched is a deed unedited, pure. But now we are in a new dilemma. Greek euphemism has taught us the value, the value-added, of silence, seen as an attempt to escape commitment, because any expression may be inauspicious. We have the ideal double-bind: to say anything will affect the deed, will leave it touched, altered, new; to say nothing is an admission that something may be wrong; that one has felt obliged to play safe, and hope that one's silence will produce the least deleterious interpretation of the deed. There is no resolution. (In October 1988 it was announced that silence may in future be taken as an admission of guilt in Northern Ireland. What previously was tacitly known, but, nevertheless, in the eyes of the law, seen as a legitimate and desirable manifestation of a commitment to the burden of proof tradition, has now been rewritten: the euphemism of silence is to be legally recognised. An ironic footnote to the legacy of Orwell!)

To talk of the distortion in euphemism requires a notion of the non-euphemistic which is surely unrealisable; any description of an idea or event adds to it, qualifies, distorts it. Even redundancy adds just that—an over-emphasis; any commentary distorts by the incorporation of its own comment. Is not the non-euphemistic already some form of euphemism? Are we not again dealing with euphemisms of euphemisms? Is it not time to begin referring to the truth of euphemism? And, as with any truth, it is a particular perspective, and therby is false as well. Euphemism has no special privilege, but neither has it any particular impropriety. It transgresses, it does violence; but it could remind us that such is always at stake each time we speak or act. We take a line. We make a mark.

But perhaps there is something significant about Greek euphemism. Could we say that its two extreme manifestations, the religious silence and the triumphant shout, manifest something special, symbolic, over and above their euphemicity? They are concentrated signs. Not so much over-determined as overloaded; they are hyperbolic euphemisms. They have taken the dicta 'to avoid words which augur ill' and 'to speak words which augur well' and expressed them at the edge of, or beyond, words. The silence sacrifices language itself in this disavowal of inauspicious words; the shout supplements and extends language in its quest for the most auspicious words. Words very much become deeds; the actions are symbols of complete dedication, of over-fulfilment. And in a way, these opposites become powerfully fused as the most conceivable manifestation, the limit of auspicious euphemism. Compared to any word-form they display a difference that makes a difference; but, of course, only within this context. It is this that allows them to acquire their particular value. Without this we would have a mere silence or shout, another silence or shout. With the euphemistic silence or shout have we not isolated something we could call symbolic?

Symbolic of the human need, no necessity, to overcome. Of humankind's immanent drive to shape its reality more to its suiting. In the face of circumstances seemingly given and beyond it, to intercede on its own behalf; to reduce pain, to increase pleasure. No matter how restrained by events, it 'naturally' attempts to exploit the moment, to act independently of other determinations. It is as if, at some profound psychic level, it has faith in the efficacy of its words, its gestures, its Five Year Plans, to change things. And it would seem that irrespective of result, it perseveres. As if this compulsion and talent to euphemise compensate for a world otherwise out of hand. A wry deception?

The necessity of euphemism ultimately symbolises a paradox. Humankind is driven to be creative. It seems determined. It has no choice. But does this not leave us in quite an unexpected position? It is that, whether we like it or not, we are daily engaged in euphemism. Rather than the exotic and the occasional, it becomes the mundane, the banal. Not the exceptional, but the normal. Not the deliberate or the evil cunning, but the unavoidable, the innocent. I cannot help thinking that it seems we have apparently always deceived ourselves in this matter. Or is that a deception? Who knows? Can we know?

Boundaries and Proper Places | 2

WE ALL know what metaphor is, one way or another. Not unlike schooling and politics, it is something about which we have an opinion, informed or otherwise. We would, I imagine, approve each of the following attempts to define its attributes, beginning with the more simple: metaphor is the substance of poetry; a poem is nothing but an extended metaphor; metaphor is about words, especially the unusual use of them—and the abuse of them—that is, when words are not used in their proper sense, with their normal and correct meaning; when words are used with cunning, deviantly, with deliberate ambiguity. That is, when the intention is to say other than what the words actually say. Yes, to construct a sentence with two meanings: one obvious, literal one which somehow does not quite make sense; and a second, the metaphoric, which although at first appearing incongruous, nevertheless makes interesting sense. The incongruity is initial, only apparent; with a touch of imagination the reader sees what is being revealed by this uncommon use of words. It throws a new light on something, it highlights a relationship, a connection, a similarity between things till then unnoticed. It can be quite trivial like a pun, a joke, or a play on words; it can be very moving, quite powerful; it can also be dangerous. There is something dishonest about it; it is an artifice. Well, that depends on its context; in its place we are not fooled by it; we take it for what it is, an imaginative play with language; we really cannot do without it. Poetry, perhaps all the arts, depend on it. After all, rhetoric does have a place, a valued place (to intrude just a touch of it here).

It is proper in its place. In a situation where it is desirable to suspend one's normal judgement of reality, or one's commonsensical use of language, for some emotional and intellecutal absorption in allusion, imagery, symbolism, indirect representation, in general, in the world of 'as if', then metaphor plays an essential role. We all can be moved by 'Busie old foole, unruly Sunne'. But if metaphor belongs there, it certainly does not belong elsewhere. Its place is bounded; the demarcation descriptive and prescriptive. It has no role in any human activity characterised by rationality. Science, philosophy, scholarship, normal human communication may well have certain features distinguishing one from the other, but they share one disavowal—a denial of metaphor. That which is logical, scientific, rational, that which seeks the truth cannot tolerate metaphor. It is anathema.

It is probably inevitable that whatever comprises a cultural commonsense is rarely articulated in so many words. There simply is little need to express the obvious; one merely sustains it by performing it, naturally as it were. It would be naive, therefore, to expect to trace declarations concerning the boundaries of metaphor in various historical tracts on philosophy or science or art down the ages. It is commonly not seen as a problem, as a matter of conscious concern. We merely repeat the tradition of Aristotle; avow metaphor in our rhetorical arts; disavow it in all other discourse.

Periodically, metaphor blatantly intrudes. Wittingly or otherwise, the fey, the reckless or the iconoclast infiltrates metaphor into rational discourse. It is through such occasions that we best come to appreciate the nature and place of the boundary and the force of its interdictory function. Such an intrusion, if trivial, is chastised as ornate, pretentious, too colourful, showing an inappropriate concern with style. If considered more than trivial, the work is condemned as polemical, irrational, unscientific, unscholarly. It is on such occasions that we are all reminded that metaphor has no place in serious scholarship. So, metaphor is defined and known positively, for what it is, the property of literature and the arts; and negatively, as what it is not, all the tacitly recognised qualities of rational discourse. It is ordered and controlled within a tight, coherent and inflexible set of binary opposites: on the one side is clustered the poetic, figurative, imaginative, speculative, intuitive; on the other side, exclusive and mutually confirming, are reason, science, knowledge, truth, rigour and the literal use of language as the neutral and transparent tool of objective enquiry. And, as with so many dualities, this opposition is impregnated with value. It demarcates the good from the bad.

Apart from these responses of exclusion and dismissal, the use of metaphors at times receives quite explicit attention. It is not uncommon for hidden metaphors in otherwise scholarly work to be exposed for what they are. For example, the language and ideas of evolutionism or mechanism may be revealed in works of social science, their derivation from nineteenth century biology or physics noted, and their misplaced role in the study of human relations challenged. It is implied that the offending language, while perfectly legitimate in its original context, acquires an illicit metaphoric quality once it transgresses its boundaries. Cross-fertilisation is, apparently, *prima facie* illegitimate, out of place. To avoid such errors, disciplines are urged to conceive their own conceptual apparatus, to shun miscegenation no matter how momentarily attractive it may seem, and to remain faithful to the literality of language and to the purity and particularity of each field of enquiry. Moral codes emulating one another.

At other times it is argued that the presence of metaphors in non-literary works encourages, if not necessitates, an anthropomorphic reification of the metaphor-concepts being employed. They thereby acquire a life and come to be seen by their authors as self-propelling actors, as causes, as subject or object of their own movement. The work of Richard Schafer exemplifies this type of concern. He sees the writing of Freud and his followers as dangerously marred, for theory and practice, by the role played by Freud's metaphors (for that, according to Schafer, is what Freud's concepts are; a label which the master himself often conceded).[1] It is argued that words like id, ego and super-ego lose their initial heuristic value and become actual prime-movers, the agents of psychic dynamics, victim or tyrant in the dramas of the unconscious. Schafer's solution

---

[1] Richard Schafer, *A New Language for Psycho-analysis*, New Yale University Press, Haven, 1976. His attempt to replace reified nouns (metaphors) by action language he explains as follows: 'In this approach, we rely on reasons—reasons that are, in essence, redescriptions that make actions comprehensible'. 'To ask "why" is to ask for another designation of an action', pp. 204, 370. Verbs apparently cannot be metaphors.

is to replace all Freud's metaphors, which appear as nouns and adjectives, by verbs and adverbs, thereby creating a non-reified 'action' or behavioural psychoanalysis.

Again and again we see metaphor confirmed and confined by the dictum that there is a place for everything and everything in its place. A consensus reiterates a profound belief in the right, as if law, soundness and legitimacy, of location, of place. Certain things apparently belong here but not there; each thing has its own proper place; certain things but not others are the property of some domain or other; some things properly go together, others do not. It is transgression which creates our problems; provided things remain where they properly belong there is no cause for worry; the pursuit of truth, beauty or progress will proceed and be judged within the appropriate boundaries and using the requisite language. These rules of the game are not normally imposed by force (other than on deviants); a consensus cuts across all domains; the rules have been internalised; one polices and disciplines oneself. Indeed, domain qualities are frequently jealously guarded; one's own cloth is a matter of pride. Nevertheless, it is still uncommon to unearth declarations like the following. Let us first consider René Wellek's characterisation of poetry, expressed with a certain élan and certitude:

> The two main organising principles of poetry, one of our contemporaries has said, are metre and metaphor: moreover, 'meter and metaphor "belong together", and our definition of poetry will have to be general enough to include them both and explain their companionship'.... Perhaps our sequence—image, metaphor, symbol and myth—may be said to represent the convergence of two lines, both important for the theory of poetry. One is sensuous particularity, or the sensuous and aesthetic continuum, which connects poetry with music and painting and disconnects it from philosophy and science; the other is 'figuration' or 'tropology'—the 'oblique' discourse which speaks in metonyms and metaphors, partially comparing worlds, precising its themes by giving them translations into other idioms. These are both characteristics, *differentiate*, of literature, in contrast to scientific discourse[2].

[2] René Wellek and Austin Warren, *Theory of Literature*, Penguin, Middlesex, 1973, p. 186.

The property and place of metaphor entails, in its obligatory binary opposition, the property and place of the non-metaphoric. To recognise and identify oneself is to distinguish oneself from one's other. Stephen Toulmin, talking of science, enacts the same gesture, once again without reluctance or embarrassment. What is unusual, however, is Toulmin's sensitivity to the possibility that a person could, in ignorance, mistake a scientific model for a (non-scientific) metaphor.

It is this suggestiveness, and systematic deployability, that makes a good model something more than a simple metaphor. When, for instance, we say that someone's eyes swept the horizon, the ancient model of vision as the action of antennae from the eye is preserved in our speech as a metaphor; but when we talk of light travelling our figure of speech is more than a metaphor. Consequently, when people say that to talk of light travelling in some sense reflects the nature of the world in a way in which to talk of eyes as sweeping the horizon does not, they have some justification. For to say that 'light travels' reflects the nature of reality, in a way in which 'his eyes swept the horizon' does not, is to point to the fact that the latter remains *at best* a metaphor. The optical theory from which it came is dead. Questions like 'what sort of broom do eyes sweep with?' and 'what are the antennae made of?' can be asked only frivolously. The former does more: it can both take its place at the heart of a fruitful theory and suggest to us further questions, many of which can be given a sense in a way in which the questions suggested by 'his eyes sweep the horizon' never could. (original emphasis).[3]

Science and poetry conjoin in the requisite vigilance, share the consensus: metaphor has its place, in art, nowhere else.

But we have a problem. Another tradition in the West presents a different face of metaphor. This is the established belief that metaphor tells us something new. It is the hallmark of creativity, of all radical innovation; a different focus, a change of perspective. The metaphor of art and only art emphasised the use of words; it was a semantics of language—the appropriateness of choice, a shift in

---

[3] Stephen Toulmin, *Philosophy of Science*, Hutchinson University Library, London, 1958, p. 39.

meaning, a play on words, a game of allusion. The metaphor of creativity highlights a thought process, a shift in cognition; not any thought or cognition, rather an inexplicable one which produces an incongruous end. Metaphor now involves the discovery or invention of new relations between things, a connection between things previously considered unrelated, a new way of interpreting the world. Typical of this understanding is Paul Ricoeur's crisp statement 'metaphor bears information because it "redescribes" reality.'[4] It is a challenge to institutionalised wisdom for more than one reason. It resonates with incongruity, often disturbingly so. It is further disconcerting because its means of achieving this incongruous thought presents a problem. How someone is able to perceive or conceive a new metaphoric insight appears beyond our traditional talents to explain—without resorting to devices like genius, intuition, spontaneity, and creativity which appear irreducible and at the same time question-begging. It is again disconcerting as the whole thing appears to demean traditional thought: it seems beyond it and inexplicable in its terms. And, for the very same reasons, it seems beyond our control: we can neither educate ourselves for it, prepare for its appearance, predict it, nor avoid it if we were so inclined. All of it anathema to those values of rationality the West has held so high. And yet, we welcome the idea of genius—but surely with ambivalence. Here, as in so many places, we remain heirs to classical Greek thought. Aristotle willingly conceded that 'the greatest thing by far is to be a master of metaphor. It is the one thing that cannot be learned from others; and it also is a sign of genius, since a good metaphor implies an intuitive perception of the similarity in dissimilars'.[5] Ricoeur, in a more restrained manner, restates the same enigma, 'a metaphor is an instantaneous creation, a semantic innovation which has no status in already established language'[6]—'or thought', we could add.

The incongruity of creative metaphor resides in its results as well. Here we face the problem of credibility and the dilemma of choice. Kenneth Burke's depiction of metaphor as a 'perspective by incongruity'

[4] Paul Ricoeur, *The Rule of Metaphor*, University of Toronto Press, Toronto, 1977, p. 22. And as he says elsewhere: 'a metaphor, in short, tells us something new about reality.'

[5] Aristotle, *Poetics*, 1459a 5–8.

[6] P. Ricoeur, *Interpretation Theory: Discourse and the Surplus of Meaning*, Christian University Press, Texas, 1976, pp. 52–53.

is apt: it reminds us of the oddity that a new metaphor will appear to be in comparison to some established belief. The more incongruous, the greater the shock, the larger the rupture demanded from current beliefs. We could remind ourselves, for example, how disruptive, offensive and senseless it must have seemed when Marx first enunciated the call for the workers of the world to unite, when Freud first postulated the sexuality of small children, when a feminist first identified everyday speech as 'man-made language', when an ecologist pointed to an industrial plant and described it as pollution. For bold new metaphors do not present us with a simple accumulation of knowledge, a mere adding of another brick to the current edifice of learning. We are not faced with a simple addition to our facts or yet another step in some rational discussion. Such things we readily cope with. No, a radical metaphor may demand we jettison an entire system of belief; that, for example, the nation-state remains the pre-eminent loyalty, that children are sexually innocent, that language is natural and neutral, that an industrial plant represents progress, a constant goal. Whether one opts for the new or stays with the old will depend on factors closer to faith than to some form of rationality. It is not surprising that so many innovative thoughts have been denounced and dismissed rather than reasoned with, evaluated and judiciously judged. A reasonable discussion, whatever that means, seems to require some similarity in viewpoint. By their expressed opinion in October 1988 it is obvious that the Law Lords of England hold a radically different meaning of treason than do the defenders of Peter Wright (and I would imagine most people). Under the circumstances a useful debate would be meaningless and impossible. But we knew beforehand that the absoluteness of definitions is a shibboleth. It is because of situations like this (and they constantly occur) that politics and the weapons of power, that the cultural mood of a period, and that timing and chance play a more significant role in the history of thought than is often conceded. If plotted, this history (and I use the singular here only for convenience—there is no such one) would therefore appear more irregular and discontinuous than regular and evolutionist.

This perspective on metaphor radically challenges the one which sees it limited to art. Innovative and incongruous insights appear in any domain; obviously so, once the emphasis is on ways of seeing rather than on some mere figurative use of language. Without using the word, Henry Poincare pinpoints metaphor with his description of scientific innovation. He refers to making combinations which 'reveal to us unsuspected kinship between...facts, long known, but wrongly believed to be strangers to one another.'[7] Robert Frost is in no doubt about its ubiquity when he says 'Poetry is simply made of metaphor, so also is philosophy—and science too.'[8] Robert Nisbet is equally succinct 'No occupation or discipline can do without its metaphors. They are ways of knowing.'[9]

Once we emphasise the pervasive innovativeness of metaphor we realise that the concept has received more attention throughout history than any crude word-count would suggest. Writings on creativity, intuition and imagination, for example, can now be seen as explorations into the operations of metaphor. The concept of imagination, for example, during the eighteenth century, attracted the attention of British empiricists like Hobbes, Hume and Johnson as well as German and British idealists like Fichte, Goethe, Schelling, Hazlitt, Shelley and Coleridge. More recently James Engell[10] has argued that the idea was the most significant bridge between the Enlightenment and Romanticism. To all these thinkers the human 'faculty', energy or force called imagination both enabled all human understanding of the world and, in particular, was responsible for generating all creative reinterpretations of the world. Their descriptions varied: some saw it as a necessary complement to reason; others as reason's most valuable component; while still others thought it superior to reason and favoured a replacement. All agreed that its truths could not be reached by means such as mechanistic logic, reasoning or deduction—rather it appeared to operate intuitively, immediately, somehow ineffably beyond our understanding, to be captured only symbolically, never to be explained.

It was thought that imagination bridged gaps, made links where none had previously existed, made whole where contraries and polarities had before held sway; it combined and connected, it showed how things resembled each other. Some of these thinkers considered such connections followed rules of association like

[7] Quoted by J. Bruner in 'The Conditions of Creativity', *Beyond the Information Given: Studies in the Psychology of Knowing*, Allen & Unwin, London, 1974, p. 210.
[8] Quoted by J.J. Arlow, 'Metaphor and the Psychoanalytic Situation', *Psychoanalytic Quarterly*, 48, 3, 1979, p. 383.
[9] Robert Nisbet, 'Genealogy, growth and other metaphors', *New Literary History*, 4, 1972–73, pp. 351–63.
[10] James Engell, *The Creative Imagination: Enlightenment to Romanticism*, Harvard University Press, Cambridge, 1981.

contiguity, resemblance and cause and effect; other stressed the novelty and variety by which such relations were created. As one commented 'Discovery of a new or unknown relationship can be nothing else but the result of placing truths, objects and ideas in some new or unobserved position.... Every different juxtaposition of ideas will give us a new view of them, that is, discover some unknown truth.'[11] Some thought the resulting diversity of imagination's work was because 'no two minds will associate ideas in the same way'; others stressed that 'no phenomenon in nature is fixed....There is no isolated Being or isolated thing-in-itself'.[12]

To many of these writers, imagination reaches its highest form in the arts. To others, however, its protean quality dissolves any specificity of domain, it transcends conventional boundaries, and makes common the pursuits of science, philosophy and poetry. Through creative imagination, Schelling says, 'philosophy becomes an artistic act and art becomes a philosophic expression.'[13] Ultimately, it seemed that imagination was able to transcend all such categories of thought because its very operation depended on overcoming and uniting the erstwhile dichotomies of self and nature, the particular and the universal, the subjective and the objective, the ideal and the real, the sensuous and the transcendental, the cognitive and affective.

Sympathy, as one vital form imagination takes, was prized as an exemplary illustration of the conjoining of passion and ideas and of the inadequacy of conventional rationalism. It not only allowed an identification with others, an essential ingredient of any human community, it also permitted the equally essential projection of oneself in the future. 'A child nearing a fire does not feel his present and future selves as two distinct things. He fears *becoming* burned' (original emphasis),[14] argued Hazlitt.

The power of imagination, however, was variously judged. At one extreme it was thought conducive to greatness: 'A man of genius forms relations between previously unconnected perceptions and thoughts because his imagination associates them with a "peculiar vigour"'. At the other its 'capricious power' was considered capable

[11] *Ibid.*, p. 70.
[12] *Ibid.*, p. 83.
[13] *Ibid.*, p. 321.
[14] *Ibid.*, p. 199.

of deceiving us and of being tyrannical.¹⁵ To appreciate imagination was in no way a call to be sanguine about the future of mankind.

Whether imagination or metaphor is considered the instigator of the creatively new, the conventional separation of art and science becomes irrelevant, because, whatever the difference there may be between those domains, the presence or absence of metaphor is not a distinguishing mark. However, such creative metaphor erects its own boundary, within which metaphor becomes the new, the very instant and instance of the new, and nothing else. The word becomes bound to the notion of creativity, and hence to incongruity. And somewhere close behind this novelty hovers an invisible barrier beyond which metaphor cannot go. It exists, apparently, only at the edge, the cutting-edge of thought.

This distinction can arise merely through definitional fiat: a metaphor is the creation and annunciation of a new insight; it thus can have nothing to do with old insights (and notice the faintly oxymoronic quality of those last two words—a symptom of what I am referring to). The original French title of Ricoeur's comprehensive opus on metaphor captures this bias well, *La Métaphore Vive*.¹⁶ In a way, the birth of the new is everything; usage wears it away. As Ricoeur says 'such inventive metaphors tend to become dead metaphors [which are 'really no longer metaphors properly speaking' he adds a few lines away] through repetition'.¹⁷ The foot of the mountain seems a popular choice in illustrating the dead metaphor, the no-longer-a-metaphor, the cliche. In no way is Ricoeur being novel or diosyncratic here. He is merely repeating the dominant western tradition since Aristotle described metaphor as 'an intuitive perception of the similarity in dissimilars'. In like manner, Shelley, 'recognising the before unapprehended relation of things.'¹⁸ And more recently, Kenneth Burke, 'a perspective by incongruity which brings out the thisness of a that and the thatness of a this.'¹⁹ The action-language of perceiving, apprehending, discovering, bringing

---

¹⁵ *Ibid.*, p. 80–81.

¹⁶ The French title seems far superior to the English. The translator apparently felt 'uncomfortable with the more literal translation'. *The Rule of Metaphor*, Toronto University Press, Toronto, 1977.

¹⁷ P. Ricoeur, *Interpretation Theory: Discourse and the Surplus of Meaning*, The Texan Christian University Press, Fort Worth, 1976, p. 52.

¹⁸ Quoted by Ricoeur, *The Rule of Metaphor, op. cit.*, p. 336.

¹⁹ Kenneth Burke, *A Grammar of Motives*, University of California Press, Berkeley, 1969, p. 503.

out, makes it difficult to think of metaphor in terms other than its moment of creation, its novelty, its incongruity. It may be this disposition alone which has implanted in the western mind the association of metaphor and poetry, where, it is assumed, freshness of imagery is at a premium. And thus, of course, the perceived connection with imagination and creativity. I imagine it is something in this ambience of thought that has promoted poetry as being the highest form of mentation. Heidegger is not alone in this belief.

But exactly what is worn away with usage? Surely it is not the metaphoricity of a thought! If a metaphor is created by a new relationship being perceived between things, then it is still a metaphor, in thought and language, even after familiarity has robbed it of its strangeness. What was once bizarre eventually becomes conventional, indeed becomes, in time, a part of our commonsense. Usage merely wears away the novelty; repetition changes it from prominence in consciousness to matter-of-factness and finally to the oblivion of habit, where it remains very much alive. The incongruity of yesterday becomes the commonplace of today. The metaphor is still a metaphor; we just no longer think, consciously, of it as one. Rather it now seems to us to be the literal, the obvious, the natural, the true, the correct classification.

It is no accident that our tradition has taken the end of consciousness as the benchmark for the end of metaphor. As a culture we have always over-privileged consciousness, or immediate awareness. The idea of unconscious thought (or unconscious intention) is still nonsensical to most people. As Lancelot Whyte said: 'Self-conscious man thinks he thinks. This has long been recognized to be an error, for the conscious subject who thinks he thinks is not the same as the organ which does the thinking. The conscious person is one component only, a series of transitory aspects, of the thinking person'.[20] Culturally we find that difficult to accept. Neither metaphor nor, indeed, anything else changes its intrinsic quality when it slips out of our sight or out of our awareness. To forget something does not end its existence. Our metaphors remain, and they remain metaphors. And the implications of this are profound. What is beyond metaphor? If a metaphor reclassifies reality today, is it not probable, or necessary, that it was a metaphor which had reclassified reality

---

[20] L.L. Wyte, *The Unconscious Before Freud*, Julian Friedmann Publ., London, 1979, p. 59.

yesterday, and the time before, and the time before. Ricoeur confronts this likelihood at one stage:

> If metaphor belongs to an heuristic of thought, could we not imagine that the process that disturbs and displaces a certain logical order, a certain conceptual hierarchy, a certain classification scheme, is the same as that from which all classification proceeds? ...Could we not imagine that the order itself is born in the same way that it changes. Is there not, in Gadamer's terms, a 'metaphoric' at work at the origin of logical thought, at the root of all classification? The idea of an initial metaphoric impulse destroys these oppositions between proper and figurative, ordinary and strange, order and transgression.[21]

When we are confronted with a new metaphor, the dilemma we are faced with is not a choice, as commonly assumed, between the literal, proper and true (these tend to slide into one another because of a 'metonymic' equivalence) meaning and some hypothetical, fanciful, conjectural world of 'as if'. The choice is not between a categorical 'is' and an imaginative 'maybe'. No, the choice is between an old metaphor and a new metaphor; between one that we are familiar with and one which, in the light of the old, seems incongruous. Metaphors are metaphors of metaphors. But the ones which we have worn away longest, which have become part of our unconscious and implicit knowledge have acquired a hegemony in our thoughts and are taken as the real. So, the most powerful metaphors in any society are not the purple ones which immediately spring to mind, like 'progress', 'growth' and 'development' in western societies today, but the ones least likely to occur to us, the ones we have hidden from our conscious selves by constant wear and tear. Nietzsche appreciated this well:

> What then is truth? A mobile army of metaphors, metonymies, anthropomorphisms...which after long usage, seem to a notion fixed, canonic and binding; truths are illusions of which one has forgotten that they *are* illusions. (original emphasis)[22]

[21] P. Ricoeur, *The Rule of Metaphor*, op. cit., pp. 22–23.
[22] F. Nietzsche, 'On Truth and Falsehood in an Extra-moral Sense', *The Complete Works of F. Nietzsche*, O. Levy (ed.), London, 1909, vol. 2, pp. 173–88.

Once metaphor is understood in this pervasive guise, the likelihood that it belongs in some privileged position or with some particular class of person evaporates. It is certainly not the distinctive quality of a high art or of a creative elite. Three hundred years ago, Montaigne knew that: 'When you hear about metonymy, metaphor, allegory and such grammatical terms, don't they sound like some very rare and fancy form of language? But really they apply to your chambermaid's chatter.'[23] What a Pandora'a Box is opened!

Are there no barriers left intact? It seems at least one powerful one remains. One could refer to it (to anthropomorphise a tradition), as the final, rearguard action of those enamoured of maintaining proper places. I refer to the well-entrenched argument that metaphor (or intuited imagination) may be highly desirable, even necessary, for radically new thoughts to emerge in any domain of activity, but it *must* not have a place elsewhere. That is, it must not be allowed to interfere with the serious work of rational, critical, conscious thought and agrument which must follow an inspiration. From that area it is proscribed. It must have nothing to do with reasoning. That is beyond metaphor's reach—insofar as one wants to maintain a purity, rigour and integrity of thought. Philosophy, that is, thinking, in all its forms and attachments, must remain free of it. We are reminded, for example, that metaphoric imagery of the Double Helix may well have been the start of the discovery of DNA, but that a lot of hard, scientific, rational analysis, in which metaphor could play no part, characterised the long and arduous quest between the initial inspiration (metaphor) and the final discovery (research). It still forms part of conventional schooling, of reprimands against inappropriate figurative language, against analogy taken as proof, in support of a logical, sequential and objective line of argument. The separation is the hallmark both of proper scholarship and of mundane mental activity.

In a surprising way, this tradition of learning has received its most powerful defence from a quarter normally associated with its antithesis. I refer to Freudian thought, because it is within that frame of reference that metaphor and its opposite, rational thinking, have been given their most coherent consideration and their most unqualified placement. With this in mind, it may seem odd that Freud has suffered as much rejection as he has (which in one form or another

---

[23] Quoted on one occasion by Jacques Derrida.

centres around the 'scandal' or 'plague' of psychoanalysis, its interpretation of sexuality) because, in so many ways, Freud both repeats the dominant western tradition, and provides it with one of its most persuasive and elaborate apologies. I refer to his understanding of the conscious, and of its opposite, the unconscious. Freud reaffirms conventional wisdom that to adult (male!) conscious thought belongs all that is rational and reasonable, and that its proper, literal use of language is the tool of a scientifically accurate representation of the external world. Such a healthy, normal and accurate vision of things, he continues, is in constant jeopardy because of the intrusion of the dark, passionate forces of the mysterious unconscious, our other-than-ourselves, primitive self. To that cryptic region belong our aberrant thoughts, our intuitive impulses, our bizarre associations, our nonsensical use of language. It is the world of metaphor, symbol, myth, ritual and fantasy.

Let us elaborate, and for convenience, we collapse three overlapping conceptual schemes of Freud into one: we take the ego and the secondary process to be synonymous with the conscious; and the id and the primary process to be synonymous with the unconscious. With the former there are no surprises; he upholds the post-Cartesian assumption that the conscious man is the rationally thinking man. As, on one occasion, he says: 'There is no need to discuss what is to be called conscious: it is removed from all doubt.' It is the part of the mind which interacts and responds to external reality through the functioning of the perceptual system. A reality principle prevails. Conscious thinking is engaged with reality testing. To this end it utilises its appreciation of time and space, and it has the benefit of language. It is linear and rational and possesses the ability to organise, combine, unify and synthesise. This conscious presents an accurate picture of the external world to the unconscious (id) in its attempt to curb if not control it. At the least, it intervenes against 'the blind efforts for the satisfaction of its [the id's] instincts' by interposing a postponement in the form of thought. As he said, 'To adopt a popular mode of speaking, we might say that the ego stands for reason and good sense while the id stands for the untamed passions.

Freud's novelty begins with his insistence that this conscious cannot operate independently of its opposite, the unconscious, the more dominant (and shocking) part of the human mind. Even in

[24] S. Freud, *New Introductory Lectures on Psychoanalysis*, Pelican Books, Middlesex, 1973, p. 109.

normal adults it becomes ascendent whenever passions are strongly experienced, or when conscious attention slips. The unconscious is active all the time; even at best it remains a 'compelling force'. And it operates solely in the interests of the pleasure principle. It is the 'dark, inaccessible part' of the mind, quite 'alien to the ego'. Freud considers that most of what we know about it 'is of a negative character and can be described only as a contrast with the ego.'[25] Logical laws of thought do not apply; it possesses no quality of time or space, negation or contradiction—all of which being necessary for normal thinking. It entertains 'no doubt, no degrees of certainty';[26] nor does it make value judgements. Its character is even more 'bizarre' because of the transformations created by repression and the compromises of censorship: condensation by which composite imagery or laconic representations of complex phenomena occur; displacement by which unexpected chains of associations result in the emphasis of incongruous items. Because of these operations, the unconscious is characterised by metaphor, symbol and analogy in visual images and language. Word-play, puns, homonyms and neologisms predominate. Unconscious thought does not mean what it manifestly says; indeed it employs everything 'scorned by our normal thinking'. Its latent meaning always has to be deciphered.

The conscious speaks literally and logically, the unconscious metaphorically and falsely; and in line with the dominant western tradition, Freud valorised the former. He parts company with that tradition only by his insistence that this ideal constantly struggles with its enemy, the unconscious, which, because of repression, is always a force to be reckoned with. Metaphors and symbols are symptoms of a rampant unconscious, and are a call for interpretation; literality is a transparent sign of reasonableness in some momentary control.

Freud deserved a greater appreciation than western culture has afforded him; he provided it with a complex system of thought which explained and upheld so many of its long established faiths. Despite its many novel and unwelcome features, psychoanalysis vindicated the righteousness of a rationality based on a conscious and literal use of language and a dependable sensory perception of external reality. Freud may not have entertained as charitable and optimistic a view of humankind, its society and its future as a naive

[25] *Ibid.*, p. 105.

[26] S. Freud, 'The Unconscious', *Standard Edition*, Hogarth Press, London, vol. 14, p. 186.

and wishful-thinking public desired, but he at least showed that one can get to know all such things. He was a son of the Enlightenment. At the same time his work explained how the more primitive and unpleasant and unwelcome aspects of life are never the products of this privileged rationality but emerge from the nether regions of the mind. If his shocked public had been willing to read further it would have discovered so many of its cultural prejudices confirmed: that, for example, the frightening fantasies of a child, the obscene dreams of a housewife, the enigmatic works of an artist, the hallucinations of a madman and the superstitious rituals of a native tribe all had something in common. They all emanated from passions, instincts and drives out of control. It would have reinforced that which it had always suspected: that if the sound and decent language of conscious rationality were jettisoned, the only alternative is the mysterious and malevolent rule of the unconscious.

Cultural traditions get support from the most unexpected sources, even from areas seen as antithetical to most things mainstream. We should not be surprised, therefore, to realise that a movement like Surrealism, though dismissed by society generally, (as its founder, Andre Breton, was dismissed by Freud, as crazy), essentially upheld, repeated and reinforced society's dominant ideas on the conscious, the unconscious, metaphor, language and rationality. Surrealism merely inverted contemporary cultural values. Wishing to create an art to be a prerequisite of a revolutionary and liberated humanity, it proclaimed an art which eschewed those fundamentals representative of conventional culture and society. It was to shun conscious rationality. It thereby rejected, in that name, all normal ideas of the sensory perception of reality, in particular of time and space, the use of literal and linear language and notions of meaning and sense as commonly understood. Its art aimed (failing to appreciate the irony of this intentional behaviour) to tap and express the unconscious. This was assumed to be best achieved by exploiting automatism, chance and arbitrariness, by representing dream-scapes and incongruous juxtapositions of symbols and metaphors, by an apparently nonsensical use of language and a suspension of all conventions of time, space and vision.

One illustration must suffice; chosen, somewhat arbitrarily, from the writings of Guillaume Apollinaire, who created the term surrealism. In *The Poet Assassinated*, the hero, Cronimantal, announces on one occasion 'Yesterday I wrote my last poem in regular verse:

Lute
Shoot!'

after which he recited his 'last poem in irregular verse'. He then proclaimed 'I'll never again write any poetry but one free of all shackles, even that of language'.

Listen old buddy!
MAHEVIDANOMI RENANOCALIPNODITOC
EXTARTIPAN + V.S.
A.Z.
Tel.: 33–122 Bang:Bang
OeaoiiiioKTin
iiiiiiiiiiiii

It was received as quite appropriate by his sole audience, the Bird of Begin, whose only reply was 'Your last line, my poor Cronimantal, is a direct plagiarism of Fr.nc.s J.mm.s'.[27]

The urge to locate and thereby constrain metaphor persists, but no consensus prevails. Confusion does, however. If metaphor belongs to the arts it cannot with ease belong to the creatively new as that demands transgression beyond the conscious. If, on the other hand, it belongs to the unconscious, no particular domain of enquiry seems privileged, or immune. From one perspective metaphor seems ubiquitous but disconcerting; from another, rare yet puzzling. From one angle we can just sight it, fleetingly, as it brings forth a new thought then dies; from another we need to dig it up, encased as it is in the crustiest of our habits, so bedded in our usage we fail to notice it as we repeat it. Prescription seems in comparable disarray. Do we shun it or seek it? Do we encourage it for its suggestive pleasures? Do we attempt to marshal it for its hidden order? Should we learn to restrain its imperialist and subversive tendencies, to contain it in some proper place? Are all such options beyond us if, in fact, we remain its prisoner? To what degree should we welcome it for its inherent largesse; prizing it for its economy of abundance, in the mood of Nelson Goodman's taut tribute: 'in metaphor, symbols moonlight'?[28]

---

[27] G. Apollinaire, *The Poet Assassinated*, Grafton Books, London, 1985, pp. 29–30.

[28] N. Goodman, 'Metaphor as Moonlighting', *On Metaphor*, S. Sacks (ed.), Chicago University Press, Chicago, 1979, p. 180.

If no consensus prevails, and, indeed, if more and more uncertainty pervades the arenas of debate, it is because these days a further factor aggravates the situation. More people appear to doubt the previously intact boundaries between domains, between the properties of human activity. In other words, further doubt about the place of metaphor is fomented because the many places themselves are no longer distinct, clear and unequivocal. How can one encase metaphor when its potential boxes suddenly seem protean, elusive, amoeboid?

Hans Loewald,[29] for example, recently attempts to restate the Freudian position on the relation between the primary and the secondary processes (the unconscious and the conscious) and language. He sees everyday mental activity fluctuating between the two processes, between the homogeneity of the primary process and the duality of the secondary process with its linked manifold between word and thing. This linking is normal adult thought, he says; repression is its unlinking. However, a certain amount of repression is always there, he argues, to produce the desirable compromise between 'too intimate and intense closeness to the unconscious...and deadening insulation from the unconscious.' Schizophrenic thought is without this link; that is, words are treated like things. On the other hand, abstract thought makes words quite independent from their thing-representations, producing a 'lifeless nimbleness all its own'. Great literature, he concludes, 'interweaves' the two processes. Metaphor slides, is restless. Yet just as we may settle for 'great literature' as its home, home away from home, somewhere between and across the conscious and the unconscious we have to face the problem which certain thinkers raise these days: do we any longer know what is literature? non-literature? As more than one person has said: 'there is no such thing as ordinary language'. Boundaries evaporate because their criteria and rationale no longer persuade.

Arthur Danto[30] faces a similar problem in his attempt to characterise the philosophy of science: 'it is difficult to draw boundaries that neatly separate philosophy of science from philosophy, from science, or even from the history of science, broadly interpreted'.

---

[29] H.W. Loewald, 'Primary Process, Secondary Process and Language', *Psychoanalysis and Language*, J.H. Smith (ed.), Vol. 3 of *Psychiatry and the Humanities*, Yale University Press, New Haven, 1978, pp. 235–70.

[30] Arthur Danto, 'Problems in the Philosophy of Science', *Encyclopaedia of Philosophy*, Macmillan and Free Press, New York, 1967, vol. 6, pp. 296, 300.

And scientific theory, he realises, goes beyond science, 'The careful elucidation of the logic of scientific deduction...draws attention to features which lie, far more obscurely, within the oldest philosophical problems and controversies: problems of emergence, of natural kinds, of free will and determinism, of body and mind, and so on.'

And it is telling to compare a recent work by Stephen Toulmin with his earlier, confident exposition, already discussed, of the difference between a scientific model and a mere metaphor. His book, *The Return to Cosmology*,[31] a significant title in itself, concerns the author's engagement with what he sees as post-modernist science in a post-modernist society. It is a science freed from Cartesian dictates, in particular the belief that science and the pursuit of truth can only be well served by maintaining the separation of mind and matter, and that the scientist acquires knowledge by objectively observing, as an outsider, the object, nature. According to a 350-year old tradition nothing may bridge that boundary. Intrinsically related is the fact/value distinction: ethical questions were to have nothing to do with this scientific pursuit of knowledge. Post-modernism rejects this, Toulmin believes, explaining his own change of mind in these terms. Science ought no longer to proceed without moral scrutiny. The scientist must see himself responsible for whatever results from his interference with nature. Such a change, he argues, allows us to return to questions rejected as irrelevant by the 'new philosophers' of the seventeenth century, and ever since. We can, he says, once again ask the big questions like enquiring into the nature of the cosmos. And for such a difficult task no domain holds a monopoly of knowledge. An ecumenical dialogue between philosophers, scientists and theologians is demanded. Toulmin insists that we now need a 'theology of nature' to help understand this 'larger scheme of things'. Towards this end he insists that politics and theory, scientific knowledge and ethics can no longer be separated. Ultimately action, concerned and appropriate action, rather than merely wise contemplation or knowledge as an end in itself, is his called-for goal; a moral judgement of Heidegger's which Toulmin is now happy to echo. Completely gone are the certitude, neatness, and ease of the early, boundary-maintaining Toulmin. He is now a more humble scholar, despite the grandeur of the task; his goals are diffuse and transcendental; his means a call for new types of dialogue, a marriage of mixed

---

[31] Stephen Toulmin, *The Return to Cosmology: Post-modern Science and the Theology of Nature*, University of California Press, Berkeley, 1982.

metaphors, hybrids and oxymorons: a theology of nature falls outside the parameters of all conventional science, of all conventional ideas of knowledge.

In all walks of enquiry it is often worthwhile to distinguish between what a person says he does and what he does, between intentions and outcomes, between a manifest and a latent message, between a form and a content. To reveal a self-deception can be instructive; it can perform an exemplary function, with significance far beyond the particular work in question. We have just seen how various authors now concede, in a variety of ways, the elusive nature of boundaries between domains of knowledge. To complement this let us now see how one writer, keen to uphold the demarcations of our dominant western tradition, fails to do so himself in the very process of pleading his cause.

In the *Encyclopaedia of Philosophy*, John Passmore[32] has the task to describe what philosophy is, and as part of this endeavour, to distinguish the philosopher from the sage. This is a distinction which Plato also made, but according to Passmore, Plato contradicted himself when he insisted that 'at the culminating point' of philosophy one 'has to abandon critical discussion and, like the sage, fall back on direct intuition'. It is clear that Passmore, speaking as a philosopher, regrets Plato's inconsistency and weakness and, we can imagine, intends not to commit similar errors himself. He immediately concedes that while there is general acceptance of Plato's distinction between philosophy and the pursuit of worldly success there is still dissensus about his distinction between philosophy and poetry. Passmore's criteria for such a separation rest on critical discussion and rational reconstruction. He admits there remains a problem: 'obviously, there can be disagreement about whether a reconstruction is rational'; whether, for example, both Kierkegaard and Kant are engaged in the same philosophic activity. To re-phrase this carefully worded sentence of Passmore, we can say 'Of course there is no agreement about what constitutes a rational reconstruction but, despite that, I use it as my benchmark of philosophy.' Now the problem Passmore confronts immediately seems a bit more serious: a seriousness partly disguised by the innocent verb 'can' he used, and partly by the author's *sang froid*. We could accept this, if Passmore were to indicate how such possible/likely/inevitable disagreements were to

[32] John Passmore, 'Philosophy', *Encyclopaedia of Philosophy, op. cit.*, vol. 6, pp. 216–25.

be resolved; how he, for example, would distinguish between Kierkegaard and Kant; and note, not just any distinction, but, according to the project he has set himself, the latter as a philosopher from the former as a sage—but he does not. It would seem that Passmore was slack in his language for a moment; his task was not to debate whether these two thinkers 'are engaged in philosophic activity'. We may all agree that they are engaged in different philosophic activities—that is not the issue. Passmore is obliged to show that one of these thinkers was engaged in philosophic activity; the other in non-philosophic activity. A more difficult task! On second thoughts Passmore may not have been slack; he could have been exceedingly careful in his choice of words: 'the same philosophic activity' carries at least two meanings (the same activity known as philosophy; the same type of philosophy). Passmore's case is helped (that is, one is tempted more easily to agree with what he has said) when meaning resonates from one to another sense in our mind, without being aware of the shift). Now, to return: Passmore does not attempt to show how this particular disagreement, were it to arise, could be resolved. Instead he indicates why it is difficult to resolve it, and presumably, why such a disagreement is likely to arise. 'Controversy on this point is all the more difficult because words like explanation, philosophy, science, and knowledge are used eulogistically.' He refrains from stating the necessity or otherwise of such use although the words 'are used' suggest it is up to the discretion of the writer/debater to employ them in a eulogistic manner or not; whereas it would seem that such discretion is beyond the individual because those words, in the western tradition, are highly valued terms; they come loaded whether we agree with the judgement or not.

Let us be quite clear what Passmore has admitted. The very term, philosophy, the word which stands for critical discussion and rational reconstruction, contradicts itself, exists outside its own domain, is a prejudiced term, is historically a rhetorical piece of language—a fact which cannot simply be put to one side while we conduct a rational debate about it. (And the same can be said for all the other terms Passmore mentions in that sentence). However, Passmore appears unperturbed; this disagreement does not create a serious problem. As he says 'But this is only to say that agreement in philosophy is difficult to secure—which is scarcely news.' That seems so reasonable: that is what philosophy is all about—debate—without necessarily reaching final agreement. But once again the sentence is not as innocent as it appears. Note the preposition 'in'—now change it to 'about', which is all that is warranted for Passmore to say: that agreement *about* what constitutes philosophy is difficult to secure is another matter altogether, and that would be news; especially to a philosopher engaged in the task of showing, philosophically, why some thinkers are not philosophers. It would mean, in fact, that discussion on the alleged distinction of philosophy and the operations of a sage cannot begin, cannot even be asked because we cannot reach a prerequisite condition for that debate—that is, we cannot agree what philosophy is. And, furthermore, if we situate that debate *within* philosophy we have dishonestly predetermined the result one way; if we situate it *outside* philosophy then we cannot determine what criteria may or may not be used to settle the debate—may we bribe? use force? Such conclusions would surely be quite newsworthy whichever choice we opt for: either philosophy is a dirty game—one only plays it with loaded dice; or it is an activity impossible to begin. It was convenient that the author used the preposition 'in' instead of 'about'!

Passmore wants to distinguish two 'forms of activity [which] go under the name "philosophy"'; the first he characterises as 'essentially rational and critical, with logical analysis (in a broad sense) at its heart; the other (represented by Heidegger, for example) is openly hostile to critical analysis and professes to arrive at general conclusions by a direct, essentially personal intuition.' He continues 'There is no value judgement involved in describing practitioners of the first kind as "philosophers" and practitioners of the second as "sages".' To deny a value judgement in a move which excludes certain people and practices from a classification to which they believe they belong and of which membership is commonly prized (and he admits the word 'philosophy' is a eulogised expression), displays a strange appreciation of what does and does not constitute a value judgement. This is more so when the side of the eulogised term also retains the associated words rational, critical and logical—the first two at least are also eulogised terms; and the other side, the non-eulogized sage, is associated with 'openly hostile to critical analysis', when the word 'analysis' may be in fact the only word there open to question by erstwhile sages. It is only this side as well which '*professes* to arrive' (my emphasis)—philosophers apparently do not. However the skewed nature of the comparison is topped by Passmore's next sentence: 'There are bad philosophers—unimaginative, pedantic men whose criticisms are captious and devoid of understanding. There are also good sages—men who bring us to a greater understanding of human life, even though they are neither systematic theorists nor careful analysts.' He did not say, nor *could* he, that 'there are bad sages...and good philosophers', because we know the structure of that expression is weighed in favour of the implicit exceptional: some bad sages imply the majority are good; some good philosophers imply the majority are bad. He could not allow that. But Passmore goes further, he over-determines the weighted comparison—only the sage receives a qualified judgement—'though neither systematic nor careful'.

Despite appearances there is no symmetry in Passmore's presentation. And despite what he says there is a value judgement in his 'neutral' descriptions. The philosopher is hierarchically valued over the sage. Language is not innocent. He is saying much more than what he says he is saying; and, indeed, he is saying the opposite of what he alleges he is saying. We assume he is talking philosophically; making moves, establishing his case of distinguishing between philosophy and the activity of the sage, and doing it more successfully than apparently Plato had done—all this within the borders of critical discussion and rational reconstruction. Yet his case is riddled with deceptions, guile, structural forms of a hidden persuasion, non sequiturs, a latent play on words, rhetoric. Yet this text, we are led to believe, is the practice of philosophy. If so, it survives, thrives, only with the help of everything that is commonly construed as non-philosophical. Boundaries seem here to be irrelevant. We have already faced the question 'how do we start philosophy?' We now need to add 'where do we start philosophy?'.

But another reading is possible. Let us suppose that the author's intentions are other than what we have been assuming. That he was not aiming to establish or illustrate what the essence or purity of philosophy is, and as part of this show how it absolutely differs from the work of a sage. That may be a literal yet false reading of the encyclopaedia article. Would it not make another sense, and a better one, if we realised that Passmore took this opportunity to show, outlandishly, scandalously yet so subtly, the *impossibility* of philosophy; that there is no such pure genre possible; that what it poses to be is actually a cunning rhetoric; he has acted as a subversive. Instead of some naked declaration that philosophy (as it is commonly understood) cannot exist, which probably would appear a little gauche in an encyclopaedia of philosophy, he, with great skill, exemplifies this message—and who knows, may at the same time, have satisfied his philosopher-colleagues. After all he has presented us with a most reasonable, systematic and careful discussion. It did, in every way, have the hallmarks of philosophy. And some people like the idea of definite boundaries; they eulogize the idea, whether the reality is reasonable or not, real or not.

Let us return to metaphor. Perhaps, after all, it has no proper place. This suggestion no longer surprises anyone, I would expect; although such a proposal at the beginning of the chapter would have appeared odd. We all thought we knew what metaphor is, but we have travelled some distance, changed our perspective, and become, I would imagine, a little less clear and certain. The thing itself has changed its colours; it has become more of a chimera: 'a thing of hybrid character', 'a bogey', 'a monster with lion's head, goat's body, and serpent's tail', 'a fanciful conception'. Elusive. And as it changes, its location does. Yet there does seem a cultural need to locate it somewhere, rather, incarcerate it somewhere or other, because while it is respected in a way, it is also, dare we say, feared! An ambivalence operates. But the desire to control it becomes more difficult as the very locations themselves acquire some chimerical quality. Boundaries tantalise us: we are regularly attracted by their lines, by what they enclose and outline; yet, when we approach, when we feel we need them most, they become hazy, they fade; we are left without anything tangible to touch, to hold on to; we are left uncertain where we are, being out of sight of our lines, we are left suddenly feeling powerless. Yet, have we been deceived again? Has the imagery used made us momentarily mistake one thing for another? Have places and boundaries become like metaphors, become metaphors, are metaphors? Have we deceived ourselves again? No. In a way, but of course, only in a way, boundaries and places are metaphors; metaphors are boundaries and places. In a way. And have we by accident (coming across it, we did not reason our way there) discovered the metaphor for metaphor? In a way. And 'in a way' is a multiform in its form: it is universal yet singular, many yet one, general yet specific, vague yet precise. And true yet false. A contradiction?

Definitions abound. The drive for accuracy a determined one. A relief, therefore, to come upon Umberto Eco who takes his appreciation of the elusiveness of metaphor as his starting point. 'The "most luminous and therefore the most necessary and frequent" (Vico) of all the tropes, the metaphor, defies every encyclopaedic entry.'[33] His opening sentence.

We could restart our enquiry into metaphor by taking its defiance seriously, by considering its refusal to be pinned down. We could begin by exploring its ubiquity, and then pursue it by investigating its apparent necessity. Our flirtation with euphemism will perhaps be auspicious: it may have eased the tight cultural reins by which our thoughts are normally held in check. We are now, I imagine, more ready to entertain metaphor from a perspective of incongruity.

We are now also, I hope, more attuned to the importance of location; to the politics of enforcing a proper place for metaphor, as for anything; and to the powerful consequences, for knowledge and even for social and political relations, of prising anything free from its established moorings—often against the efforts of vested interests.

---

[33] Umberto Eco, *Semiotics and the Philosophy of Language*, Indiana University Press, *Bloomington*, 1986, p. 87.

The Metaphoric Modes 3

WHEN LÉVI-STRAUSS proclaims that binary opposition constitutes the basic, universal operation of human thought he highlights something that cannot be too readily dismissed. That it has been derives, I suspect, from the feeling that it demeans the richness of the western intellectual tradition. Yet our literature is riddled with dualities and dichotomies—and not least in the area that interests us here—the nature of thought and metaphor. Western thought is commonly distinguished from its primitive counterpart[1] by a refrain of couplets: rational v. irrational, scientific v. mythic, logical v. analogical, segmental v. holistic, inferential v. symbolic. The many writers still attempting to wrest themselves from such twin-jaws are a living testament to the grip of dichotomies.[2] The current solution often merely entails arguing that such

---

[1] The meaning of 'primitive' has altered over the centuries, and as it has, it has acquired a pejorative sense. Initially, it referred to 'original', its opposite being 'derivative'. Crude, immature, inferior are the current associations. 'Counterpart' in this setting has many bearers: as complement and opposite to modern, rational, western man we have woman, child, illiterate, tribal, even Third Worlder (see the reference to note 2). This chapter is based on an earlier article of mine, 'Metaphor, Thinking, and Thought', *Etc: A Review of General Semantics*, 39 (2), Summer 1982, pp. 134–50.

[2] One example will suffice. See *Modes of Thought, Essays on Thinking in Western and Non-Western Societies*, R. Horton and R. Finnegan (eds), Faber and Faber, London, 1973.

binary opposites are present, but with different emphases, in all types of society.

I want to assert that all thought is metaphor. Aristotle's well-known and already discussed description serves adequately as a beginning: 'metaphor is the perception of similars among dissimilars'. But all thought is just that: it classifies, perceives or creates relations, makes connections, pulls together significant similarities. Reality is a complex of differences. To talk or to think about it we have to identify and separate, we have to dismiss certain dissimilarities as incidental for the particular purpose, and emphasise, bring out in our thoughts, relations of similarity, similarities of relations. To think, to order, is to relate or classify in one way or other. Aristotle's perception was in so many ways an impressive one; but, as we have seen, it has since helped shape the dominant western tradition, which assumes this metaphoric activity restricted to the creation of new insights.[3] But as Ricoeur and others have pointed out: if metaphor is responsible for the reclassifications of reality, it ought to be held responsible for the original ones as well. Most metaphors are old; it is just because we are struck with the novelty of the incongruous or new that we often remain transfixed there. These are merely the highly prominent tip of the iceberg.

Even accepting the notion that we must include as metaphor all those lifeless ones we handle each day without awareness of their status, it is still understandable that a reader may balk at the proposal that *all* thought is metaphor. It seems so easy to conjure up some snatch of mundane thought which, while certainly including elements of metaphor surely cannot be reduced to it. Much more seems entailed in any train of thought. This is so—provided the meaning of metaphor is curtailed as severely as it normally is. Aristotle, after all, proposed four types of metaphor, using the term both generically

[3] We have already discussed (in chapter 2) the influence of Aristotle on the western tradition of considering metaphor as the creatively new insight. What has not been mentioned, however, is his equal influence in the cultural belief that metaphor concerns words, the particular use of words. That it is a form of thought (let alone all thought) is probably the minority view still. A sign of change is the publication *Metaphor and Thought*, A. Ortony (ed), Cambridge University Press, Cambridge, 1979. And more pointedly Max Black's chapter 'More about Metaphor' in which he refers to 'metaphorical thought' as 'a neglected topic of major importance' (p. 32). In this article Black seems to display a far greater respect towards metaphor than in his earlier and very influential one, *Models and Metaphors*, Cornell University Press, Ithaca, New York, 1962.

and specifically, as whole and type. With some variation, they have been translated over the years as metaphor, metonymy, synecdoche and analogy. New formulations, new metaphoric 'perceptions of similars among dissimilars' have abounded since, in particular during the past 200 years. Gérard Genette[4] elaborates several of these overlapping but distinct typologies; an exercise which leads him to press two points. He regrets the urge to track down the *master*-trope (*centrocentrisme* he labels the futile search); he likewise regrets the modern tendency to restrict the classifications of rhetoric to either one form only, metaphor, or to two, metaphor and metonymy. In this regard, he highlights the influence of the Russian Formalists and Roman Jakobson in particular. The work of both Lévi-Strauss (and thus structuralism) and Jacques Lacan (and thus 'French' psychoanalysis) are significantly informed by the dichotomy of Jakobson, who sees all language and thought as composed of two structural modes, that of metaphor (associations of equivalence) and of metonymy (associations of succession or contiguity). Genette's grievance is legitimate: a worthwhile understanding of language or thought demands elaboration beyond any two-fold typology; yet in no significant way have we broken the grip of binary opposites.

I propose a seven-fold typology of metaphor: in other words I argue that all thought is explicable in terms of seven processes. Together they constitute a grammar or structure of thought (the precise label is incidental) which seems both universal and inherent. Such a structure can never be observed (in any sense of that term); it manifests itself only content-laden; 'dressed' as it were with language, action and other culturally shaped qualities.

As Freud used the expression 'dream-work' to distinguish the structure which creates the dream, and as linguists refer to language as the system from which speech emerges, so the seven modes of metaphor may be conveniently considered as the 'thought-work' from which all thoughts, in their manifold expressions, derive. As 'thought-work' sounds awkward we could refer to this system as 'thinking', and restrict the word 'thought' to its manifest, creative expression. I do not always follow this advice here.

The order of the seven has no significance. There neither is nor can be one master-trope, without reducing thinking, accordingly, to

[4] Gérard Genette, 'La Rhetorique Restreinte', in his *Figures III*, Paris, Editions du Seuil, 1972, pp. 21–40.

The Metaphoric Modes

one dominant mode. There is also no privileged sequence; no two modes are naturally more closely related to each other than to the rest. It seems desirable, maybe politic, to persist with the long tradition of using 'metaphor' in two ways; as the generic label for the complete set, and as the specific term for one of the modes. The latter I will tend to call metaphor (proper) if precision demands it. The descriptive explanations I give are necessarily loose, while the accompanying examples have to be restricted, yet indicative of the pervasive range of application (an impossible task!). Some examples may seem to fit equally well, if not better, under another mode. This is appropriate, as any metaphor (proper), for example, can be re-thought as an homology, a synecdoche or as a metonym. The reason for such interdependence will become clearer later. Finally, we must remember that we are presenting here the process of thinking *in words*, a metaphoric translation to begin with.

Metaphor (proper)

The relating or classifying of two or more things because of some common property. The precise point of similarity may or may not be immediately recognised. And it is often disputed: thus our changing classifications, our jurisdictional disputes, our language innovations and our social institutions.

Naming words, typologies and concepts (old and new) all constitute metaphor (proper), e.g., table, plant, energy, social mobility, perception, black holes, odyssey, learning, ruling, anxiety, love, red, cold war, twilight years, development, fuzz, science, illness, in, out, up, down, growing, stable, quiet.

Many metaphors (proper) circulate less than others. We are rarely in a position to know at the time a fresh metaphor appears what its life-history will be: it can vary from being evanescent and individualistic to durable and universally reified. Book titles often capture new insightful relations: *The tyranny of distance*, *The naked ape*, *The selfish gene*. So do political manifestoes.

Homology, isomorphism, analogy

Appreciation of the repetition of a relationship; the repetition being responsible for the relationship having significance. Aristotle's original description of analogy is an adequate paradigm of this mode of thinking: A is to B as C is to D. A metaphor (proper) can be re-thought and re-expressed as a homology if the particular quality of similarity is recognised and emphasised.

Likewise, a homology can generate its own metaphors, e.g., a common homologous thought (not often expressed in language as such) as 'we' is to 'they' as 'known' is to 'strange' as 'clean' is to 'dirty' as 'good' is to 'bad', generating the metaphor 'dirty foreigner', a paradigm of ethnocentrism.

The discovery of personal homologies is one notion of self-identity. Likewise, in the therapeutic situation, the analyst looks for repetitions in the analysand's language or behaviour. Isomorphic repetition is proposed by some scientists as the dominant characteristic of nature.

Translation, transformation, transcoding

An equivalence created or perceived between any phenomenon in one form of expression and its translation into any other form of expression. It is because of this mode of thinking that language itself can legitimately be seen as metaphoric, because words and the things they may refer to are understood as 'equivalent'. Obvious examples of translation include 'corresponding' expressions in any two (or more) forms of thought, language, affect, mental images, social behaviour and art. Translation exhibits an irresolvable ambiguity: being a 'replication' of the thing translated, or a 'distortion' of it. Many writers refer to the inevitable 'falsification' or the 'creativity added' necessarily involved in any translation, including the type most readily recognised by the term—translating from one language into another (even a paraphrase in the same language is different—see, of course, the prosification of poetry). That is, translation, as with all metaphor, is best seen as both true and false. It is the same and yet it is not.

René Magritte, the 'thinker-in-paints', captured the paradox succinctly with his painting, 'This is not a pipe'.[5] Gregory Bateson[6] has warned us that a map is not a territory. But, as he continues 'we cannot get away from the tangles' produced by any such transformation between 'the report and the thing reported'. Each time we 'reproduce' in another form we 'produce' something new. The inevitable paradox of transformation: we cannot act our words, nor verbalise our

---

[5] Magritte's paradox is discussed more fully in subsequent chapters.

[6] G. Bateson, *Mind and Nature: a Necessary Unity*, E.P. Dutton, New York, 1979, pp. 30–31.

The Metaphoric Modes 61

acts; yet we have to, and assume them to be equivalent. This is metaphor.

It is the interpersonal translation of language-based thought in 'communication', however, where we are most aware of the difficulty of transcoding. We must postpone a discussion until later, but we can say here, at least, that any theory of language, thought or communication which assumes some notion of transparency or exact replicability misrepresents the situation. It is not merely the polysemy and ambiguity of language which beset us; nor even the concealing to the author as much as to the listener, which Freud in particular explored (making him in the eyes of one writer 'among the world's major theoreticians of translation').[7] Ultimately we are faced with the simple inevitability that translation changes that which it translates. It is for this reason that the same author can say 'Even repetition is never the same, is never duplicated exactness, if for no other reason that each repetition represents an accumulation'.[8] Yet we constantly have to translate, and assume some notion of equivalence. Humboldt's axiom captures the dilemma: 'All understanding is at the same time a misunderstanding, all agreement in thought and feeling is also a parting of the ways.'[9]

Political activists of all persuasions face the unenviable task of 'translating' ideologies and platforms into actual social programmes.

Exchange

Exchange is the metaphor of value. It is the thought process which creates an equivalence in value or worth or cost between otherwise disparate things. Whereas in metaphor (proper) it is a perceived quality in common which classifies two different things, and in homology it is the perceived repetition of a relationship, and in translation it is the transcoding of a quality into another mode of representation, in exchange it is the deeming of one thing as of equivalent worth to another that creates the relation between the two. It is a relation of exchange because such a dual equation or

---

[7] P. Mahony, 'Towards the Understanding of Translation in Psychoanalysis', *American Psychoanalytic Association Journal*, 28 (2), 1980, p. 472.
[8] *Ibid.*, p. 464.
[9] *Ibid.*, p. 465. In fact, Mahony is quoting George Steiner quoting Humboldt; and Steiner continues 'Or as Fritz Mauthner puts it, it was via language, with its common surface and private base, that men had "made it impossible to get to know each other".'

investment of a quality of value, and only such an investment, allows the replacement of one by the other.

Lévi-Strauss, in particular, has established the quite fundamental role exchange plays in any process of social relations. He sees it as the inevitable and irreducible building-block of all social systems.[10] For him, the paradigm is the exchange of brides for cattle. It would be a mistake, however, to consider exchange as a social operation only of macro-systems. For all intra-psychic and inter-personal relations to endure and change, the bestowing of value on all aspects of human endeavour, including, of course, human affect, remains indispensable. Metaphor does not merely classify and reclassify reality in the conventionally cognitive sense; it, just as necessarily, classifies by value and worth. This necessity arises from the human impossibility of total possessiveness;[11] a feature which parallels the impossibility of grasping entire reality as one thought. Selection, choice, differentiation is endemic to the human condition. Thought has to be partial in both popular senses of the word.

Exchange can be seen as a paradigm of all politics. The individual forsakes potential rewards, at any one time, for the satisfaction of others, by an appreciation of some equivalence between the expected expenditure of effort and the lack of forsaken rewards on the one hand and the assumed rewards on the other. Certain things are 'worth the effort'; others are not. One thinks of surrender in terms of a receipt. We cannot be concerned here with investigating the possibility of persistent personal patterns, or with the probability of occasional changes of values, or with those moments of uncertainty, or, of course, with the likelihood of never knowing with any precision the actual exchange of values one has chosen. None of these issues, no matter how resolved, alters the proposal that one inherent mode of human thinking is that of value exchange. And as with any of the seven modes, it is closely related to, but distinct from, the others.

Of course, humans are obligatorily social. Exchange relations, from those of infancy to the most complex of social ones, knit

---

[10] See *The Elementary Structures of Kinship*, Social Science Paperbacks, London, 1970. Lévi-Strauss appreciates the complexity, ubiquity and necessity of exchange once it is understood as something more than 'simple', mechanistic exchange. It may be 'direct or indirect, general or special, immediate or deferred, explicit or implicit, closed or open, concrete or symbolic' (pp. 478–79). As he says, 'social life is the collective form of symbolic thought' (p. 496).

[11] *Ibid.*, pp. 496–97.

The Metaphoric Modes

individuals and groups together and operate on the same principle of some equivalence in the giving and receiving of valued rewards, including material benefits as well as more elusive satisfactions such as self-respect, security, love, admiration, belongingness, lack of anxiety and the whole range of human gratifications, short and long term, positive or negative. Whether spontaneously or with calculation, whether apparently clear or unfathomable, whether habitual or novel, all social activity operates on a process of metaphoric exchange. As Lévi-Strauss noted, social life is the collective form of symbolic thought. No two things are the same: despite this, just as we have to classify by perceiving similarities in dissimilarities, so do we have to exchange by perceiving equivalent values among things otherwise dissimilar and unequatable. A bride (or groom) is not 'worth' six cattle or anything; nor is a book, or one's labour, 'worth' any particular amount of cash. We deem them so and we have no option but to do so. Everything is valued, and it is we who value them. Some, of course, are in a position to impose their values on others. They set the price.

Contradictions, Opposites

Certain things are related because of being considered opposites of each other. They relate because they are tied together. They exist only because of their mutuality, this co-existence, this pairing. Alone either term loses its value; it acquires a sense by being seen as 'naturally' related to that which it is not. In that sense, opposites are defined negatively, in terms of the essential other. Seen as a pairing, an opposition loses much of its dual quality; it is one, in opposition.

Binary opposites are perceived in a variety of ways: as opposites, oppositions, contradictions, contraries, dualities, dichotomies, negations, paradoxes, ironies. They are similar and different, but, it would seem, they all belong to the same mode of metaphorising.

As with all the seven modes, contradictions/oppositions pervade both our mundane and specialist arenas of thought, for example, nature/culture, body/mind, birth/death, right/wrong, yes/no, in/out, up/down. The nature of their mutual exclusiveness and the extent of their very interdependence and identity is, of course, debatable. And what is disconcerting to certain people is that what is in opposition varies from time to time and place to place. Much of politics involves the formation, confrontation and shifting of opposites.

Synecdoche

Synecdoche is the perception of identity between part and whole, whole and part. Since Aristotle there has been so much discussion of this form that it warrants no extensive elaboration here; the most frequently quoted example being the mast (of a sailing ship) standing for the whole ship. Synecdochic thinking seems to operate in a slippery fashion: a part may represent a whole, a part becomes an equivalent of the whole, the part is the whole. But there is nothing idiosyncratic about this; sliding from 'as if' to 'is' is symptomatic of the entire metaphoric process, of all thought.

One common type of synecdochic thought is triggered by sensory perception. We see, hear, touch a small part of something and our thinking completes the whole; (and Jakobson was right when he reminded us that cinema,[12] of all the arts, depends so much on this function—a mouth, hand or shadow tells us all). But we constantly operate synecdochically on the non-sensory levels as well. All diagnostic thinking—in medicine, psychoanalysis or in public policy to mention only a few areas[13]—works by relating parts ('symptoms') to conceptual wholes. Again, so much intellectual debate and change centres around conflicting classifications, here the synecdochic one of to *what* whole (system, theory, structure) does any particular thing relate as symptomatic part. Varying consequences for both individual and society, for example, will depend on the synecdochic thinking which relates, say, mental illness to the breakdown of religious traditions, to the neurophysiological system, to the family structure, or to particular social systems.

Synecdochic thinking could get a bad press because the caricature of it is in caricature and stereotyping. Groups are identified by some one 'characteristic' feature which becomes the total quality of the group, and into which all members are fitted: all Xs smell, or are avaricious or are effete, or are boastful, or are friendly. Blacks are black; one synecdochic part dominating self- and other-identification. It tells us all, we have classified them. We may know its dangers, but we have to use this form of thinking every day, and whilst in no less a blatant way than in offensive caricature, it passes unnoticed. Many of our metaphors can be re-thought as synecdoches;

---

[12] R. Jakobson, 'Aphasia as a Linguistic Problem', *Fundamentals of Language*, R. Jakobson and M. Halle (eds.), Mouton, The Hague, 1956, pp. 78–79.

[13] See chapter 5 for a study of public policy. Psychoanalysis as a therapeutic, of course, is based on the interpretation of the analysand's metaphors as symptoms.

The Metaphoric Modes

we refer to a whole while thinking of it in terms of one of its parts. Let us consider one that has been recently 'exposed': 'man' has been classed as such, and opposed to 'woman', on the basis of one part, the genitalia. This part has represented the whole and has determined the exclusiveness of the two classifications. Feminism challenges this synecdoche, redefines or dislocates the opposition and reclassifies social reality; constructing new metaphors as it goes along. Group identity and membership constitute a synecdochic element in all politics.

Metonymy

Metonymy has also had a long history in western consciousness. It rests on relations of contiguity; things that seem to go together because of their proximity, be that spatial, temporal or conceptual.

It is the 'naturalness' of most metonymic relations (no matter how they have in fact been culturally determined), like all used or dead metaphors, that makes this common form of thinking pass unnoticed—it appears to be 'commonsense', the 'real'. It is when our accustomed contiguities are unexpectedly disturbed by the introduction of the incongruous that we become aware of our conventional metonymic thoughts; we do not normally think, for example, of a game without rules, of a judge without probity (but not a politician!), of a city without noise, of an effect without cause.

One technique of humour is the breaking of metonymic associations and chains; and, in a different way, our metonymic thinking is exploited by advertising as it juxtaposes a product 'naturally' with the appropriate, culturally valued rewards, e.g., status, sociability, health, charm—pleasures contiguously fused together.

Contiguity by temporality in all its diverse guises, in the narrative, in history, in the secrecy of private life, is to many people the hallmark of metonymy. Jackobson's depiction of the realist novel as being wholly constituted in it is well known. Let me add Genette:[14]

> Without metaphor, Proust said (roughly or thereabouts), there are no true memories; we could add for him (and for everyone): without metonymy, there is no chain of memories, no *history*, no novel. (Original emphasis, my translation.)

It is impossible here to illustrate with any adequacy the ubiquity

---
[14] Genette, *op. cit.*, p. 63.

of the metaphoric modes. However, any reflection on the system of law, for example, would reveal the pervasiveness of metonymy as well as of metaphor (proper), synecdoche and opposites. Evidence for the prosecution rests almost entirely on the construction, and for the defence, dismantling of metonymies. The outcome of accepting one or the other pattern of contiguous clues, of course, establishes guilt or innocence. This is an interesting illustration because it seems to bridge in metonymic thinking a contentment in relating phenomena contiguously and a desire to impose a *causal* relation on the material. The study of cause and effect has long been seen as part of metonymic thought; and it is plausibly so, because the sequential aspect of temporality fits our fundamental notion of causality, that is, that cause precedes effect, that the past influences, determines, conditions or explains its future. Simple causality, therefore, consists in establishing a temporal relation of metonymy and labelling the preceding elements 'cause'; although as A.J. Ayer has pointed out: 'if A is a sufficient condition of B, B is a necessary condition of A, these are just two ways of saying the same thing, that A, as it were, carries B along with it'—a relation of contiguity![15] More sophisticated interpretations of causality see metonymic relations determined by conceptually bonded contiguity rather than by the more obvious, spatial or temporal proximity. Things otherwise 'distant' or unrelated become 'close' and metonymically tied each time a new theory (a metaphoric reclassification) occurs. Politics and economics become contiguous only after a Marxist or some related theory of the state is applied. Dreams and parapraxes were unrelated before Freud. In this sense, metaphor (proper) and metonymy are closely interdependent. Once again, a preoccupation of intellectual debate centres on the question of just what is metonymically related. There is power in the choice of the appropriate story.

This classification of seven modes of thinking is like any metaphor; it illuminates similarities despite dissimilarities. They are different yet the 'same'. In a way, they are seven faces of the one thing—but there is no master face, no beginning, no end. Given any metaphor, we can rethink it in other ways. It is no longer surprising (although initially disturbing) that basic modes of thinking so easily spill over and reshape each other; now it seems anomalous to imagine that thinking could be compartmentalised in mutually exclusive

[15] A.J. Ayer, *The Problem of Knowledge*, Penguin, London, 1964, pp. 171–72.

The Metaphoric Modes

units. Because the embankments are so porous, the verbal definition of each mode is necessarily imprecise; indicative rather than definitive. Likewise, no overall definition of any exactitude seems possible—beyond something like modes of relating or classifying; otherwise we would have created another, 'total' mode of thought. We must rest content with 'the seven modes of thinking'.

In one way or other, each mode has been seen for what it is, for its metaphoricity, by many thinkers. For example, both Freud and Lévi-Strauss, in entirely different ways, almost—and without awareness—put their fingers on every one of the seven.

Furthermore, reference to these authors prompts us to say now that 'thinking' or 'thought' extends beyond popular notions of conscious mental operations (whatever such an expression may mean). We can refer to unconscious thought (and we explicitly do so in a later chapter). We can, as well, infer thought from behaviour. We perform our metaphors in action as much as we think them or verbalise them. As we have said before, we live our metaphors.

To the extent that the metaphoric modes are universally applicable (and I can think of no way to confirm or deny this assertion), then the conventional grounds for distinguishing the form of thinking of the modern westerner from the primitive, the scientist from the artist, the rationalist from the mystic, collapse. In fact, all such conventional dichotomies are challenged. There may well be differences, as for example, there obviously are in terms of metaphoric *content*; that is the various *specific* metaphors in use. But this shifts the nature of the conventional debate; and, in particular, questions the use of rationality, logic, conceptual abstraction and sequential, language-based reasoning as the delimiting criteria. However, one significant point needs to be made immediately. Nothing that has been said implies that all humans use the seven forms in something that could be considered equal weight (however one could measure that!). Jakobson's observation,[16] although limited only to metaphor and metonymy, is still pertinent. He suggests that 'under the influence of a cultural pattern, personality, and verbal style, preference is given to one of the two processes over the other'. The same interesting reflection may apply to the seven modes; but little along that fascinating path of investigation can be attempted here.[17]

---

[16] Jakobson, *op. cit.*, p. 76.

[17] However, chapters 7 and 8 develop critiques of the power of oppositional dualites in western thought and practice which, it is argued, do not appear to have the same tradition in India.

Many other aspects of the subject have also to be neglected, because the remainder of the book is concerned only with exploring the implications of my perspective on metaphor *for social theory*; in particular in reconsidering questions of language, communication, modernity, social planning, radical politics and the effects of a western discourse on the non-West. There are connections as we will see.

With such a preoccupation I have felt obliged to ignore many of the significant works on metaphor appearing in recent years.[18]

---

[18] A brief recreation of some works, however, seems desirable. I will leave the reader to decide for himself in what ways my work agrees, disagrees or is incommensurable with the following writings.

I have always found the two essays by Derrida a stimulating challenge: 'White Mythodology: Metaphor in the Text of Philosophy', *New Literary History*, 6, 1, Autumn 1974; 'The Retrait of Metaphor', *Enclitic*, 2 (2), 1978.

Other recent books would include: D.E. Cooper, *Metaphor*, B. Blackwell, Oxford, 1986. E.D. Kittay, *Metaphor: Its Cognitive Force and Linguistic Structure*, Clarendon Press, Oxford, 1987. G. Lakoff, M. Turner, *More than Cool Reason: A Field Guide to Poetic Metaphor*, University of Chicago Press, Chicago, 1989.

A Question of Language   4

ALL CULTURES hold certain beliefs so emphatically, so absolutely, that any alternative appears inconceivable. Such beliefs seem forged by the fires of commonsense and hammered into a quality of myth. Not mythic as a tale constantly told, rather as an eternal faith constantly enacted, never requiring articulation. It is just there, unobtrusive, the primary and absolute foundation for all and any subsequent edifice of knowledge. Western culture, it would seem, has always held one such mythic belief about the nature of and in particular, the relationship between, language and thought (although I am in no position to state categorically 'always'; it just seems that this surely has been the case!).

This fundamental belief, of course, is that thought is primary both temporally and ontologically. Accordingly, language comes second, being merely the form of expressing the prior thought. As one writer, recently defending this Aristotelean tradition, as he and others refer to it, said 'Language is the means of expressing thought, not of having them'.[1] A simple, unambiguous and unproblematic statement of relation. Language certainly can have its own complexities,

---

[1] Z. Vendler, 'Words in Thoughts', *Thought, Consciousness and Reality*, vol. 2 of *Psychiatry and the Humanities*, J.H. Smith (ed.), Yale University Press, New Haven, 1977, p. 48. Vendler sees himself as continuing the 'Aristotelean' tradition as distinct from the 'Platonic' one which, he argues, 'reduces' thought to language.

This chapter first appeared in a radically different form as 'Metaphor, Thinking and Thought', *Etc: A Review of General Semantics*, 39, 3, Fall, 1982, pp. 242–56.

richness and, even, an inherent value, but its function is circumscribed. It is the means only to ends created elsewhere, in and by thought; its role is to facilitate, articulate, translate these primary ends. One thinks, mentally, and then one's physical tools, speech and pen manipulating language, record it either for one's own future use or for broadcasting it to others. The skill to be acquired and admired is to express the thought as accurately as possible. We learn language for it to be as true a mirror as possible of the objective world out there, but more fundamentally, of the internal world of thought inside us.

Corollaries flow. In education we are drilled (and this time I use the tense with confidence) to use the language, orally or in writing, to express our intentions as truly as we can. Our thoughts, in other words (forgive the telling pun), are taken to be the product of a conscious, intentional mental activity. 'Is this what you mean to say?' we are asked; 'express your thoughts more clearly' we have recorded on our written efforts at school and university. I think therefore I write (or speak) is our Cartesian-style declaration of faith. Language in the service of. We know our educational essay to be successful if it be marked by our teachers as 'clear, logical, methodical, rational, sound' (the intellectual qualities considered Cartesian according to the French dictionary, *Petit Robert*.[2] 'Confused, mystical, obscure' being the antonyms provided in the same entry). On this issue, our western educational standards are firm, unequivocal. And yet could there be a sign of confusion? Is the pedagogical judgement directed to the expression or to the thought 'behind' it? It would seem that in practice we care little about consistency in this matter. Is this because the issue is of little importance? I think not; it seems more likely that we know with such certainty that thought is prior and language its necessary expression that we can afford casually to call one by the other; to see, metonymically as it were, the contained in its container. An admonition to tidy up one's thinking is followed in time by a check on one's rewritten expression. We know one, apparently, by the other.

Our basic assumption about communication also follows, as it seems axiomatically, as part of this cultural gestalt. The unquestioned assumptions that communication occurs between people, and that

---

[2] *Le Petit Robert 1, Dictionnaire*, Societe du Nouveau Littre, Paris, 1979, p. 260, my translation.

this exists as a necessary inevitability, automatically follows from the belief that language is the expression of thought. If language translates this private mental phenomenon called thought into something available to the senses, and if, as we believe, it is merely a factor of care, skill and training that determines whether such thought is accurately expressed or not, then the likelihood that communication, a communion of thought, can and does exist between people is no longer in doubt. Any reasonable attention by both parties will ensure an accurate sharing of thoughts. If difficulty is encountered, the fault and its remedy are evident. The specific imagery is varied: one could talk of a faulty line, crossed wires, a leak in the container, an incorrectly coded message and undoubtedly many others; but the sense is unvaried—the difficulty lies not in the incommensurability of the thoughts or in the possibility that what may be eminently reasonable to one party may be outside the conception of the other; but it lies, and must lie only, in the mechanisms and processes of transmission—in the language employed. Adjust the language, if necessary clarify the meaning of particular words, successful communication can be eventually achieved. Communication, and by that is meant invariably 'successful' communication, becomes 'natural' to human society; it is the norm and expectation of social intercourse. Its evident strengths are exploited, its industry becomes manifold, language becomes a technology, the paradigmatic technology circumscribing the totality of human intercourse. Its recognised shortfalls are also exploited, creating in its turn further technologies of language measurement, diagnosis and rectification. Once again it becomes merely a matter of procedural tinkering, technical adjustment and more rigorous consensual coding. Any mystery is denied; the possibility of certain thoughts not being successfully communicated to others because of entirely different world-views is ignored; not because of any wilfulness, but because it is structurally excluded from consideration. To suggest, as certain contemporary writers do, that successful communication is in no way guaranteed and that the related processes need to be considered afresh and less naively, is commonly greeted as a scandal, a waste of time, and nothing more than the symptom of an old and now tiresome sceptical point of view.

This conventional understanding about communication can be extended. If interpersonal dialogue can be achieved, provided attributes of care, skill and goodwill are present, then there seems little reason to doubt the eventual success of inter-cultural communication. The situations are qualitatively the same. The patient and rigorous acquisition of language-skills becomes the sole requisite (we should not be misled by exhortations to 'study the culture as well' as a desirable supplement to any foreign-language learning; in neither principle nor practice do these qualify my statement—languages, it is indubitably believed, are translatable.) This is all that is required. The rest follows. Once we have mastered the exchange rate in words, the culture and mind of any people lie transparently in front of us. Apparently underneath some veneer of difference, we all think alike. Thought is universal; we just express this common commodity in different ways. This does not deny that we have different beliefs and customs, but our thinking about these is comparable. Thinking alike is, in time, knowing alike. The task again is a technical one only. What follows is the belief that knowledge is universal. The question whether we can attain truth or not is a matter aside, and probably one of constant dissensus; what is not open to debate is the continued application and perfection of one universal schema of knowledge. Thought is basic and primary in all ways: only its expression, in language, differs. We, therefore, can and must continue to translate and communicate in the quest of one common, ultimately the best, knowledge. Babel, after all, was a confusion of tongues not of minds. It is understandable, therefore, that it is the West which has produced a utopian dream of a universal language, Esperanto—the ultimate facilitation, by elimination, of translation. A consensual world in thought and language: the former a prerequisite for entertaining the latter. Many non-utopian thinkers, however, indeed, many of our finest representatives of efficiency, management and modernisation, see the continuing diffusion of English (the 'language of science') as a more likely historical outcome, and one achieving an equivalent mediating universal function with no cost or sacrifice to the English-speaking world (pragmatism at its best).

But let us draw back from such future scenarios, and remind ourselves again of the most significant implication of this Aristotelean tradition. This material base, this tool, vehicle, carrier we call language may legitimately be expressed in all its idiosyncratic guises; a Spanish literature, for example, may differ from, let us say, a Chinese literature: the very differences may be taken as symbolic of literature's fanciful property. But such freedom of creativity has its resolute and permanent boundary; when language expresses serious thought, when it is the vehicle for scholarship and knowledge then its idiosyncracies must evaporate. Science and learning are expressions of thought, not of language. We can entertain nothing else; as if, for example, a Spanish physiology could be distinguishable from a Chinese physiology! The notion is laughable. And if we were to need an exemplary reminder of its impossibility, which we do not, then we think of the fiasco called Lysenko, and the foolish endeavour to establish a particular, Russian, Marxist science. The West rarely needs such reminders; consensus normally reigns: there is thought, primary and universal and then there is language, culturally diverse, the vehicle of expression of this thought.

But scandals do erupt and do scandalise. In 1968, for example, when Jacques Derrida presented a paper on 'Differance with an "a"' to the French Philosophical Society,[3] a member of the audience, clearly speaking for more than just herself, strongly objected to Derrida's play on words, and even his creation of the word 'differance' with an 'a' which he had admitted as untranslatable. Whereas, she continued, 'the tendency in French thought has been, at least in principle, towards a thinking that lends itself to universal translations'. In his reply Derrida noted that 'I would perhaps agree with what you have said of French philosophy, with this reservation: French philosophy has not been able to separate an unequivocal language from a universally transmissible thought; it just thought it could'.

Derrida was not speaking as a prophet. The twentieth century has witnessed a remarkable series of attacks on the so-called Aristotelean tradition. And the assault has come from a wide variety of sources: from philosophers such as Wittgenstein and Heidegger, from anthropologists and their linguist colleagues like Edward Sapir and Benjamin Whorf, and from socio-linguists who have argued that different abilities in utilising thought seem causally related to varying levels of language use in different social classes. Reinforcement has come from several more engaged sources of criticism: from certain Marxists analysing the linguistic base of bourgeois domination of the oppressed classes; and from feminists who emphasise the male constructed and biassed nature of language, and the manner by which this maintains a masculine hegemony. Women are kept oppressed, in part,

---

[3] 'The Original Discussion of "Differance" (1968)', *Derrida and Differance*, Parousia Press, Warwick, 1985, especially pp. 136–38.

by women being obliged to use and reproduce a male language and, hence, a male system of thought which subordinates women as a gender in all its manifestations. And we could add as a further source of dislocation, the many linguistic cultures struggling to maintain or recover their freedom from a dominating nation-state imposing a foreign language on them. The Bretons in France and the Tamils in India can be cited as representing the two ends of the battle, one having been submerged and the other attempting to forestall that fate. All such movements insist that language is primary: it determines one's thoughts, culture and one's very identity. Their protagonists know that the education and communication policies of the nation-state in the name of a national unity are too accurate a prediction for their own future well-being; a unity being obtained through the destruction of all internal sub-cultures.

It is likely that this century will end with the Aristotelean tradition still dominant throughout the western world. But it is certainly being challenged. Increasingly representative minorities argue its reversal, that language is dominant, it shapes thought. Certain implications follow.

There has been a shift, one readily senses, from one of optimistic, unitarian, if not totalistic universalisms to one of atomism, separateness and relativism as well as one of challenge, questioning and frustration. Sapir and Whorf, for example, considered that the North American Indian tribes they studied had created different world realities in keeping with their different languages. Translation between these tribes becomes a difficult proposition as their entire world systems seem incompatible. Such an argument inevitably casts a shadow on all the conventional notions of communication, translation and the very reasonableness of knowledge based on universalisms: of ways of thinking, of absolute and homogeneous concepts, of truth, of knowledge, of judgement, of any comparison—indeed, ultimately, of most forms of enquiry as we have known them.

What is also involved is both a creative outpouring of imaginative, new thinking and, yet, I suspect, an element of frustration experienced by some as they face the new intellectual/political (and that union seems quite contemporary in its urgency) tasks confronting them. How does one radically alter the existing order given the new perspective on things? How feasible does it appear, for example, for women to 'overthrow' an entire system of language and set of social relations? Even if, hypothetically, we were to assume willing co-operation from all quarters? How does one handle tradition, either by rewriting it or ignoring it? Does one start again with a clean slate? Surely not. Such problems can be crystallised in what often appears to be the first necessary steps towards such a programme of liberation. How does a woman begin to define herself once she breaks from the traditional and hierarchical duality, masculine/feminine? What is woman once she refuses an identity determined by that which she is not—man? The problem is identical to that being faced by certain 'Third World' thinkers who are attempting to create for themselves an identity cast free from the one shaped by the West, one that makes them nothing other than the Other of the West. How does he make his next move when Ashis Nandy in New Delhi says 'India is not non-West; it is India'?[4]

Frustrations and dilemmas deepen once we reverse the conventional order; once we concede that, rather than 'speaking our thoughts' with language but a tool, we 'think our words' when language becomes the dominant partner. A significant shift seems entailed once this new perspective is adopted. The Aristotelean tradition fits well our modern, post-Cartesian, rational view of human activity: intentional in our behaviour, conscious in our decisions. Improvement appears within our grasp; we merely have to polish techniques, invent further technologies. It all seems manageable, eventually. But, reverse that order and we easily slip into a less positive mode. We see ourselves as more passive recipients of factors beyond our control. We are not surprised or offended at references to expressions like 'the prison-house of language'.[5] Our conscious intentions, the paradigmatic hallmark of conventional self-identity in the West, are dislodged and to some degree replaced by notions of the unconscious. A 'we are thought' replaces a 'we think'. Without succumbing to some fatalism, we are presented with entirely new sets of problems. We have to imagine new scenarios in which we are less in control.

The present century has been the epoch during which representation as the only valid means of signification has been destroyed. We think immediately of the innovations in the plastic arts and in

[4] Ashis Nandy, *The Intimate Enemy*, Oxford University Press, Delhi, 1983, p. 73.

[5] The title of a well-known book by F. Jameson, Princeton University Press, Princeton, 1972.

literature, and then of photography and film. Likewise with language; no longer seen as merely serving the practical function of representing our thoughts, it gains a life of its own. Once it has become detached, once it has acquired a modicum of autonomy, we are obliged to look at it afresh, no longer a tool but a force in its own right. Its materiality is now noticed; its size, weight, sound, look, resonance. We realise that language has to have an impact on its recipients quite independently of any intentions of its user. We may, personally, with full consciousness, author certain aspects of our language use, but other components seem self-authored. We share language, it becomes a joint enterprise, in which we can take only a limited responsibility. We need to hunt for a new vocabulary: what do we call all those 'messages' and 'signals' given out by language which we did not intend? 'Message' too readily implies authorship and intentionality; 'signal' suggests some explicit and definite information which we could specify, some preconcerted and intelligible sign. In coining novel terms or in giving new meanings to particular words we experience the reality and the difficulty of the problem. We discover each time that language is not an open, elastic and neutral kit of tools able to be reworked or reset to meet any need. Anything does not go. It comes to us pre-packaged: set to be used in certain ways, open and available for innovative exploration in others, and in some areas closed, inhibiting if not prohibiting certain articulations. It is as if we are to discover for ourselves, by trial and error, and by a desperate grappling with our lexical skills, as much as by what we receive from 'theory' or from precedent, the operating rules of language and our relationship to it.

Nevertheless, having moved this short yet vital distance from complacent acceptance of language as a malleable tool of representation, we become dissatisfied with any simple reversal of that convention. If language does not represent our thoughts, perhaps we should question any glib application of reflecting or mirroring imagery elsewhere as well—such as the equally uncomplex assumption that thought reflects our language. Both need to be challenged. Let us illustrate this in one exemplary area. Feminists have by now surely proven their insight that language is not a simple, neutral tool of expression for all and any of our consciously deliberated thoughts no matter how radically unconventional they may be. It is, they have shown, a man-made language, and because of this it allows or forces us to think and say certain things and inhibits us from saying

A Question of Language

and thinking other things. In a way, language can never be the same again—though caution warns us that history is never smooth and unidirectional; besides, even now, the new appreciation is a minority one. But it seems foolish to replace one unproblematised myth by another. Surely language is more than *just* a man-made instrument, and surely we may have more than one relation to it.

'It' may be the clue. Perhaps it is not singular to begin with, and this in two ways. It may be wrong, for example, to assume that language constitutes a system in any strict sense of that term. It may not be homogeneous, complete, entire, uniformly marked out and off. On the contrary, it may be composed of heterogeneous parts, of congeries, of both enclosed and open boundaries. It also may be plural. Language may be a misleading simplification, and in its place we, perhaps, ought to think languages. This should not alarm us as we do something like this when, depending on a context, we imply by 'language' some one perspective only, to the exclusion of others. We may, for example, be implicitly referring to some arena of related vocabulary, such as the language of politics or the language of art. We may be concerned with some specific function such as language as communication, or as a symbolic system, or as a code. Each label constitutes a language with attributes, points of entry and parameters different from each other. Certain languages may be related in some way to the rest; some may not; some may be incommensurable. We have no reason to believe that all these various languages and our investigative concerns fit neatly together to compose Language, a language in all its conceivable totality, now and in the future. Consider an imperfect analogy: we do not create one total, whole language by assembling all the various national languages of the world. We can surely conceive of more than one form of Babel.

Let us turn to consider thought. If the twentieth century has liberated language by insisting on some degree of its autonomy, and if, as I have said, we should avoid a simple reversal of thought and language, then we have to concede that the former as well has some independence from the latter. An infant, before any acquisition of language, surely can think. It is telling, maybe, to appreciate the etymology of the word infancy, 'without speech'; not, mark you, 'without thought'. By now it is not merely Melanie Klein and her followers who are pushing back the threshold of human mental and emotional life further and further. So, it may be useful to suggest and illustrate here, hypothetically, the range of metaphoric thought an infant accomplishes before it acquires language. Metaphor (proper): food is pleasure, hunger is pain; analogy: homologies of oral satisfaction, such as the dummy being the breast of the absent mother; translation: the sound of laughter is the emotion of joy or excitement; exchange: the giving of the child's trust, dependence and recognition of the mother in return for maternal love, protection and care; opposition: self/others, presence/absence (see Freud's fort-da analysis); synecdoche: the breast is the mother, the mouth or hand is the bodily self; metonymy: physical warmth, emotional comfort, affective contentment are contiguously related; or metonymy (causal): crying (in its various manners) and maternal attention are sequentially related.

We think in a wide range of ways: with our bodily actions, our emotions, through the medium of paint, or music and beyond. Some rendition in stone considered artistic, and a slap in the face considered violent, are as much thoughts as any verbal utterance or written treatise. When we relate, we think: we consider, realise, reach a decision, have an opinion, react, initiate, intend. We readily imagine thoughts mediated by words, but language has been too privileged by our conventional ideas of thinking. Henri Poincaré describes scientific activity—to many people a paradigm of thinking: as making combinations that 'reveal to us unsuspected kinship between...facts, long known, but wrongly believed to be strangers to one another'.[6] Not only is this a very clear description of metaphoric thinking, it also describes a process independent of language. And Einstein's 'discovery' of the general theory of relativity: on the basis of the scientist's own (quite emotional!) description of the event, the author considers that particular creative insight to be an example of 'Janusian thinking', which he explains 'consists of actively conceiving two or more opposite or antithetical concepts, ideas or images simultaneously, both as existing side by side and/or as equally operative or equally true'.[7] Language seems in no way a necessary component of thought here.

To decide that one dislikes a particular occasion, to ponder the linguistic asymmetry between the expression 'old master' and 'old

[6] Quoted by J. Bruner in 'The Conditions of Creativity', *Beyond the Information Given: Studies in the Psychology of Knowing*, Allen & Unwin, London, 1974, p. 210.
[7] A. Rothenberg, 'Einstein's Creative Thinking and the General Theory of Relativity: A Documented Report', *American Journal of Psychiatry*, 136, 1, 1979, p. 39.

mistress', to determine whether an azure or indigo blue fitted better some shape or mood, to perceive a behaviour as paradoxical, to vote 'no', all seem instances of thinking, constitute a variety of means by which we classify, relate, or determine; and, surely, they prompt us to think it better to refer to a plurality of 'thoughts' rather than to one constantly homogeneous form of thinking. By now, it also seems obvious that to insist that language is always or never related to thought is reckless. No constant relationship, whatever it may be, seems privileged. For a moment we understand the appeal that the Soviet cognitive psychologist, Vygotsky, has attracted. He constantly stresses a dynamic interaction:

> The relation between thought and word is a living process; thought is born through words. A word devoid of thought is a dead thing, and a thought unembodied in words remains a shadow. The connection between them, however, is not a preformed and constant one. It emerges in the course of development, and itself evolves.[8]

And yet something is unsatisfying. Is it that he is blithely repeating too much of the western myths about human endeavour and its attributes? He follows a conventional path in considering thought as only a language-based (and language in its narrowest sense) phenomenon as well as denying a role to words other than its representative one. Words are to have no life of their own. And, it would seem, the process of relations is an evolutionary one: humans go through stages of development; presumably more words, more complex thoughts. We are being presented, once again, with the optimistic story of man's (the implicit model is masculine I have no doubt) gradual but certain maturation into rational thought. 'Concept thinking' is his final stage of growth. As he describes it:

> To form such a concept it is also necessary to abstract, to single out elements, and to view the abstracted elements apart from the totality of the concrete experience in which they are embedded. In genuine concept formation, it is equally important to unite and to separate: synthesis must be combined with analysis.... A concept emerges only when the abstracted traits are synthesised anew

[8] L.S. Vygotsky, *Thought and Language*, M.I.T. Press, Cambridge, Mass., 1962, p. 153.

and the resulting abstract synthesis becomes the main instrument of thought.[9]

What seems striking about this statement, in so many ways admirable, is that, contrary to the author's intentions, the role of language seems quite unnecessary! It also seems an admirable description of metaphoric thinking from the simplest of examples (see Piaget's grandson who would make steam-train noises whenever his grandfather puffed on his pipe) to what is considered the most sophisticated (see the description of Einstein). Ultimately, Vygotsky's work displays an inherent naivety. He seems unaware of the problems involved in his language—or is it in his thoughts? He concludes his book:

> Thought and language, which reflect reality in a way different from that of perception, are the key to the nature of human consciousness. Words play a central part not only in the development of thought but in the historical growth of consciousness as a whole. A word is a microcosm of human consciousness.[10]

Vygotsky's work, unintentionally, highlights our need to take the next step. We have already problematised the relationship between language and thought; we now need to problematise the very concepts of language and thought. In each case, the move is towards multiplication and complexity, away from an essence and singularity. As we have said, change of perspective changes the agenda and the possible responses. We suddenly realise that what we are dealing with is the problem of metaphor. Therefore, in this sense there is no such thing as thought or language, only one or other specifically characterised (whether consciously or, more likely, unconsciously done) type of language or thought; that is, one or other metaphor of thought or language. In no way does this imply that either of those 'things' become ethereal, a mere figment of the mind—or language. What it does mean is that there is no such thing possible as Language or Thought as one essential, universal, absolute thing—as our common use of those words, the concepts of those words, inevitably imply. What we are, in fact, referring to when we use those words is one or other of the many abstracted characteristics we may have

[9] *Ibid.*, p. 76.
[10] *Ibid.*, p. 153.

perceived/discovered/invented/created (or inherited) in either of them. How many kinds of language or thought there are or may be one cannot say; none, however, is central or the proper one from which the others have deviated as exceptional. That is, there is no such thing as pure thought or pure language (certain aestheticists are apt to describe poetry in some such terms). A thought will always come dressed (and therefore marked by and difficult to distinguish from) as words or emotions or bodily movement or physical action or sound or music or plastic arrangement. We can repeat the same for language: any word, even a surreal fabrication, will send out non-linguistic waves as well. Likewise, an ideograph or a hieroglyph.

The implications are significant. If we cannot entertain an idea of purity here, then we can never conceive of the possibility of a universal thought or a universal language—ones that are neutrally, objectively and equally applicable in time or space. There is, in other words, no conceivable universal mind, creating 'a universal thought and employing a universal language. (Esperanto, or English, may one day become the world's sole language; neither, however, would constitute a universal language. There is a world of difference!) No pure, universal knowledge or truth is the only conclusion one can reach. Everything is touched, coloured, shaped and, at the same time constrained, by culture, by human artefacts which can never be other than local.[11]

So, when we say language or thought we are really saying the X metaphor of language or the Z metaphor of thought. And what we have said for those two 'concepts' applies equally for metaphor—that is, the 'concept' of metaphor which, as applies to all concepts, is the metaphor of metaphor. No metaphor is pure or universal. It also must come clothed in language or behaviour or act which is necessarily cultural, and so culturally limited, and relative.

It should now be clear why we cannot accept the Aristotelean tradition or its current reversal. Both language and thought possess

[11] That is, not universal in character, but one of many. I use the word local for effect; I could have said regional, national, etc. In fact all those terms are inadequate. We require a placement notion which would represent irregular geographic distributions, like, for example, designating the regions, in which, say, English is spoken. That would constitute a cultural locality. Likewise we need a term to refer to historical localities: that historically limited time within which certain thoughts held some sway somewhere. For a fuller understanding, one would then want to join the temporal and the spatial contours.

some autonomy, some internally generated creativity; but at the same time, each remains to some degree under the influence of the other. Questions of primacy and simple causality no longer arise. In the circumstances they are meaningless concerns; pointless to pursue not only because determinations go in both directions, but more so because the very idea of the 'other', or the 'itself', is in confusion. Causality or directionality make sense only when there is 'sufficient' separation between otherwise related units; here, the boundary, to the degree there is one, is within not without each entity. In other words, language is in thought, and so is thought in language to some indeterminate degree. Internal boundaries, a self-causation which is different from self-determination (as it is commonly known), is the awkward-sounding and paradoxical position we reach, and express in a struggle against language (we have no appropriate words for it) and against thought (it sounds a senseless contradiction within conventional western reason). We also have difficulty in understanding and accepting the idea because we cannot visualise it; we cannot mentally construct a material model for it—and our western tradition depends so much on sight as a mode of comprehension and confirmation.

To say that language is thought and thought is language (to some degree, because to be *in* the other constitutes, in a way, *being* the other) is a perfect illustration of metaphoric thought and expression. This is no accident. And such a metaphor is the essential step in understanding we now need to take. Metaphor is primary and necessary, not secondary and derivative. Our tradition has just hidden this from us. It took the other path by asking for internal clarification: the quality of thought was sought within thought, the quality of language within language. Having created two essences, two things, it asked which is primary? What and how are the relations between the two? The idealist-inclined rewarded the mental operation as primary; the materialist-inclined, language, as it 'belongs' to the sense of speech. But a philosophical preference for either ideas or matter is quite irrelevant. Neither thought nor language has primacy over the other because neither can exist before or without the other. The oldest of philosophical divisions is no longer needed here—if, indeed, it is needed anywhere.

To say that thought is language and language thought refers to that element which is essential to both and to each other. The hinge

metaphor is the "hinge" between language and thought

hinge
image

illustrates this well. Both a door and a door-frame can operate as intended only if each is linked by a common, pliable connection, the hinge. This joint transmits or translates the one unit into the other; it is essential to both but belongs exclusively to neither. The metaphoric operations, the modes of relationships and associations, constitute the hinge between language and thought. If we were to imagine words organising themselves into associations, structures or patterns free of external restraint (as a hypothetical exercise) we would see them fall along lines of close contiguities, be that syntactical, semantic, by shape or sound; along lines that cluster as synonyms and homonyms; along lines of opposites such as with antonyms; as parts of wholes; as distant yet telling associations and homologies. A play on words is the order of language; words replace, translate, exchange, imply, follow from, suggest, stimulate, cancel, oppose, challenge, destroy, fabricate and invent each other. These inherently linguistic operations (which can never exist in anything beyond the hypothetical and heuristic scenario as here)—these metaphoric operations—constitute the hinge. So, what would commonly be seen as the aberrations of language are actually its basic quality: jokes which turn on a twist of words, riddles which live by the same laws, the pun, rhyme, children's nonsense words, rhyming slang, graffiti ('uranium spoils your genes'), advertising, headlines, titles, Joycean or Rushdien creations, insightful oxymorons ('trained incapacity'), Lacan's attack on psychiatrists as (the)rapists, technological and scientific amalgamation-words like television, and submarine; and transplants over domains like economic growth. The modes of metaphoric thought transfer and are transferred through these specifically language-based metaphoric operations. This is the hinge. And at some moment of translation, of interplay, of movement from one to the other we have something that is clearly neither thought nor language. It seems to belong to both, or to nowhere. And would it be too reckless to suggest that it is the hinge which creates the possibility of the (swinging) door and doorway, not the opposite? Does metaphor determine language and thought and the constant traffic each way?

At the same time that language is thought, language is *not* thought as well. This is the deceit of metaphor, which is true and false together, of necessity. For, to declare some metaphoric equivalence between language and thought, as between anything, focuses attention on some common attribute and turns attention away from all

else. Let us now change perspective and consider the difference, which is most easily done by highlighting the passage from thought to language (and its reverse) as translation. And, as we have already said, translation changes, there is slippage and accretion, things lost and things added—translation can never be a transparent reproduction of some original. Magritte's pipes said it all!

We can only infer, of course, what the process of thinking entails. It seems to be a simple, laconic affair: an image, one or two words, a mélange of the two appears sufficient to do the trick. What has been written about 'inner speech' appears its suitable approximation. As Vygotsky describes it: 'Inner speech must be regarded, not as speech minus sound, but as an entirely separate speech function. Its main distinguishing trait is its peculiar syntax. Compared with external speech, inner speech appears disconnected and incomplete'. He adds later 'When the thoughts of the speakers are the same the role of speech is reduced to a minimum.... A mere hint, Tolstoy realised'.[12] Thinking is a private affair, between intimates (our several selves)—it can dispense with extraneous, redundant, cautious repetition, with grammatical requirements. It is direct, one is tempted to say intuitive, and, in its brevity, it may be adequately clear to the 'insider' while, hypothetically, appearing to an 'outsider' as incomplete, ambiguous even meaningless. (Of course, as psychoanalysis has shown, the 'self' may be both on the 'inner' and the 'outer'; we remain, in part, strangers to ourselves.)

It is not surprising, therefore, that the dream, so personal, is also considered laconic. Freud's interpretation of the dream-work can be our second suggestive model of thinking. The dream's economy comes about, not only because of the unconscious motivation to compromise and disguise otherwise disturbing thoughts by the use of condensation (metaphor) and displacement (metonymy), but also because all the associative operations of images, symbols and word-play have no need to explain themselves to any 'other'. Here, thinking can dispense with rules of language, can collapse several thoughts into one, and can dispense with the necessary linearity of language. Consider the effort and time needed to reproduce a dream in words, in language which is extended and redundant and which, despite effort, remains a pale, inadequate recreation of a vivid experience. Is the situation much different when we wish to communicate

---

[12] Vygotsky, *op. cit.*, p. 141.

to others any thought of our own? We have already discussed how unlikely it is that the comfortable and comforting ideas of conventional notions of communication hold true. Language, we have said, should not be thought of as a perfect tool of expression of some universal thought. Let us now extend that argument.

Any use of language, it has been argued, is, by necessity, some form of compromise between a 'private language' of each and every user and an idealised language system, the 'public language' of the community. Language becomes 'psychologised' as each user furrows its own linguistic groove. To some degree or other, language is always a personal symptom (as well as other things). As Karchevskij pointed out, there is an inevitable struggle between the two languages: between a psychology and an ideology (as it were).[13] He points out two consequences: an individual can never express himself entirely in the language of an other; and the language 'system' constantly changes through the operations of synonymity and homonymity between the two languages. Changes occur, as it were, through constant language exchange. We can draw two further conclusions. In the constant transmission of private languages, no matter how mediated they may be by some public language, we have to expect transmutation of thought as a regularity not an exception, and all under the guise of a common language. Furthermore, not only ought one not expect to say what one wants to say but one cannot be expected to know when and how one is not saying what one wants to say. Thought cannot be guaranteed its translation, and criteria for such a detection are lacking: we have not advanced towards communion if, to our enquiry whether another party meant X when they said Y, they reply 'yes'. Heidegger's influential aphorism that language conceals as it reveals resonates in several directions.

Despite the best intentions, when we use language we hint rather than signal. Nothing is more aware of this abyss between thought and expression (verbal or otherwise) than the craft of the psychoanalyst. Freud's work has understandably been referred to as a major theory of translation. The challenge—transcoding back from the manifest language to the unconscious thought. Once again, metaphor, in all its modes and manifestations, is seen as the bridge. An interpretation may be reached but a gulf, a doubt and a gamble

---

[13] See W. Steiner, 'Language as Process: Serge Karchevskij's Semiotics of Language', *Sound, Sign and Meaning*, L. Matejka (ed.), University of Michigan Press, Ann Arbor, Michigan, 1976, pp. 291–302.

remain. It is telling to read Vygotsky again, who apparently unware of Freud's work, expresses the task to be confronted: 'To understand another's speech, it is not sufficient to understand his words—we must understand his thoughts. But even that is not enough—we must also understand his motivation.'[14] And yet, as we will discuss later, we have to act as though successful communication occurs; we have to assume that what is said by others is meant as we mean it. We take translation casually in our stride; we act as though language were thought, thought language. We have no time to consider slippage. Trusting, we think, speak and act transparently. Suspicious, we read a difference. Neither way carries a guarantee.

And this for very good reasons. We can never remove ourselves, as thinking individuals or as social creatures, from the absolutely fundamental dilemma of the copula, from the paradox of being, from that most innocent sounding of all verbs—to be. Reality and life, in their entirety, are enclosed, and it cannot be otherwise, in the enigma of 'to be': we know something is this and is not that; we act as if A is B and not C. Everything is predicated on an 'is!'. And little do we ponder, and little good would it do if we did, what this very being means; what is and is not entailed when we identify something as something else—thoughts we just have and act upon every moment of our days. We do not normally stop to concede that this so basic, rather this totally basic proposition, this proposition of all propositions, is ambiguous. Being is both positive and negative, it is and it is not. 'To be' hides its not-being; we forget that every 'is' also admits its 'is not'. To glibly or solemnly declare 'today is hot', 'that politician is corrupt' or 'this book is expensive' (to choose relatively innocent predicates) leads us blandly to take these propositions as total, homogeneous, exclusive, as if nothing else is permissible simultaneously. But 'to be', in fact, is 'to be' in part and 'not to be' in part together. Being is the absolutely primary and unavoidable metaphor. We begin, necessarily, with metaphoricity and we can never escape it. Our entire knowledge rests on nothing other than an 'as if', but that is thought and expressed as a categoric 'is' which we forget conceals (rather openly) its 'is not'. When we think of something as something else we metaphorise, we designate a similarity, while we forget a difference; we are thinking being.

The copula, being, the connection/connecting, has always been a profound philosophical problem. Exactly what is 'is' will never be

[14] Vygotsky, *op. cit.*, p. 151.

answered, or rather be answerable, if for no other reason than that one needs to have the answer to 'is' before we can begin to answer 'what it (i.e., 'is') *is*. We can never really begin. We can appreciate the pitfalls however: we know the ease with which 'being' becomes 'Being' in one theological form or other; that it becomes the expression and thought of an essence, a totality, an absolute. We encounter this daily when we witness what we call stereotypical responses to such declarations as 'she is a feminist/anti-feminist/non-feminist', 'he is a Marxist/capitalist/Catholic/conservative', 'this is a poor country/modern society/democracy/dictatorship', 'this is economic growth/inflation/stagnation', 'this is proven/science/truth'. The problem is not merely the definition or characterisation, be it single, multiple, good, bad, closed or open, of the predicate in each case—this is recognised by many (though ignored, selectively, also by many). The more neglected problem is the copula each time which determines our responses to *that* particular person, situation, phenomenon: when a Jew is exterminated or a black incarcerated or an anti-feminist shunned, the copula as a totalising Being is in operation. But, let us not sink into a patronising attitude towards a recidivist bigotry. We are talking also about you and me. Most scholarship, most of our knowledge, most of our politics are performances of Being. Domestic and international politics would suffer atrophy if Being and its exploitation were erased from their rules of the game. When an economist diagnoses a situation as stagflation, an educationalist determines a child's IQ, an historian traces the spread of capital, a sociologist demarcates urban growth, a social planner recommends an anti-poverty programme, a trade unionist campaigns against declining real wages—should we stop—all are quotidian instances of our inevitable engagement with Being—as is that last sentence.

This is not a problem with a cure, a disease with a remedy, a fault with its rectification and redemption, a danger and its avoidance. The copula with its Janus-style two faces, metaphoricity with its similarities and difference—both being two descriptions of the one thing—is inescapably present always. Thought and the use of language cannot begin without classification, without relating, linking, qualifying. This is metaphor; this is employing, no matter how unconsciously, the copula: something is taken as something else, with all the ramifications of thought which are thereby entailed, and with all the human behaviour which may accordingly follow such a judgement. Likewise, no human intercourse could begin or sustain itself were it not that one exchanges something for something else which is considered an equivalence—be that a material possession, a service, an allegiance, a love, a contract. Without such primary and proper and essential copulations life could not exist. There is no opposite to metaphor—other than death, mental and/or social. It is unavoidable.

The problem lies with the belief that there is an alternative to all this; that the cure is there and always has been, provided one is rigorous and consistent in one's work. This is our traditional belief that language is nothing other than the expression of universally applicable thought; that there is a proper use of language which provides us with the literal meaning every time, a convention we ought not contravene; that classifications and relations between things are products of objective inquiry which are not changeable willy nilly but which may be revised periodically only in the light of further knowledge; that the copula is the expression of true propositions announcing the persistence of proper qualities. That some things, by their nature, possess certain qualities which belong there and not elsewhere; that, therefore, such characteristics are not open to variations and change, they are not social constructions, they are the established discoveries of rational or scientific enquiries. We all know, or at least we should (this belief would continue) what is, for example, politics, or art, or literature, or beauty, or science, or terrorism, or poverty or health and anything else, and in our discussions we would do well to keep these different things separate; let us always begin with a precise definition and proceed with a 'clear, logical, methodical, rational and sound' language of universal enquiry. It would be anathema for this tradition to read that 'Every society decides what content to give to its politics and what to keep out of politics' to quote a recent statement by Ashis Nandy.[15] Politics can have only one content, it would insist; anything else is either a mere rhetorical device to be ignored, or an intrusion of alien affairs, to be deplored. Such literality in one form or another is the hallmark of our western tradition; it concerns itself with correctness, both of language and location, with a search for single truths, with uni-homogeneous, monolithic, absolute definition, with rigorous

---

[15] Ashis Nandy (ed), *Science, Hegemony and Violence: A Requiem for Modernity*, Oxford University Press, Delhi, 1988, see 'Introduction: Science as a Reason of State', pp. 4–5.

boundary maintenance, with consistency, with universal application—all, in one way or other, that we have learned to understand as commonsense. And to repeat, metaphor ought have nothing to do with such matters—it rightly belongs, indeed, it flourishes in the arts, or it periodically illuminates in innovative thought, or it lurks, deviously, in our unconscious fantasies.

Literality breeds a certain rigidity of thought, often an intolerance and dogma. But in isolation such criticisms can sound merely carping, over-moralistic, liberal (a virtue with limitations). So, let us elaborate. Gregory Bateson,[16] in his pioneering work on schizophrenia, noted, inter alia, that patients diagnosed as such were unable to pass an office door with a notice 'Knock before entering', without knocking and entering, whether they had any need to do so or not. He argued that schizophrenics are unable to 'read' metaphorically; everything has to be taken literally. Bateson explains: 'the schizophrenic's error is in treating the metaphors of the primary process with the full intensity of the literal truth'...(for) 'in the primary process, map and territory are equated; in the secondary process, they can be distinguished. In play, they are both equated and discriminated.'...Although 'his utterances are rich in metaphor', the schizophrenic's use is peculiar. It is '*unlabelled* metaphor' (original emphasis): in receiving or transmitting a communication, he is 'unable to handle signals which assign Logical Types to other signals'. Because of this incapacity, he does 'not know what kind of a message a message is': he will, therefore, respond 'with a defensive insistence on the literal level when it is quite inappropriate, e.g., when someone is joking'—or when he passes a door with a sign saying 'Knock before entering'.

If, for present purposes, we accept Bateson's account, I want to suggest that the literality of the dominant western tradition I have been discussing portrays some comparable, albeit diluted, schizophrenia. With a certain degree of tentativeness, I would like to go further and suggest that this cultural schizophrenia is especially marked in our institutions of higher learning. Members of the academy take more to heart the western strictures against anything believed to be anti-rational such as all notions of metaphoricity. Associated with that they cultivate a professional concern for 'accuracy' of definition, caution in analysis, neutrality, formality and redundancy in expression, and 'reasonableness' of finding.

[16] Gregory Bateson, *Steps to an Ecology of the Mind*, Paladin, St Albans, 1973, pp. 163–66, 177, 181–83.

Their language and thinking become reified, and no matter how abstract, concrete. All this promotes the transmission to subsequent generations of this particular cognitive/psychological disposition, the extremity of which Bateson describes as schizophrenia. On the other hand, the man in the street faces no such comparable demands and expectations. He is more liable, therefore, to be more indifferent, even negligent, in his thinking. He probably cares less for inconsistency, ambiguity and ambivalence. Despite other problems, he is less prone to commit certain literalist errors in his thinking.

The literalist appears to have inherited from Aristotle an antipathy towards contradiction. It may range from disapproval to fear, but anything resembling contradiction (seen as a fault in logic or reasoning) or paradox or dilemma or ambivalence or ambiguity, is either dismissed as an error, or shunned, or unnoticed. It is, preferably, not to be handled. What is and what is not being said here is a matter of delicacy and risk. I am not proposing to distinguish a literality, imbued with clarity and precision, from a metaphoricity commending some mystique or confusion. I do, however, express a regret that a misleading simplicity, which can lead to nothing other than inappropriate or crudely shallow and dangerous interpretations and responses, holds so much sway as to be seen as the right, the proper, the correct, as the sign of reason at work. It is not a matter of a choice between a simplification and a sophistication; it is that the former, despite its apparent appeal of neatness and orderliness, ought to be seen as a travesty of truth, a misapplied thinking process, and a guaranteed danger to useful discourse. Literality breeds solutions destined to fail, as it is cultivated through a blindness of insight, a crippling of intellect. A literalist, cultured to see paradox as little more than a poetic device, is oriented towards simple 'either-or' judgements and decisions; something is known either to be X or not to be X; it is not imagined possible to consider the two. One is not disposed to think 'both-and' or 'neither-nor'. The dualism of the copula, the together 'being' and 'not being', cannot be readily grasped with such an orientation: if one knows that something *is* X, then that is all believed needed to proceed. It has to be ignored that something *is not* X at the same time. A literalist thinks totalities, monolithic homogeneties. Of course, one may consider multiple variables and create typologies; but the thinking actually remains the same: each typology now becomes the new totality, pure, exclusive, bounded, as any name suggests: a doctor is a doctor is a doctor is a doctor. Or one may create a duality to allegedly handle the complexity of a name: one may divide the doctor into 'personal' and 'professional' compartments, but each domain remains exclusive to itself, untouched by the other. The personal cannot at the same time be professional—without infringing the law of contradiction. The situation is normally safe: a literalist would not entertain the very conceivability of such an infringement. It is because of this disposition alone that applied social science, social planning and social engineering fail. It cannot be otherwise. Any thinking which necessitates the division and location of human beings and situations into types and categories, all necessarily divided from each other for distinct handling, treatment and consideration—no matter how compassionately and sensitively executed—has to make as many if not more errors of judgement and misappropriate and counter-productive policy decisions as successful, consonant, applicable ones. The human condition is infinitely classifiable; neither planners, governments nor expert consultants can ever place under consideration such complexity. The literalist tradition believes it can because it believes it knows how to handle such diversity by complex internal and exclusive divisions. Being is unproblematic to it; the only problem it faces, and it is seen as manageable, is to know what are the most fitting distinctions to make. To divide is the skill of the literalist. But this ability has its limitations.

There is a danger, every time we employ a metaphor, and the more fruitful it is, the greater the danger, that sooner or later we take the world shaped in this way to be the only true world, to be reality, given, universal, eternal. While this disposition will always hang over us, it is not necessarily one that characterises our literalist tradition through and through. Undoubtedly, certain classifications, oppositions and metonymies linger on as eternal truths, but, it seems to me that, on the contrary, 'modern times' can generally be credited with a steady turnover of ideas. Literalism, therefore, is not essentially to be understood as a commitment to some set of ossified, rigid beliefs about the nature of humans and their society. At this level of thought, one of tangible description, there are, perhaps, few sacred cows. An open-minded, competitive jostling of ideas operates. But the literalist fallacy remains steadfast; the changes, no matter how frequent, are superficial and of limited value. Nothing has been learned by the experience of change; they have not 'learned to learn' in the words of Bateson. One division, one classification has been replaced by another; one belief has replaced another belief; one faith is changed by another. It may be that one day, X is considered right; the next, Y is considered right and X is now dismissed as wrong or irrelevant. The colour of the balls may be myriad, but only one, at any one time, is juggled. What has not changed is the belief in faith and a faith in certain beliefs.

They have not learned to realise that they have merely replaced one metaphor by another, one perspective by another; and, because of this they do not realise that there is no reason to assume that the new metaphor is any better than the one just replaced—on the contrary, those adopting a new idea automatically assume its superiority, presumably because of its newness. They do not reflect upon the idea that this new thought (metaphor), being yet another human construction, and thereby being some interactional product of themselves and the 'outside' world, is likely to bear some homologous relation with their previous thoughts. In place of some such self-reflexiveness, from which they could have learned something about their own disposition, they tend to explain a new idea in terms of an improved technique or more careful an analysis. They fail to appreciate the idea that being a metaphor, the new thought will have necessitated the suppression of differences just as much as the old thought did; they will, in other words, once again need to treat the new idea with care; to remind themselves regularly that it is both true and false rather than wasting their time comparing it, in a crudely digital fashion, to the idea just replaced. They do not question the language being used, to search for its own hidden agendas, for its own associations and oppositions which may seduce the user along paths unintended and undesirable. They never learn, in other words, that every use of language is necessarily at the same time an abuse of language. In their innocence they fail to see slippage, they fail to challenge, to work with and against, and to work the differences. The new idea is treated as one would a billiard ball, complete in itself, distinct from other balls, independent except for moments of impact, the sole mode of interaction between foreign and sovereign bodies; impersonal and unchanging over time, a bodily atom, to be manipulated freely and wholly through the agency of its user. It is not just that literalists have an inordinate faith in the language of their ideas, which in a way they have; but more significantly they have too great a faith in themselves; they believe that they are in control, like the best of nineteenth century rationalists, that everything is in place, in order, their order, and that through their reasonable and rigorous manipulation, they can comprehend this comprehensible world. What they achieve is a caricature of knowledge bearing little relationship to social reality, and one that if used as guidelines to social policy can wreak havoc on human lives—the damage done to the so-called Third World by economic theories and modern technology being their most notorious but little noted product. It can all make good sense on paper; it is all 'literally' sound and true, but it should remind us that thinking can be dangerous. Thinking, no matter how rationally and logically done, can achieve nothing more than fanciful and even grotesque language-worlds which will always bear a questionable relation to reality. But literalist thinking miscues most, just as the schizophrenic miscues when he knocks and enters the room each time he passes. So much of our western knowledge is as superficially close to, yet removed from, life as the unproblematised reading of the notice on the door.

It is time to draw this discussion to a close, without pretending that we have closed off the topic. Language and thought ought no longer be considered two distinct phenomena with some unambiguous relationship. Somewhere they fuse, become each other; the meeting point, the mediation and the constant transmissions seem beyond any complete comprehension, yet undoubtedly appear to reverberate with metaphor: that is, with a specifically limited number of modes of association (I do not take my seven types as necessarily the final word) and a related play of associations within language itself. Separately and together, language and thought have no beginnings, no origins, no proper place or fixture, and no finality in the flow of metaphoric association. There is neither certainty nor closure: the very metaphoricity of 'being', the inevitability of similarity *and* difference, of 'being' and 'not being' at the same time guarantees that.

Seen in this light, we can say that the operation of thinking is beyond our conscious control and awareness; it is an unconscious process. And, as Piaget says: 'the concept of the unconscious itself is completely general; it is not all restricted to the emotional life. In any area of cognitive functioning, all the processes are unconscious. We are conscious of the result, not of the mechanism.'[17] Consciousness

---

[17] Quoted by N. Gould in 'The Structure of Dialectic Reason: A Comparative Study of Freud's and Lévi-Strauss' Concepts of Unconscious Mind', *Ethos*, 6, 4, 1978, p. 191.

may provide the setting for thought, the theme, the attention, the retention, the possibility of planned replication and likely more, but it (and I use the words 'consciousness' and 'unconsciousness' with care and warning) does not do the thinking. Obviously I cannot accept conventional ideas of rational thought, nor the Freudian dichotomy of a 'primary process' characterised by metaphor and a 'secondary process' characterised by language-based rational thought. Nor can I continue to privilege such valorised terms as induction, deduction and causality. Without specifically identifying them as examples of certain metaphoric modes, Arieti's explanation puts them in their rightful perspective.

> In induction, the mode of *contiguity* makes us associate A and B because we have observed that B has followed A many times. The mode of *similarity* makes us associate all A's with all B's. The mode of *pars pro toto* causes us to extend to the whole series of A's and B's what we have observed in the segment of the series. (original emphasis)[18].

Rationality rightfully loses its aura as the acme of mature, sound and reliable thought (if not the hallmark of western greatness) seen in this light. It is nothing more than part of the armoury of metaphor, and this carries no guarantees with it. Metaphor is just a metaphor, a thought is just a thought. But we can do no better. We can, however, constantly shift between believing our necessary self-deceptions, in order to exploit the thought in mind, and disclaiming them for what they are. Culturally we need to remind ourselves that we metaphorise for good and bad, so there may be little virtue in hanging on to, let alone deifying, some stale thought or expression we, more likely than not, inherited. Our literalist tradition, unfortunately, believes otherwise. And it seems to live and proselytise its faith from pulpits of authority.

---

[18] S. Arieti, *The Intrapsychic Self*, Basic Books, New York, 1967, p. 193.

II

The
West
and
Modern
Times

Social Policy and its Rationality

5

BY NOW, certain readers may concede some useful role of metaphor in the various academic disciplines of the social sciences, but be still reluctant to admit any place for it in the day-to-day practicalities of business or public office. So, let us now consider the activity of social policy, an area normally characterised by rational investigation, commonsense, various expertise and economic constraints. The greyness of government administration and planning seems the last place to demand grand theory or abstract models let alone metaphor.

Donald Schön has written persuasively about the significant role 'generative metaphor' plays in the domain of social policy.[1] His contribution is an admirable one, so much so that my more radical understanding of the role of metaphor in all thinking, and therefore in social policymaking as well, is best presented through a critical commentary on his work.

[1] D.A. Schön, 'Generative metaphor: a perspective on problem-setting in social policy', in *Metaphor and Thought*, Cambridge University Press, Cambridge, 1979, pp. 254–82. Specific references to details of the article will be footnoted in the text as they occur. This chapter originally appeared in a shorter version in *Knowledge: Creation, Diffusion, Utilization*, 7, 2, Dec. 1985, pp. 191–215.

Schön sees metaphor as central to how we think about things, make sense of reality, and set our problems. This particular way of seeing he labels 'generative metaphor', which is both the process of thinking and its product, a particular perspective. In the domain of social policy, it directs us to the problem-setting end of the task, which then largely determines the solution to be sought.

Such problem settings are mediated by participants' stories or descriptions of the situation; descriptions that crystallise, consciously or otherwise, around organising metaphors that sew the now-related items into a sense. Social services, for example, may be seen as 'fragmented' and, as with a broken vase, deemed bad. The solution, which 'under the spell of metaphor appears obvious,' is coordination. If we realise that we are herein thinking metaphorically, we can more easily be aware that our perspective is a partial one of emphasising certain similars the metaphor creates at the expense of ignoring certain dissimilars. We can then, perhaps, view the situation in a different perspective, i.e., say within the metaphoric perspective of 'autonomous', which is not necessarily bad, and for which the solution 'coordination' is far from being good. Attention to this inevitable metaphoricity thus enables us to 'recognize descriptions as descriptions rather than as reality' (p.280) and alerts us to the 'dilemmas' of conflicting frames that cannot be resolved by any simple recourse to facts, as the facts will be different for each metaphoric perspective. Rather, the dilemma needs to be 'dissolved' by constructing a new frame that integrates or coordinates the old. The mode of inquiry involved here, Schön argues, is again closely related to metaphoric thinking.

His first illustration is a simple, technological one of researchers attempting to improve the performance of the first paint-brushes made from synthetic fibre. Efforts to imitate natural bristle—for example, by splitting the bristle ends—failed. But intuitive metaphor that saw the brush as a kind of pump produced the solution. This new perspective forced the researchers to look for the first time at the spaces between the bristles; spaces that were now seen as channels through which the paint is pushed or sucked by the constant flexing of the brush. This insight led to producing more flexible synthetic bristles with a performance comparable to natural bristle.

The life-cycle of this discovery, Schön says, is that at first the researchers feel that brushes and pumps (A and B) are similar, without knowing in what way. Later they are able to formulate an analogy between the two; that is, to describe relationships between the restructured perceptions of A and B. Only later still are they able to construct a general model for which a redescribed A and redescribed B are now instances. That is, they have created a new technological category, a 'pumpoid' (which also includes mops and washclothes).

Schön's major illustration comes from housing policy. Here, as everywhere, problems are not given; rather, they are constructed by humans to make sense of complex situations. He delineates the dilemma created by the two housing policy metaphors dominating American thinking in recent decades. One, 'urban renewal', sees the once healthy city community as now diseased and blighted. Its solution is to replan and reconstruct the community as a whole, with 'new homes, new schools, churches, parks, streets, and shopping centres' constituting a balanced, integrated redesign of the entire area. The second views these environments as 'natural communities', with established supports, formal and informal, providing comfort and belonging. Such areas are seen as 'comfortable, homelike and picturesque', no longer places of disease and decay. Instead of rebuilding and relocating, the goal is now to reinforce and rehabilitate.

Thus, two sets of naming and framing present two problems, each with compelling, even obvious solutions—but contradictory ones. Furthermore, the solutions have strong normative connotations, as in each case the moral judgement attached to the labels (disease and natural community) is carried over to the living areas under consideration. This 'normative dualism', Schön suggests, is common in social policy through the inevitable operation of generative metaphor, even though we commonly are unaware of the process. 'When we see A as B, we carry over to A the evaluation implicit in B' (p. 265).

'Critical inquiry', that author continues, is now needed in order to become aware of the differences hidden in the similarities expressed in each metaphor; to determine in what precise ways certain things are similar and others are not; to consider for the first time things ignored by the existing perspectives. 'Questions such as these call attention to what is metaphorical about generative metaphor.... Then our diagnoses and prescriptions cease to appear obvious and we find ourselves involved, instead, in critical inquiry' (p. 268). In other words, being conscious that we are inevitably thinking metaphorically results in 'frame awareness', even when this necessitates the difficult task of unearthing the metaphors being used (they are not always conveniently transparent in words such as 'disease' or 'fragmented'). This awareness is likely to bring us into 'more explicit confrontation with frame conflict'; a situation that cannot allow simple compromise as the solution because we are dealing with 'ends which are incommensurable' (p. 269). Schön's solution lies in 'frame restructuring'; that is, a further conscious application of generative metaphor, this time to integrate the conflicting frames by constructing a new problem-setting story. This dissolves the dilemma, because the 'conflicting purposes are redescribed so that they no longer conflict.' To best achieve this, participants need to become involved 'in a particular concrete situation—experiencing the phenomena of the problem', thereby attending 'to new features and relations of the phenomena, and in renaming, regrouping and reordering those features and relations. . . . The participants themselves are also redescribed in ways that capture different features and relations to each other' (p. 270).

Schön's example of frame restructuring is the so-called 'sites and services' solution to the housing of the poor in many Third World cities. Squatter settlements were considered illegal by municipal officials who insisted on nothing other than public housing programmes no matter how inadequately they coped with the problem; yet the former continued to flourish and be defended by the squatters themselves. Sites and services was a 'complex co-ordination of the two perspectives. . . . The competitive game formerly played between municipal officials, in which officials seek to control and punish while squatters seek to evade control, gives way here to a collaborative game in which officials and settlers both win' (p. 273).

Schön's argument joins description and prescription. He insists that we are constantly engaged in generative metaphor in social policy, but normally intuitively and unconsciously. Awareness enhances our willingness and ability to create new problem settings and solutions, in particular when we are faced with conflicting, incommensurable purposes. He rejects as 'radically unsatisfactory' solutions such as 'extended instrumentalism' (trade-offs) and 'institutionalised competition' (the bargaining table or the marketplace). Frame restructuring, a reinterpretation of the situation that dissolves the conflict, is his desired option; and this is a highly conscious re-application of generative metaphor.

I agree with Schön that metaphor is unavoidable in the creation and formulation of social policies, because, as I have argued, I believe that metaphor underpins all thought. I also agree that awareness of this situation is desirable, because knowing what we are actually doing has two benefits. First, we are alert to the metaphoric nature of the problem as set; that it is a perspective about some similarity, which has to ignore the differences in the complexity of reality for its value as metaphor to act. Second, we can assume that alternative metaphoric perspectives also exist potentially, and that these will create different relevant facts, different relations, and ignore different differences. Both implications follow once we 'recognise descriptions as descriptions rather than reality' in Schön's apt phrase.

Sometimes two or more metaphors of a social phenomenon may be cumulative; that is, they can coexist complementarily. More often, two metaphors are mutually incongruous; one cannot be easily considered while the other is under discussion. Such incongruous metaphors can, however, be brought together once some third metaphor is created that actually integrates them. Many examples at all levels of discourse could be cited here; however, one will suffice: the many and various efforts these days to synthesise a social theory embracing Marxism and Freudianism. Sometimes two metaphors are conflicting or contradictory about the same apparent subject matter. They can be jointly discussed, but both cannot be pursued simultaneously, as the respective policy implications exclude each other. One negates the other. To characterise a situation as both autonomous and interdependent could be an example of such conflicting analysis. This contradiction cannot be resolved; it may, however, be dissolved by a third metaphor that replaces the first two, or by a radically new one that actually integrates the contradiction. Finally, two metaphors may be incommensurable; that is, each is meaningful within mutually exclusive epistemologies. Here, the possibility of an integrating third metaphor is even more rare. However, we could perhaps suggest psychosomatic analysis, diagnosis, and treatment within western medicine as an illustration of such an endeavour.

Judgements such as contradiction, conflict, incompatibility, and incommensurability are relative only to some moment of understanding and to the current boundaries of knowledge. Theoretically and practically, what is incommensurable one day may be compatible the next, provided a new integrative metaphoric insight has been acquired. These distinctions, which are by no means offered as definitive, call into question the ease with which Schön reaches certain attractive conclusions. More on that later. For the moment we need to be concerned with foundation descriptions of what metaphors are and what is entailed in their use.

Let us commence with Schön's apparent worry about the 'obviousness' of metaphor, for this anxiety betrays a mistaken appreciation of what is involved. Note his repeated concern: 'Under the spell of metaphor, it appears obvious that fragmentation is bad and coordination, good. But this sense of obviousness depends very much on the metaphor remaining tacit' (p. 255). Later, in discussing 'normative dualism', that is, 'when we see A as B, we carry over to A the evaluation implicit in B,' the author says,

> It is typical of diagnostic/prescriptive stories such as these that they execute the normative leap in such a way as to make it seem graceful, compelling, even *obvious*. A situation may begin by seeming complex, uncertain, and indeterminate. If we can once see it, however, in terms of a normative dualism such as health/disease or nature/artifice, then we shall know in what direction to move. Indeed the diagnosis and the prescription will seem *obvious*. This sense of the *obviousness* of what is wrong and what needs fixing is the hallmark of generative metaphor in the field of social policy. But that which seems *obvious* to the unreflecting mind may upon reflection seem utterly mistaken. Insofar as generative metaphor leads to a sense of the *obvious*, its consequences may be negative as well as positive (pp. 265–66).

And finally, in reiterating his solution, he says,

> In order to dissolve the *obviousness* of diagnosis and prescription in the field of social policy, we need to become aware of, and to focus attention upon, the generative metaphors which underlie our problem-setting stories (p. 266, my emphasis throughout).

To be obvious carries an indictment: to be 'plain and open to the eye or mind', to be 'perfectly evident', to be 'palpable' (Oxford English Dictionary). It connotes a slack if not irresponsible satisfaction with the mere appearance of things. But worse, one has been fooled: what is obvious only *seems* obvious (notice Schön's use of words). Careful reflection (the hallmark of a thinker) produces, not the obvious opposite of obvious, the 'unobvious', but the 'truth'! What is obvious is apparently false to Schön; what is not obvious he takes as accordingly true. He has aptly but unintentionally illustrated the operation of 'normative dualism' in his 'diagnostic-prescriptive story' of social policymaking! And it seems obvious!

As we have seen, the seven modes of thinking are distinct yet related. Together they form a loose system in the sense that thought proceeds from one aspect to another as if necessarily entailed. To think at any length about anything means to think about its classification, its contiguous attributes, its opposites, its parts, its translations, its worth, and its analogies. Together these comprise internally coherent knowledge about the subject, be that a matter of mundane affairs or profound scholarship. Each entailment obviously follows.

So, to think of the metaphor 'fragmentation' allows us to think of, for example, its relations by opposition, such as monolithic, complete, or total; its relations of contiguity, such as weak, incomplete, or divided; its synecdochic relations, such as fragmentation being a localised symptom of a 'larger' phenomenon, for example, inattention, carelessness, or uneven development; its isomorphic relations, such as a fragmentation here being linked to a parallel fragmentation there; its translation in other forms, for example, structural fragmentation appearing as sectional independence or as parochial sentiment; its exchange value, such as greater dedication or transfer of loyalty being the cost or price of maintaining or altering the current situation. Whatever particular thoughts we have about fragmentation, certain other thoughts will automatically follow, and certain further thoughts, equally automatically, will not follow. This is inevitable. It is likewise inevitable that judgements of worth will be an integral part of any such resulting system of thought. We are foolish to assume that cognition is immune from evaluative judgements or, indeed, from our passions. We will approve of some and, possibly though not necessarily, disapprove with equal passion of their opposites.

So, whatever is 'obvious' in our understanding of social reality is not so because we have been duped by our hasty and innocent intuitions, but because our thoughts, conscious or unconscious, operate necessarily in such a way. Whatever we have thought will seem obvious to us; what others think may not. At times we may have 'second thoughts': and see, for example, certain synecdochic or metonymic implications in a fresh way. Once we have done this, it will now seem obvious to us. We have not stopped thinking metaphorically, we have merely changed our metaphors. Just as grief may be seen in western cultures as an obvious metonym of death, so may relief. If we accept grief, further obvious entailments about appropriate or likely states of mind and behaviour follow; if we accept relief, a different set will just as obviously follow. At times we may lose faith in some accustomed metaphor; until we find a new one, nothing seems obvious. Most of the time we deal with obvious situations. Anything else would be intolerable.

When we are concerned with human affairs in particular, we are not dealing in truths or falsehood; rather, we are constructing a system of understanding, with some degree of simplicity, which makes sense to us. Profound or creative thought merely rejects conventional metaphors for novel ones, replaces something obvious with some new perspective that once discovered, becomes obvious. Intellectual debate, and political conflict, revolve around competing metaphors. The choice we make determines subsequent interpretations of the situation and the nature of our operations in it. We live our metaphors.

For example, 'mental illness' can be seen as a synecdochic symptom of a variety of causal wholes. If it is seen as part of a personal psychic malfunction, the appropriate (i.e., obvious) recourse is to some form of psychotherapy; if as a product of spiritual decadence, it calls for a priest; if as a result of alienating urban living, it calls for imaginative town planning; if as a byproduct of hard times, it requires improved employment opportunities, a better wage policy, and less alienating working conditions; if as a sign of the entire socio-economic system, it demands a revolutionary political solution. How we define the initial problem directs us to the course of action to be espoused. All judgements and all actions that follow will be in one way or another consistent with the informing metaphor. It sets the agenda, imposes constraints on actions to be entertained or ignored, and determines the normative judgements to be made, and even the appropriate emotions to be felt.

Schön's unease seems to derive essentially from the commonly held notion that metaphor is some intuitive hunch about analogies, seeing one thing as something else, even though it is 'really' not. This he contrasts with something like conventional rational thought, his 'critical inquiry'. Although he considers the use of metaphor to be often advantageous, he emphasises the dangers entailed because we can be beguiled by them, especially when we remain unaware of their effects on our thinking. We must be careful with metaphors, but apparently not with rational thought. We must get out of them as quickly as possible; thus, his warnings about prescriptions seeming obvious only while metaphors remain tacit. But, on the contrary, they will be obvious even when quite explicit, and will continue to be obvious until the moment we reject that metaphor and replace it with another, which in turn will carry its own obvious entailments. We are not being tricked, 'under their spell', by some deviousness that is dispelled by a shaft of conscious, rational light. If we replace 'fragmented' by 'autonomous', we have not moved from guileless intuition to cool rationality: We have simply changed metaphors— for good and/or bad.

Of course, metaphors have negative as well as positive consequences; this is only saying that thoughts are fallible. As any perspective excludes other perspectives and ignores all those differences that the insight on similarity has, we are necessarily left every time dealing only with partial interpretations. That is just a more detailed way of explaining why thinking about one thing prevents us from thinking about another thing. All this applies equally to metaphors Schön ends with under the label 'frame restructuring'. Whereas he is overly wary about the initial efforts to set problems, he becomes overly complacent about the quality of the final solution. There is, however, no essential difference. Each is a metaphor; each will present obvious implications; each will be incomplete. He should have realised this, for early on he had the wisdom to say 'when we see A as B, we do not necessarily see A any better than before, although we understand it differently than before' (p. 266). The same applies when we see A as C, D, or Z. Thus, Schön's example of sites and services for Third World shanty settlements may be a successful policy; but if it is, it will be for reasons lying outside his argument. It may have ended a conflict, for example. We don't know.

Schön's complacency is, however, more fundamentally entrenched in his analysis, and again it appears to reflect his implicit faith in 'critical inquiry' as something distinct from the ambivalence of metaphor. It begins with 'frame awareness' and 'frame conflict', which he believes will end the charms of tacit metaphor. His explicit imagery of this process is 'literary criticism' (p. 267), a reading of the participants' stories to unearth the metaphors informing their scenarios. He admits this is not necessarily an easy task. But by his own elaboration he seems to ignore certain lessons that so much modern literary criticism has taught us. Reading a text is not a one-directional operation; the reader is part of the text. Hypothetically, therefore, two readers will give us two readings. In addition, the metaphors unearthed are not necessarily coherent ones; when crystallised they may reveal a co-existence of partly compatible, partly incompatible metaphors, which in turn are likely to be metaphors of even deeper, older ones. For example, underlying a public's imagery about social problems may be deeply hidden metaphors about 'progress', a faith so entrenched in modern western cultures that it often remains unnoticed. Without tapping these deep traces of beliefs, can the reader fully appreciate surface ones about housing, health and schooling? No end exists to any textual analysis; all we can do is call a halt, somewhere, for good and bad.

The participants' stories should, also, in a real sense, be taken as fiction. Getting closer to them is not necessarily getting closer to reality. Schön seems to assume that one is the other; otherwise he would surely have qualified his implicit optimism when he says 'and our interpretation is, to a very considerable extent, testable against the givens of the story' (p. 267, my emphasis). What is the quality of the test? Checking our metaphors against their metaphors for compatibility is certainly worthwhile, but is this what Schön has in mind? And what about the possible creation of two or more metaphors, each equally compatible with the participants' stories? There is no benchmark to test for the 'best'. It is undecidable in these terms. In all, Schön presents this complex process of reading and interpretation as too facile an operation, and thereby assumes a ready success. His optimism is unwarranted.

But what is involved in his 'critical inquiry' that makes it different from metaphoric thinking? He highlights two operations. One challenges the appropriateness of existing metaphors—a paradigm of rational inquiry. But Schön seems unaware that this is done by further metaphoric techniques; for example, by deliberately searching for metaphoric relations of contradiction and paradox. In what way is this fragmentation not fragmentation? That is, in what way is A *not* B? In what way is this environment diseased yet *not* diseased? We do this with any metaphor once we become dissatisfied with it. We could, for example, ask in what way is a paint-brush *not* a pump? One answer could be that the former leaves brush-marks (at least by weekend handymen), whereas pumps do not. If we then isolate (by obvious synecdoche) the factor of difference—the presence of bristles—we may conceive of (by a new metaphor) a bristleless brush, the paint-roller (and a new category, 'brushoids'). If we were to consider a further difference—contact with the surface to be painted—we may then conceive of a paint-spray (and so 'paintoids'). All are varieties of metaphoric thought, whether some want to call it 'critical inquiry' or not!

The other operation highlighted is that of immersing oneself in the minutiae of the participants' stories once again, this time to achieve 'frame restructuring'. Participants and inquirers retell their stories in detail, 'capturing the juxtaposition of events in time, the "next, next, next" of temporal experience, [conveying] the richness of the situation' (p. 278). In a footnote Schön refers to an earlier discussion on these 'figural' strategies of representation that 'group features on the basis of their temporal and/or spatial juxtaposition in a situation, rather than on the basis of fixed properties which they share'. He believes that such strategies 'play a crucially important role in many kinds of generative processes' (p. 283). He is certainly right; what he describes is metonymy, that metaphoric mode based on spatial, temporal, or conceptual contiguity that has often been recognised as the hallmark of narrative and that we use regularly in our daily lives to describe our lived experiences.

It is a descriptive style that comes easily to us, making it an appropriate means by which inquirers can immerse themselves, second-hand, in the details of participants' lives. It provides them with a different level of insight, away from the generality of embracing metaphors such as fragmentation to the specifics of sequential events. Understandably, the stories will be larded with affect as much as with event: The metonymic 'next, next, next' unfolds an emotional as well as an institutional process. From such 'thick descriptions' the inquirers will finally be obliged to generate new ('restructured') metaphors that relabel the situation. Whatever that interpretation may be, a leap from specifics back to generality must be undertaken.

But even if all this 'critical inquiry' is nothing but metaphor, as I suggest, there is no magic involved. Yet in a variety of ways Schön reflects a time-honoured, ambivalent reverence for metaphor. First he warns us of its allurement, its enticing obviousness; then he sternly reminds us that it might be wrong. Now he becomes the innocent captive of it: the metaphor generated by frame restructuring he sees coordinating and integrating the existing, conflicting metaphors, dissolving the contradictions, and apparently solving the social problem. But how? Why? Assuming the inquirer is successful in discovering a third way, a new way of 'renaming, regrouping and re-ordering (pp. 276-77) a situation, its quality is no different from that of the metaphors it replaces: it is simply another one with its particular perspective and its entailed virtues and vices. It is not necessarily better, and it is certainly not necessarily more in accordance with fact or reality. It may integrate the earlier perspectives, but it may not. This will depend on the nature of the existing metaphors (how incongruous, contradictory, or incommensurable they are) and on the sheer ingenuity of the new one. Nothing guarantees such apposite inventiveness, and I agree with Aristotle that a genius for metaphor cannot be taught.

Finally, suppose for the moment that such a remarkable creation does emerge; an integrative perspective is achieved that dissolves the conflicting frameworks and solves the problem at hand. We can confidently await new problems, because the coordinating metaphor also has to ignore certain other differences. Merely being the third metaphor does not alter any of its metaphoric attributes. That is how it has to be: there are no final solutions, no total metaphors, no embracing comprehensiveness.

We can now turn to the lacunae in Schön's account: two omissions that reflect both a restricted notion of metaphor and an ingenuous appreciation of social policymaking. In a way, both weaknesses could be crystallised by reference to literary criticism. For by omitting the metaphoric modes of translation and exchange, Schön reduces his study of policymaking to something more akin to the writing of fiction, to an exercise in social theory, or to an essay in sociology. Social policy is an intellectual and artistic exercise like any of these, but it is also much more. More precisely, metaphor is involved in all these enterprises, but in strikingly different ways.

Social policy necessitates, at some stage of its enactment, the metaphoric operation of translating language-based solutions into human performances. The writing of a novel or an article on anthropology does not. A word is not identical to a deed, so policymakers have to create some imaginative leap of equivalence between word and action to accomplish their task. In facing up to this, they will first be confronted with the awkward question of what is 'meant' by the words they have been using. If, for example, they believe that fragmentation is the problem for which co-ordination is the solution, they will now need to determine what will 'constitute' co-ordination. Do they mean (intend! intend to do!) to regularise, to methodise, to systematise, to standardise, to centralise, to orchestrate, to marshal, to grade, to connect, or simply to reduce to order? Because of the polysemy, ambiguity, even indeterminacy of language, there can never be one evidently correct answer—and there is nothing exceptionally tricky about co-ordination; consider simple notions like 'to reduce', 'to improve', to help, 'to have'.

Some decision, no matter how arbitrary, will need to be taken, here or further along the track of meanings ('but what do we now mean by "standardize"?'). Ultimately, co-ordination, as newly defined, will have to be translated into one or more specific policies; policies that are necessarily deemed in the boldest of metaphoric ways to capture, epitomise, exemplify co-ordination. As with any metaphor in any context, this transformation is likely to be a banal, conventional one; it may, however, be original and, at first acquaintance, seemingly incongruous. Whatever its merits, it will have taken the leap from one genre of language to another, and declared them equivalent; that is, a detailed list of regulatory instructions now is the concept co-ordination. Finally, with its actual implementation by people putting these instructions into operation, the policymakers construct their last and most dramatic translation.

In a certain way, translation seems the most radical of all metaphoric modes. Its equivalence or similarity expressed is based on the greatest illusion: that a bodily expression, for example, is an emotion, a photograph, a known person or place, a political action an ideological dictum. It is also here that while the differences are the most pronounced, they are most in need of being 'overcome'. As with a map, it is and it is not its territory. We would be lost without the illusion working to some degree.

Only with this step can the enormity of the social policy challenge be appreciated. Words are translated into deeds enacted by people, deeds that in turn are intended to transform a social problem into a social solution. Words become acts, become values: translation effects a chain of metamorphosis.

That this metaphoric translation so often actually fails to produce the intended goals ought not too readily be laid at the feet of 'incompetent' or 'unconcerned' policymakers. Their task is daunting and chancy. Indeed, the very exercise of pinpointing the moment of error (were it to fail) is a hazardous if not futile one. Was the original metaphor misconceived? Or its first translation? Or its final, enacted form? No reliable benchmarks exist to guarantee the success of each imaginative step; nor in retrospect, to determine the particular point of 'aberration'.

More significantly, the inevitable limitation of metaphor in social policy, and by that I mean the limits of thinking about affecting change in any human situation, should now be quite evident. Policymakers cannot, as can fiction-writers or scholars, merely play intellectually with the similarities entailed in any metaphor and ignore the differences that it ignores. Social environments can never 'fit' a metaphor, they are too complicated for that: an alcoholic is not just an alcoholic, a broken home is not just that, a depressed environment is not just that. It is because of the richness of reality that all social policy must, in one way or another, always fail, or at least fall short. By restricting social policy metaphor to its language-based intellectual processes, Schön abstracts it from its most demanding and ultimately self-defeating moments of translation into social operation, allowing himself a degree of unwarranted optimism and complacency. It is foolhardy to expect much from any policy whatsoever. Perhaps we should see social policies as little more than moments in the continuous history of a situation, as constant, ever-so-human beginnings rather than periodic ends. In this regard, one limited comparison with scholarship or art is appropriate: We do not expect any opus, no matter how fine, to settle matters.

Schön's second lacuna is his neglect of exchange, a metaphoric mode in social policy as unavoidable as that of translation. This focuses on those judgements of value, worth, price, or cost that all participants make, one way or another, and which further determine the nature of the final agreement. Metaphors are negotiated. Options are weighed by all concerned parties, each calculating the conceivable alternatives in terms of likely rewards and forfeits.

No interests are permanent, exclusive, exhaustible or universal. They are sensed each time by participant parties when faced with a particular set of new demands or opportunities. Such an 'ad hocism' is not merely because of the complex variables involved, but because no external standard can exist to provide any permanent measure of values. Rather, the *specific* values seen to be involved on each particular occasion are balanced against each other. This is achieved by the exchange mode of metaphor. Just as we use our perception of similars (such as seeing a brush for a pump) to comprehend, get a handle on a new situation, so do we use our judgements of value (such as security being worth a particular effort, or a new car being worth a certain expenditure of money) to determine choices, priorities, competing options. In each case we simplify reality, cognitively and evaluatively, by condensing a problem into a manageable form. In each case we declare an equivalence: X is Y (X is treated as if it were Y), X is worth Y (X is exchangeable for/by Y). Again, in each case we have the option of maintaining our conventional images and judgements or of creating novel ones.

In public decisions more than one party is involved in making these judgements, and some form of agreement has to be reached. By restricting metaphor to its one mode of cognitive perception, Schön removes value-choice, its competition, and its politics from his picture of social policy, thereby reducing it to an intellectual exercise in which a kind of collective imagination, unrestrained by other concerns, reaches ideal solutions. His 'frame restructuring' may reconcile, on an intellectual level, conflicting models; his co-ordination may dissolve cognitive paradoxes; nowhere does he suggest the necessary corollary of coordinating the conflicting interests and values of the various parties. He ignores the politics of devising metaphors that satisfy the several parties' notions of equitable exchange. In this sense, Schön's image of social policymaking is mythic. It depicts a situation of an intellectually ideal solution being received by a consensual public unconcerned with its segmental impact on them. A Utopian commonwealth is the apparent, sole interest. Just as he assumed his frame restructuring inevitably incorporates the existing conflicting metaphors by some perfect comprehensiveness, so does he assume, again naively, that it will also be received as an undifferentiated benefit to all. There exudes a comprehensive equality. It would seem that everyone gains the same, loses nothing, and is equally satisfied on both counts. His radically different solution based on an equally radical 'regrouping, renaming and reordering' of participants' roles and relations, magically fails to generate any questioning of the price of this change, let alone any differential response. This Elysian state is comparable to the Sumerian and Andaman myths referred to by Lévi-Strauss,[2] which 'remov(e) to an equally unattainable past or future the joys, eternally denied to social man, of a world in which one might keep to oneself.' He adds, 'To this very day, mankind has always dreamed of seizing and fixing that fleeting moment when it was permissible to believe that the law of

[2] C. Lévi-Strauss, *The Elementary Structures of Kinship*, Social Science Paperbacks, London, 1970, pp. 496–97.

exchange could be evaded, that one could gain without losing, enjoy without sharing.'

Social policy involves a variety of parties that will be affected, in one way or another, by any proposed change. With varying degrees of care, each will evaluate proposals in terms of two sets of exchange calculations. First, what kind of equivalence in value will exist between their present situation and the imagined future ones? Do they 'compare'? Are the gains worth the losses, for example, in power, status, self-respect, security, leisure, convenience, friendship, and effort entailed? Judgements of exchange value are made, no matter how intuitively; acceptance of or opposition to the proposed changes follows accordingly. Second, in what ways are such foreseeable costs and benefits comparable to value exchanges affecting the other parties? Although theoretically separate, the two metaphoric judgements will affect each other: One may be more willing to accept limited rewards—even negative sanctions—if all parties are to suffer 'comparably'. Wage restraint agreements operate on such assumptions and calculations. Of course, expectations are not necessarily fulfilled.

The role of the 'wise' social policymaker now becomes clearer, albeit in its far greater complexity and difficulty. The task is to generate metaphors that not only integrate the conflicting images of the situation but that also allow some favourable redefinition by each party of its value position relative to existing judgements of itself and each other. If all were to believe they gained, so much the better. Schön's example of sites and services was apparently successful on these terms: 'The competitive game formerly played between municipal officials [and settlers]... gives way here to a collaborative game in which officials and settlers *both* win' (emphasis his). Yet Schön fails to show that he appreciates the significance of this. This may be the goal, but it is not automatically achieved with any frame restructuring, no matter how integrative of the old it may be. For example, if municipal officers were reluctant to redefine and revalue their role from one akin to 'policing' to one more like 'welfaring', then the sites and services scheme would not have resolved the problem, irrespective of how well it integrates the existing frame conflict theoretically. The sought-after metaphor needs to be 'remetaphorisable' in terms of values, positive and negative, to suit the exchange calculations of each party. A policy will not be agreed upon by all participants for the same reason; this misconstrues the nature of consensus anywhere. Rather, a policy will be accepted for different reasons; that is, when participants are able to interpret variously the informing metaphor in terms favourable to their own value judgements. These are not fixed (although existing value-norms are obstacles to be overcome as well as avenues to be exploited), they are potentially redefinable through the imaginative creation of complex, flexible metaphoric systems—systems that are necessarily fusions of value, cognition, and affect.

This politics of value equivalence and distribution is in no way separate from the actual operation of all the other metaphoric modes, that is, from the entire process of policymaking. Indeed, astute participants attempt to define the initial problem-setting in exchange terms favourable to themselves. The more astute attempt, from the same beginning, to incorporate the values of others as well. The most astute are those who, throughout the entire process, reduce political disagreement by constantly incorporating the values of others in metaphors consistent with their own. Imagination and flexibility in the creation of novel relationships, roles, and values, for themselves and others, are the qualities most conducive to success. On the other hand, a bloody-minded intransigence is often the face of an infertile mind.

The role of the good policymaker (or the family therapist as a cognate actor) is clearly one of extreme difficulty.[3] Indeed, successful social policymaking is perhaps a mark of higher creativity than that of the conventionally lauded artist, intellecutal, or innovative scientist—if for no other reason than that only the former, perhaps, has to face the entire range of metaphoric challenge.

Having said that, it is now more understandable why so many policymakers eschew as many of its challenges as they can. Thus, the pervasiveness of the two processes Schön refers to as 'extended instrumentalism' of the trade-offs and 'institutionalised competition' of the bargaining table or marketplace—both of which he rejects as 'radically unsatisfactory'. Certainly, each of these alternatives makes caution and conservatism the virtues supreme in all circumstances. Each must implicitly assume that the status quo is not unreasonable; that is, that the problem faced is not a serious one (or is too serious to consider) and is sufficiently coped with by a

---

[3] It is interesting to note that so much of family therapy literature and practice operate notions of metaphor: firstly in attempting to capture the key problem of a family, and then to formulate a preferred model to aim for.

marginal adjustment. Within that perspective the role of the policymaker is to avoid all difficulty and to reach an agreement as quickly as possible. Minimal adjustment is the likely sought-after solution. Needless to say, many problems are left untouched or unimproved. We should realise, however, that metaphor operates here as well, although in a different manner. Proponents of these approaches are implicitly saying that whatever is the metaphor underlying the problem, it is best left tacit; not only is there no need to know, its knowledge may be disruptive to their present task. They content themselves in changing, metonymically, the unexamined current situation by minor ad hoc exchange adjustments. In certain ways, this resembles Kuhn's 'normal science', the practice of unreflective investigation within the confines of a customary but non-articulated epistemology. As such, each has a role to play—but a limited one. For it would surely be odd to judge this form of uncritical and unimaginative policymaking (or science) as superior to one that aims to be self-aware, and to use one's sensitivity and compassion imaginatively to re-perceive our social reality and to attempt to restructure it according to such new insights and judgements. An awareness of the pervasiveness of metaphor will alert participants to both the possibilities and difficulties involved. But metaphor provides no panacea. The quality of its product is without guarantee.

Nothing ensures inspired thought or that such a thought will translate into successful policy. Indeed, we have no way of judging 'success'. There cannot be any absolute benchmark for evaluating social policies. One can never step outside metaphor's parameters to judge it 'non-metaphorically'; and metaphor is impervious to judgement within itself—except, tautologically, in terms of itself. Of course, we can continue to make retrospective seat-of-the-pants assessments of palpable failures and successes. It is not a matter of 'anything goes', of any metaphor being as suitable as any other. Such a situation, however, does not justify recourse to 'commonsense' as the exemplary arbiter. That overexalted criterion, as we have seen, rests on only one manoeuvre: judgement of the new in terms of some 'consonance' with the old; the stale, dead metaphors of our habits being reified into basic truths.

Judgements can and should continue to be made, as Rorty, Feyerabend and others,[4] have reminded us, but without a pretence that

---

[4] This is a major point constantly being made by such authors. See, for example, R. Rorty, *Philosophy and the Mirror of Nature*, Blackwell, Oxford, 1980, especially the

the criteria used are universal, immutable, 'scientific', or unquestionable. We do this already in most areas of our lives, including our aesthetic judgements, with adequate though necessarily mixed results. We can and we do sometimes change our minds. There seems no need for a flurry of Jeremiahs forecasting the end of any discrimination whatsoever.

What has been said about the problem of 'success' can be repeated about the social 'problem' itself. What determines that we have a 'problem' to which social policy need respond? Again we must concede that we lack definitive criteria for such an apparently simple task. We may suggest such things as the presence of contradiction, conflict, or disparity between, for example, expectations and actual conditions, or between a past and a present situation. But none of these can be taken as social facts that unequivocally present themselves to us, as if some things are problems and other things are non-problems. It is pointless attempting to find an essence of the word, it has none. Policy theorists, preoccupied with debating criteria measures of success, fail to concern themselves with any comparable search for the very possibility and necessity of their employment—the definition of a social problem. As if it were 'given'!

Of course, we will settle for something—we have to—but this reflects our social, psychological, or political need to act rather than the unquestionable rightness of the judgement. Judgements both change and vary, and there is little point in attempting to test their validity. Ultimately, the decision is more arbitrary than not; loosely based, I suspect, on perceived differences rather than positive identities. What degree of determination will derive from current cultural values, or their sudden change, and not from epistemological principles. When we dispute the characterisation of a situation, say, between that of fragmentation and autonomy, we are in no way settling a dispute over whether a problem exists or not. We are assuming there is one, and are engaged only in naming it as '*this* problem' or '*that* problem'. Any situation whatsoever can be labelled, and determined accordingly, as a problem. Our particular values and the strength of our moral indignation will shape that outcome—rightfully so. Ultimately, problems are political problems, in all senses of that term.

---

last two chapters, pp. 315–94; P. Feyerabend, *Against Method*, New Left Books, London, 1975. Needless to say, Feyerabend was misrepresented by most of his critics. In turn, I criticise both authors in the last chapter of this book.

Awareness of the metaphoricity of our thinking, and of the osmosis between our observations, values, and affects, should alert us to the essential indeterminacy of what is a problem, of what is its successful solution, and of what is the quality of the steps to be taken in between. Such knowledge in no way undermines the possibility and necessity of valued decisions being made. It may, however, make us less complacent about conventional judgements, more ready to entertain new ones, and less troubled by uncertainty.

Let us now place the problem of social policy in a broader setting. The process of creating and implementing public policies is not a 'natural' way of life; it is a specific cultural disposition established only in recent centuries and in restricted parts of the world, essentially the West. We cannot explore here the very specific conditions that helped to generate this development; but we may assume such a story would relate the growth of science, rationality, technology, and bureaucracy to some urge to control and change the social environment, and to a strong belief in our ability to do so. The collusion between knowledge and power (in its broadest, positive, and creative sense) that Foucault emphasises seems likely to be central to such a history.

Our western engagement in social policy rests on a faith in causal thinking, in the belief that one can imagine certain thoughts or conditions that will cause other thoughts or conditions to be affected. This type of thinking is, of course, that of metonymy—relating things by their contiguity, be that temporal, spatial, or conceptual. In particular, causal thinking relates a 'before' to an 'after' in some determining sense. Social policy goes two significant steps further than, say, a causal interpretation of past history. It translates thoughts and language into social actions, at the same time projecting these translations into a future. Metaphor is in the service of constructing a change in social reality. Such grandiose exercises in metaphoric thought are replete with hazards, with maybes as we have seen. There is nothing sure about it; it lies squarely in the realm of human imagination. Our faith is surely founded on quite unfirm ground! Yet our modern western culture coaches us differently. We are led to believe in its rigour, its truth, its efficacy. It is hailed, at one and the same time, as one of the great distinguishing features of modern western politics, and as something universal, natural and all human. Mankind, we are taught, at least all reasonable mankind, plans for its future, aims to better itself, controls its social as well as natural environment and is concerned for its fellow humans. By such deeds we deem ourselves rational, practical, charitable and humane. But what is privileged in this way of thinking? Is it any more reliable than any form of metaphoric imagination? Are our planners and their specialist consultants more relentless in their logic, more sustained in their application and more discerning in their judgements than any batch of local poets?

Nor should we be too ready in affirming the positive value of our tradition of social policy by reference to its results. The task of making any reasonable and judicious evaluation of the last 200 years of planning in the West would be an awesome one. With such a caveat I would, nevertheless, suggest that our failures have outstripped our successes in planning our urban environment, our housing, our education, our employment, and our physical and mental health; and that many of the most demanding problems today are the result of yesterday's planning. We need to be constantly engaged in rectifying our own mistakes. And in attempting such an evaluation we would need to distinguish (if we had the ability to do so) the results, both good and bad, of human intention and judicious calculation, from unintended consequences, accident, chance and the mere passing of time. The extent of our failure, whatever it may be, reflects not merely incompetence and corruption (both of which are significant factors in our planning process) but the difficulty and inherent chanciness of social policymaking and implementation. It is this, the inevitable product of the metaphoricity involved in the process, that we continue to ignore.

To believe that things can be made better is certainly not unreasonable. We could, however, be more honest in admitting our limitations and conceding our relative ignorance despite the years of ritualised obeisance to the practice. We could, also, dampen our guileless enthusiasm in exporting this fundamental belief and practice of ours to cultures in which it has never been a tradition; we could mute our criticisms of their often poor replications of such western practices by appreciating their very good cultural reasons why their hearts are not in it as much as ours. One's very cultural and personal identity can be polarised around this issue. We could even encourage the non-western world not to repeat our mistakes. We may, if we look hard, even learn something from them.

We could, in sum, continue our tradition of social policy, but with less uncritical faith in it. At the same time, we could bestow greater recognition on those few imaginative, creative social planners who undoubtedly exist somewhere in anonymity. Aristotle, after all, appreciated 'the genius for metaphor' and, as Schön so rightfully helps us to see, that is all that social policy is. But that is quite a lot!

Perhaps one day a new Magna Carta may be drawn up: a new consensual arrangement reached between politician, planner and citizen in which we all acknowledge the limitations of our past efforts to plan change, in which we all concede the intrinsic difficulty in successfully planning the smallest of things, in which we all denounce a superstitious faith in reason, and in which we pledge ourselves to foster our imaginations for all those chancy leaps in thought we will constantly need in our future, more modest efforts to create a better world.

This new Magna Carta is unlikely to be drawn up if for no other reason than that our education system at all levels will continue, I am sure, to do nothing to stimulate respect for and use of the imagination. It will repeat, it would seem compulsively, the modern myth, the unquestioned reverence for a reason no matter how arid, forlorn and blind that may be. Our education will continue to do it credit.

The Reiteration of Modernity or Do I Repeat Myself

The shape of oral narrative is not linear. It does not go from the beginning to the middle to the end of the story. It goes in great swoops, it goes in spirals or in loops, it every so often reiterates something that happened earlier to remind you, and then takes you off again, sometimes summaries itself, it frequently digresses off into something that the story-teller appears to have thought of, then it comes back to the main thrust of the narrative. Sometimes it steps sideways and tells you about another, related story inside a story inside a story, then they all come back you see. So its a very bizarre and pyrotechnical shape. And it has the appearance of being random and chaotic, it has the appearance that what is happening is anything the story-teller happens to be thinking, he just proceeds in that contingent way. It seemed to me in fact that it was very far from being random and chaotic, and that the oral narrative had developed this shape over a very long period.[1]

IT IS a cliché of social science that modern society is complex. And that complexity is usually snown in its division of labour, the specialisation of its multiple roles, in

[1] S. Rushdie, 'Talk', *Kunapipi*, 7, 1, 1985, pp. 7–8.

the fragmentation of its social structure, and in the accompanying weakening and dissolution of its integrative forces and consensus; in all, in its differences, its sheer atomisation, its individualism, maybe its alienation. Whether this state of society is admired or admonished, appreciated for its sophistication, freedom and individual expression, or condemned for its loneliness and disenchantment, the explanatory language is roughly the same; merely the judgement varies. To call ourselves modern is to label ourselves complex and different; an idea like 'simple modernity' would be seen as a blatant contradiction.

Tangential if not contrary to this image I would like to suggest that our complexity arises from our repetitiousness. To be provocatively brief, we are complex because we are so much, so 'monotonously' the same; so similar to our collective past, so similar to each other, so similar to our future. Repetition produces a strain—the difficulty to distinguish; the ease with which we mistake one thing for another, the lack of clarity that comes from enacting a confusion with certitude, the benumbed consciousness when our most novel gestures are nothing more than our automatic pilot misquoting.

But now I must be reasonable again, and proceed with an element of care. The concept 'modern' is a western one, and one, ironically, with an ancient history, being used in the fifth century to distinguish the (its) present which had become officially Christian, from the Roman, pagan past.[2] Ever since, again and again (repeatedly!) the term 'modern' has been used to express the consciousness of a time which views itself as 'new' as compared to an 'old' now past. To call oneself and one's culture modern is, therefore, to distinguish oneself from a past, to declare one's difference, one's novelty, one's breach. The western world obviously prides itself on being modern. Is it possible that we insist on this identity because, at some level of our consciousness, we secretly doubt it? Do we suspect that, beneath it all, we are still what we were, that we really have not changed, that we continue to do what has always been done?

The idea of repetition, the notion that we repeat ourselves, is not a new one. But it was Freud (after Nietzsche?) who gave it currency for our times; who, therefore, indirectly told the modern world that it was not necessarily as modern as it assumed.

[2] J. Habermas, 'Modernity—an Incomplete Project', *Postmodern Culture*, H. Foster (ed.), Pluto Press, London, 1985, pp. 3–4.

It was in his mid-career, in 1914, that Freud explicitly introduced the idea in a discussion on the analytic situation which aims 'to fill in gaps in memory' through the interpretation of associations. But Freud noted that in many cases 'the patient does not *remember* anything of what he has forgotten and repressed, but *acts* it out. He reproduces it not as a memory but as an action; he *repeats* it, without, of course, knowing he is repeating it'[3] (original emphasis). And from Freud's essay on 'this compulsion to repeat': 'We soon perceive that the transference (the relationship the patient develops towards the analyst) is itself only a piece of repetition, and that the repetition is a transference of the forgotten past not only on to the doctor but also on to all the other aspects of the current situation'. Consequently, Freud realised 'we must treat his illness, not as an event of the past, but as a present-day force.'

Freud's therapeutic psychology was a search for, and then a 'working-through', of infant fantasies which, being repressed, continue to repeat themselves in an endless variety of transformation. Transformation is seen as two-faced: it is the same-but-different. The drive or compulsion is to repeat, to recreate the same; the difference is the mode, the circumstance, the form, the bearer.

By the end of his career, Freud sees repetition *itself* as the driving force: to repeat becomes its own compulsion, the ultimate self-deception, the assertion of control over what one, in fact, *has* to submit to; the gradual mastery of one's own fate. One overcomes death, by choosing it in one's own right. As Freud said 'the aim of all life is death'.[4] Peter Brooks, commenting on *Beyond the Pleasure Principle*, adds 'Repetition can take us both backwards and forward because these terms have become reversible: the end is a time before the beginning... . The organism must live in order to die in the proper manner, to die the right death'.[5]

What we are confronted with is a challenge to our conventional western notions of time, of the relations between the past and present and the future, of directionality, of the opposition, permanence and change. The symbols of our time, any time, are those we enact without knowing; they have no obvious origin; we repeat

---

[3] S. Freud, 'Remembering, repeating and working through', *Standard Edition*, Hogarth Press, London, 1955, Vol. 12, pp. 150–51.
[4] 'Beyond the Pleasure Principle', *Standard Edition*, 1955, Vol. 18, p. 38.
[5] Peter Brooks, 'Freud's Masterplot', Literature and Psychoanalysis: The Question of Reading: Otherwise, *Yale French Studies*, Nos. 55–56, 1977, pp. 280–300. This quotation is from p. 289.

them to begin with, the new starts as the old. A certain timelessness is glimpsed. The repetition, returning in transformed guises, can no longer suggest a clear movement away or ahead, a development; rather it demonstrates the pervasiveness, endurance and strength of the thing repeated. The symbols we repeat, individually and collectively, are metaphoric through and through: they are of no one particular time, belonging to the then and to the now; they belong to no one particular place, being of there as much as of here; they are, as well, neither new nor old; rather, they are both new and old. Timeless, placeless, ageless. Living is *the* symbolic activity. And each life, as each moment of life, being the same but different.

A sameness prevails so long as distinctions are difficult to be made; so long as differences are either minimal, or unclear, or inconstant or unmapped. Any society will display some uniformity and consistency because, as it is normally articulated, there is some degree of cultural consensus, a normative order, which is explained by the processes of socialisation and education and by the sharing of cultural idioms, artefacts and rituals. This popular image is one essentially of a hierarchically imposed catechism of cultural values, into which, as a vortex, we are sucked, propelled, eventually to be ejected, moulded appropriately. A passing down by generations is its vertical model. It is childhood that counts; it is then that the job gets done.

All this may or may not be so, but I want to emphasise something else in the creation of our sameness. It is that people pass their lives, unconsciously, forming each other. And they form each other, and in turn are formed by the other, in one patterned way. They make each other like themselves. And it is this, in particular, that we constantly repeat. Repetition is the return of the similar: we 'similarise' each other.

This is done in quite specific and reinforcing ways. To begin (somewhere) we project ourselves on to the world. People both perceive their environment, human and material, and respond to it, according to their own psychic state. That is, the 'external' world is constructed and acted upon to match one's 'internal' world. In a variety of ways we see the world as we see ourselves, and we act accordingly. Freud referred to projection as a 'primitive mechanism'... (as) internal perceptions...projected outwards in the same way as sense perceptions; they are thus employed for building up the external world, though they should by rights remain part of the *internal* world'⁶ (original emphasis). Other writers feel less anxious about such a crossing of boundaries. Gaston Bachelard, for example, naturally expects a house and its dweller mutually to create each other. 'Our soul is an abode.... The house images move in both directions; they are in us as much as we are in them, and the play is so varied'.⁷

We also project and make the world in our image in our tendency to attribute qualities to others which we refuse to recognise in ourselves. By this process of denying ourselves we make others as we are; and, as a result, we become more attuned to those characteristics of our own, now projected on to others. By our own repressions we make ourselves more sensitive to the world, at least to a world defined according to our own disowned sensibilities.

Together, the two processes bridge gaps otherwise separating ourselves and others; they make the world understandable, very much in our own terms. They collapse otherwise clear boundaries separating our internal and our external world, ourselves and others. We believe we know each other, and we certainly act on that assumption, the more similar we believe we are.

At the same time, we operate a series of opposite processes which complement the bringing-together of our projections. We constantly internalise and identify with what is outside. Especially that which gives us pleasure in the external world we introject and make it part of our psychic world. Freud considered identification 'the earliest and original form of emotional tie with another person'.⁸ 'For example, if a boy identifies with his father, he wants to *be like* him' (original emphasis).⁹ In its extreme form, we may idealise another. 'We love it on account of the perfections which we have striven to reach for our own ego.'¹⁰

These processes with which we all, of necessity, operate, constitute a constant exchange, a repeated giving and taking of parts and wholes between individuals. They diminish distance; the sharpness of physical boundaries has no cultural, emotional, psychic parallels. They conjoin to endlessly produce, reinforce, and reproduce a process of human resemblance. To some degree (and the extent is likely to remain permanently beyond our talents to gauge) we

⁶ 'Totem and Taboo', *Standard Edition*, 1955, Vol. 13, p. 64.
⁷ Gaston Bachelard, *The Poetics of Space*, Beacon Press, Boston, 1969, xxxiii.
⁸ 'Identification', *Standard Edition*, 1955, Vol. 18, 105.
⁹ 'Dissection of the Personality', *Standard Edition*, 1955, Vol. 22, p. 63.
¹⁰ 'Identification', *op. cit.*, p. 107.

constitute each other, we repeat each other. Within any social setting, when we address our fellows we in a way address ourselves; and these are 'no mere metaphors', as Bachelard commented in appreciating the ways 'inhabited space transcends geometrical space'.[11]

Modern man (a masculine conception) prides himself on his uniqueness and on the originality and freshness of his initiatives as he trail-blazes his way through a new and virgin life. Likewise modern society prides itself on its constant innovations, its place of unparalleled and creative excellence in the global scene, one which the less fortunate societies, still encumbered by rigid adherence to traditional ways, aspire to. Such a pride is so conscious and overt, so articulated, that modern western man endlessly repeats his own self-advertisement: that he does not repeat. Our manufactured culture, as distinct from our psychic culture, celebrates our novelty. Our cultural artefacts acclaim linearity. It is not an accident that the narrative dominates western fiction, and that biography and autobiography were born here as well, and flourish. That, structurally, they follow the one pattern of the laying out of a story line, one step after the other, a development, a study of an evolution, a growth, a determined path of change. It is the revealing, the unfolding, the creating of something new. Our academic histories as well. The serious and the leisure cultures emulate each other. The form, a constant simulation. A history will trace a birth or a death, a rise or a decline in the manner of a novel. Things follow from each other, replace each other, move on from each other. Each journey its purpose; its completion its sign of success.

The western need for this repetition, this constant re-enactment that we do not repeat, surely declares, as it hides, a vulnerability. We quickly become defensive when our rules are broken; when, for example, Jean Luc Godard makes films which fracture this hallowed sequence. An anger is displayed instantly. And when he conjures up a telling joke, people smile, but diconcertingly: once asked rhetorically whether films surely had to have a beginning, a middle and an end, he replied: 'yes, I suppose so; but not necessarily in that order'.[12] The anger is not dissimilar but the moral indignation greater when Michel Foucault's anti-histories are accused of

[11] G. Bachelard, *The Poetics of Space, op. cit.*, p. 46.
[12] Quoted in Godard: *Images, Sounds, Politics*, C. MacCabe (ed.), London, Macmillan, 1980.

breaking all the canons of a linear scholarship. There is no need here to illustrate further how our vulnerable culture responds to any anti-lineal bent. Instead I want to remind readers how this narrative disposition, how this denial of repetition, how this mythic characterisation of the West has inevitably led to the creation of the image of the underdeveloped Third World, and to a particular ideology/science of development packaged as programmes of assistance, to the consensual scenarios of their futures and, it would seem, to their inexorable destruction as unique civilisations.

The social science of development is a western creation. That the vast majority of nationalist leaders in Asia and Africa has espoused this cause in no way detracts from its origins. Nor the westernness of its conception: 'development', 'modernisation' or any alternative expression is drawn from features deemed characteristic of societies already 'modern', that is, the western world. Despite denials, development is westernisation. It cannot be conceived otherwise. There is, apparently, only one line of historical change for the entire world: all societies must travel the same path, that which the western world has already trodden. The non-western world is therefore behind it historically; it now has to catch up. In this sense we unconsciously label it the *pre*-western world.

Whatever is seen to stand in its way is an obstacle which, historically, conceptually and morally, must be removed. The image of the line, as simple and as crude as that, dominates the literature, no matter how sophisticated it may otherwise be. More tragically, it dominates the policies of scientifically-backed and economically-relevant change. Change has to be one-dimensional: it is either forward or backward. The lineal metaphor inhibits entertaining other dimensions, allowing moral judgements to be made without equivocation: that which encourages development is morally good, that which impedes it is morally bad. Consequently, it is ethically legitimate, no matter how unfortunate, to sacrifice impediments—for the future, common good.

Triage is born:[13] the scientifically and rationally engineered path

---

[13] In French, the word 'triage' means sorting out, a selection or choice. I have taken it from its use by Shiv Visvanathan in his critical analysis of science and the violence of development in the Third World. See, for example, his chapter 'On the Annals of the Laboratory State', in *Science, Hegemony and Violence: A Requiem for Modernity*, ed. by Ashis Nandy, Oxford University Press, Delhi, 1988, pp. 257–88. As he introduces the term: 'Lurking quietly within modernity-as-a-scientific-project

of progress takes place only by the conscious discarding and rejection of that which has to be sacrificed. In any world-view which sees only one line of change as possible, which thereby suppresses any notion of repetition, of the trace and place of the old, it is inevitable that an historically–discardable element exists at each moment of development. It is both sound and necessary to destroy this element. Stalin's sacrifice of the peasants is, therefore, *conceptually* no different from the policies executed by the states of the Third World, and monitored by the experts of the international (western) agencies. A next step in progress necessitates, rather just is, a replacement of an old stage. This is the western line—espoused by liberal and Marxist alike.

This excessively metonymic view of global history, a step by step narration of one and only one possible story, destroys differences and traditions, and create caricatures of a homogenised world culture—modernity. We must all end being the same, presumably because everything we must do is to be original. And so, a powerful western thought in its pervasive attempt to create and control a world thought bears a contradiction—but effectively hides it from itself, and others: at one and the same time, it prides itself on its uniqueness, on its belief that it never stands still; that at any moment it has only a future and no past; and yet this state of constant creativity, this maelstrom of instantaneous, innocent newness can only be reached by others by the most abject of imitations. Lives, civilisations are being destroyed in the service of this metaphor. Metaphors can hurt.

If this is a contradiction, let us not succumb to convention and see in it signs of some imminent change brought about by the strain of incompatibility. Part and parcel of this western tradition of linear and non-repetitive development is the firm belief that contradictions cannot endure; that they constitute both the urge and mechanism of change. It is well known that such is the Marxist understanding of historical change, but it is rarely appreciated that a comparable understanding underpins all liberal interpretations of change as well. Terminology may vary from writer to writer but the underlying

---

is the idea of triage. Triage has been the silent term mediating between the ideas of vivisection and progress... the obsolescence of those one is indifferent to.... . Triage is the dispensing with of the Other', p. 272. Visvanathan is not responsible for the particular use I give it, especially relating it as a necessary component of the idea of modernity seen as a line and newness.

assumptions, the basic incompatibility of opposites, permeates all theories of change, and in particular, studies of the Third World and their development to modernity. Incongruity apparently cannot be sustained, collectively or individually; further change to restore a balance, to remove the gap, to recreate a fresh congruence is set in train. Certain economists even propose strategies of 'uneven change' on the assumption that further change (development) would thereby be self-generated. It would seem that stability, nay permanence, within the social group as within an individual personality, rests on a fit, an integration, a neat congruence between all its component parts. Alter this balance and we introduce the irritant called lack of fit, incongruity; strain and tension are set in motion; a change to restore some new equilibrium is guaranteed. The incompatibility of contradictions and thus their generation of change has a long history in western thought; it may derive from the Aristotelean attack on logical contradiction. But it certainly fits conceptually our lineal tradition, our temporal sequentiality, our faith in one and only one thing at a time, the purity of each phase, the impropriety of the hybrid, the path without trace, a future without its past.

But we do repeat ourselves, and we are inconsistent and contradictory. Indeed, nothing seems more probable a state, and one more likely to endure, than one observed by Alvin Gouldner:

> There are, therefore, some things we do because we deem them morally obligatory though, nonetheless, ungratifying—for example, visiting a kinsman whom we dislike—and others we do because they are gratifying even though morally improper.[14]

All change is uneven. The rhythm, tempo and phases of change vary from item to item within any society or individual. And, of course, at any one time, more than one story/history is being unfolded. Together they explode any notion of linearity or of some one, internal integrity. Indeed, the very expression 'uneven' loses its value and significance as it implies a reference to some evenness. That is neither present, potential nor possible. Incompatibilities, contradictions are the normal state of affairs, in stability and change. In themselves they are a catalyst for nothing. Pitrim Sorokin,

[14] Alvin Gouldner, *The Coming Crisis of Western Sociology*, Heinemann, London, 1971, p. 238.

a social theorist perhaps too neglected during the past half century expressed it well:

> In man and society there exists at any given moment the rational and logical with the irrational and illogical, supersystems and congeries, consistency with contradictions, integration with disintegration, synthesis with accumulation of disunited and undigested values.[15]

And what takes off at any one moment; what we take up, necessarily, are only bits and pieces; bits and pieces of our past we repeat and thereby constitute as elements of each new event. We are, out of necessity, *bricoleurs*. What seems impossible to conceive is that it could be otherwise: that we could start fresh, new each time we move, with no reference to our past; or that we remain or build in totalities, wholes, pure systems. We fit together our bits and pieces; they do not slip into some proper place already preserved for them. The fit is that of a rough-and-ready handyman not that of a theorist. After a while, the fit will seem quite congruous.

We can and do change our views about things, however. Potential viewpoints are multiple. We can reject the congruent associations we have become accustomed to, for example, for a 'perspective by incongruity'. Kenneth Burke describes our options and the dilemma well:

> Any performance is discussible from the standpoint of what it *attains* or what it *misses*. Comprehensiveness can be discussed as superficiality, intensiveness as stricture, tolerance as uncertainty—and the poor pedestrian abilities of the fish are clearly explicable in terms of his excellence as a swimmer. A way of seeing is also a way of not seeing.[16]

And we can begin anywhere. Alvin Gouldner, in the work referred to above, criticised the conservative disposition of Talcott Parsons by suggesting that he (Parsons) would call a partly filled bottle half-full, rather than half-empty which Gouldner, as a concerned

---

[15] Pitrim Sorokim, *Social and Cultural Dynamics*, American Book Company, New York, Vol. 4, 1944 p. 142.
[16] Kenneth Burke, *Permanence and Change*, Hermes, Los Altos, 1954, p. 91.

radical, would prefer.[17] Of course neither is epistemologically privileged. And, it is interesting that a third option was ignored: that the bottle was *both* half-full *and* half-empty. This third option has a fascination and a disquiet about it. We could imagine, for example, a fine work or art being woven around its doubled point of view; it would appreciate its richness, declining to see it as a tautology or as a pedantic redundancy. But can we imagine a social scientific treatment of it? One that would do its justice, rather than one which would dismiss it as mutually self-cancelling, or one too readily cowed by the enormity of its implications? Can we imagine a social policy being constructed around it? I am no longer sure about any categoric distinction between art and science—as distinct from being able to allocate most things into one or other basket if presented with only two options—but I am inclined to think that social science, as a 'genre', has yet to earn our respect until it can rival art in richness and subtlety of insight and treatment. Until it does it remains a bore, an irrelevance, a danger.

And the potential viewpoint is endless in range; Burke would be the last to suggest there being only two options open to us. In this regard it seems fitting here to give the last word to Italo Calvino, from in fact, his very last words. His final 'memo for the next millennium' was on multiplicity.[18] 'Knowledge as multiplicity' he saw as the thread linking modernism and the post-modern, and a thread he hoped would continue. I quote at length.

> I have come to the end of this apologia for the novel as a vast net. Someone might object that the more the work tends towards the multiplication of possibilities, the further it departs from that unicum which is the *self* of the writer, his inner sincerity and the discovery of his own truth. But I would answer: Who are we, who is each one of us, if not a combinatoria of experiences, information, books we have read, things imagined? Each life is an encyclopaedia, a library, an inventory of objects, a series of styles, and everything can be constantly shuffled and reordered in every way conceivable.
>
> But perhaps the answer that stands closest to my heart is

---

[17] Gouldner, *op. cit.*, see his critique of Parsons on the grounds of his optimism and conservatism, esp. pp. 182–98.

[18] Italo Calvino, *Six Memos for the Next Millennium*, Harvard University Press, Cambridge, Mass, 1988, pp. 125.

something else: Think what it would be to have a work conceived from outside the *self*, a work that would let us escape the limited perspective of the individual ego, not only to enter into selves like our own but to give speech to that which has no language, to the bird perching on the edge of the gutter, to the tree in spring and the tree in fall, to stone, to cement, to plastic....

The labyrinth, for good reasons, has been employed as a useful counter-symbol of our times, of our quests, both in their relative blindness as well as in their persistence and struggle. It is, without doubt, a timely reprimand for our culture, propelled, as it believes it is, along some cleared path. I would like to propose the detour as a further exemplary metaphor to jostle our lineal culture. It is commonly seen as an unfortunate, time-wasting deviation from some direct route due to a temporary encumbrance, blockage, breakdown. Something to be avoided, a delay, an interruption to a direct travelling between a start and an end. It is a rupture to any sense of purpose; as if a detour may never serve an end, may never act as a means. The detour is therefore in all ways exceptional; breaking the norm, being an irregular occurrence only, and forcing a deviation from any path of expectation. It fits no schema, no normal way of things.

But let us reconsider the space and time between a beginning and an end, a journey, a life, a history, a case, a fiction. In what way does the middle act as an expedient, a facilitator, a necessary link between one end and the other? In what way is it necessary? Which means, of course, it being the shortest way/time possible, each and every step a moment of necessity fulfilling some promise, causing the end to be drawn closer, putting into effect the intention, the germinal seed of its start. Which means further, of course, that one may not add or subtract one jot from that necessary march of development without somehow marring it: by introducing a redundancy or a distraction, or by omitting a vital element in its growth. In what way, in other words, is a start or finish dependent on, or even related to, what happens in between?

Surely we have to concede that things that happen (is 'befall' too unreasonable a word?), and even those numerous mini-goals we daily plan and implement, are nothing more than asides, ephemera, glancing touches to our more significant qualities. They contribute little to matters like our birth, our death, our place in some order of things. All those myriad moments that happen 'in the middle' are incidental to our beginnings and ends. We could forget or delete each and every one of these moments and it would make no difference overall. They are not necessary; the order of things exists independently of their workings.

Let us admit it. In any story or history everything is detour. The word may still (if we wish) denote an unnecessary aside, but then everything becomes an unnecessary aside: there is nothing necessary as there is nothing central. We may as well wander, and indeed, that is what we do—*it* is the order of things. We just deny it, insisting that it all has purpose, that we continue in one direction, that we act with efficacy in the name of some goal (be it no more profound than more wealth, power or pleasure). The journey, all journeys, are detours; nothing *follows* from a start nor *leads* to an end. The shortest distance between two points is an unnecessary detour. If we were to prune a story, a life, of its inessentials we would be left with a beginning immediately followed by the end. The tombstone says it all. But then again, there is nothing essential (and remember that is the only feature being discussed) about those two dates. Even the end bears no meaningful relationship to a beginning. It is, in fact, not the story's, or life's or the beginning's end—as a possession; it does not belong to anything, it stands for nothing, it represents nothing other than a cessation, an ending of a perspective, which, if one wished, could be replaced by another perspective and its beginning.

We could, however, consider the detour for just what it is; and its telling and exploration become the entire rationale of a history. Nothing is then necessarily irrelevant. Any moment, any aside, acquires a value for its own sake, on its own merits. The worth of a passing interest, of a distraction, becomes the sole criterion. (And the measure of such a worth?) Time is no longer of any consequence, nor is the question of route a relevant one. The journey has no order, nor any one ordained mark to gauge an order. In this sense (to speak with caution) we move rudderless, without compass, without pilot. We are nomadic; stopping, starting, changing course at apparent random. And it is our permanent state. And as we go, the 'we' changes: in mood, in pace, in spirit, in talent. Whose fiction is it, in this multi-authored history called our life? Our psyche has a nomadic quality as well.

Traditional oral story-telling as Rushdie retells it establishes itself as the normative form, not only of our folk fictions, but of our lives, our epochs, our civilisations. But Modernity has to deny this; it disturbs its line.

So complexity arises in our times, not mechanistically from the structural differentiation which exists, but from the many, competing and inconsistent ways we operate our social environments. This is best illustrated when we consider the variety and idiosyncracy of the human response to attempts to impose one and only one order, such as in 'total institutions' like monastic orders, asylums, armies and, of course, concentration camps. Primo Levi[19] subtly and poignantly exemplifies human richness in his portrayal of his German Lager experience. The rules of the most ruthlessly dehumanised regime still, unknowingly, confronted limits to its control, beyond which people left their own marks. Even under these circumstances, it would seem, we each continue 'to live our own metaphors'.

But we need to go further in detailing the essential quality of our complexity. I have already referred to the manner by which repetition, the new constituted in an old, ensures remarkable similarities yet differences over time. Is something to be taken as the same or not is at all times an understandable question. Likewise I have referred to the means by which our projections and internalisations succeed in part in making the world similar to ourselves. To some degree we constitute all that which we are not. Together they compose human societies which are disturbingly yet innocently deceptive. So much seems to be alike—but is not.

Such irreducible human complexities are aggravated by our necessarily limited ability to read each other, to interpret a situation. What I have discussed elsewhere as inherent linguistic obstacles to communication must now be extended to encompass the totality of any cultural system. In brief, societies are complex because of the inconsistency, inaccuracy and uncertainty of interpretation. We translate each other unevenly. Irrespective of 'clues' we misread as often as we read well. I am not referring to semantic or hermeneutic errors, but to something more basic, more simple yet more chancy. The inevitable ubiquity of metaphor, the inescapably symbolic nature of human society determines this chanciness, this fallibility of response.

When René Magritte, the self-proclaimed 'thinker-in-paints', created his now well-known work, 'This is not a pipe' (Ceci n'est

[19] Primo Levi, *If this is a Man*, Abacus, London, 1987.

pas un pipe), he represented in oils one of the most constant and inevitable dilemmas we all confront daily. Of course the word 'pipe' is not a two-dimensional drawing, no matter how naturalistically executed, let alone a 'real' pipe. The three represent the soundest, indeed, the best of translations of each other; but they are not the same. No matter how interchangeable each may be for certain purposes, we are incapable of exchanging one for the other with other goals in mind, trying to smoke one for example. One is the other, in a way, while it is not the other in other ways. So Magritte's painting is both true and false, or neither true nor false. But is it the word or the 'pipe' which is at fault, which is misleading? And further, would there be any conceivable way of re-writing/re-drawing the relationship which would dissolve the problem? Clearly not; the dilemma is eternal. If we were to insist on an unequivocal separation between the two, life would be brutal and spare, bereft as we would be of the use of representation, translation and sign. But if we were to deny all distinction we would end up attempting some very strange and unpalatable things.

There are no rules by which we know when a translation is appropriate or not. We intuitively cope, flexibly, with many of these predicaments, but so often we have to take a punt. Stanley Fish once cleverly illustrated this with a *New Yorker* cartoon in which a 'wife' says to her 'husband': 'You say you're sorry, you look sorry, you act sorry, but you're not sorry.'[20] We have no guaranteed way of reading signals, verbal or otherwise. And we cannot determine whether we are being deceived or not. Which message do we privilege if we believe we are receiving conflicting messages? The cartoon-wife may or may not have been right in rejecting three modes of signal for an unspecified fourth. She will never know.

When Gregory Bateson reminds us that a map is not a territory—but that in a way it is—he is not describing some esoteric paradox, but one *sine qua non* of any cultural system.

If somebody steps on the 'Old Glory' the response may be rage. And this rage will not be diminished by an explanation of

---

[20] Stanley Fish, 'With the Compliments of the Author: Reflections on Austin and Derrida', *Critical Inquiry*, Vol. 8, Summer 1982, pp. 693–721, in particular pp. 699–700.

map-territory relations. (After all the man who tramples the flag is equally identifying it with that for which it stands.)[21]

In our daily social engagements we are regularly confronted by such dilemmas. They may even constitute a 'double-bind' for which there is no safe answer; whichever decision we opt for can carry a negative sanction. An object or action will always present to us its double: we are perpetually faced with the basic problematic: do we take it at its face value, as it were, in its materiality, nakedness, or do we treat it, and respond accordingly, as a representation? The point here is not, yet again, to remind us of the multivalence of meaning and therefore the difficulties of interpretation. What is at issue is more fundamental and inescapable. What is to be taken symbolically or symptomatically and what is not? Things do not necessarily come labelled—with a sign saying this is a sign. But if they did we would be scarcely better off as, of course, we would really need a sign saying this is a sign saying this is a sign. Let us pretend for the moment we can hunt down that final sign; our problem still remains. That metaphoric opposition of sign and not-a-sign, of map and territory, of the material and the symbolic, of the sensible and the intelligible—all such oppositions are *both* true *and* false. Necessarily, like all metaphors. That flag is also just a piece of cloth, or as Mircea Eliade has reminded us 'A tree, by virtue of the power it manifests, may become a blessed haven, without ceasing to be a tree.'[22]

Milan Kundera[23] tells us how kitsch began as a theological solution when the early church fathers announced that god ate and drank but did not defecate. In a way we inherit this theological disposition to simplicity: we tend to think and we like to think that things are either one thing or the other; we prefer to avoid the awkwardness and discomfort of double-identity for the appealing truth of one-dimensional kitsch. With a cavalier aplomb we take the other as either a surface phenomenon or as symbolic of something else; rarely the two. Mistakes abound; and they are aggravated

[21] Gregory Bateson, *Mind and Nature: A Necessary Unity*, Dutton, New York, 1979, pp. 30–31.

[22] Quoted by J.E. Cirlot in his introduction to *A Dictionary of Symbols*, Philosophies Library, New York, 1962, xxxi.

[23] Milan Kundera, *The Unbearable Lightness of Being*, Faber and Faber, London, 1984, pp. 248–49.

when two parties concerned take opposite senses. A recent, dramatic illustration of this is Salman Rushdie's confrontation with Ayatollah Khomeini: the one seeing the *Koran* as a book, the other seeing it as a sacred object. That situation is irreconcilable. Whether our perspective has been stimulated by a Freud, a Barthes, an Eco or by any other semiologically inclined theorist, we are still, by necessity, unprepared to think of symbolism with flexibility. Not least in the political arena.

However, as disengaged theorists we are in a privileged position: once we appreciate that human reality can rarely if ever be adequately understood in terms of our dispositional either-or alternatives but demands an intuitive feel for both-and and neither-nor qualities as well, we are in a position to understand, at last, the ambiguity, uncertainty, misunderstanding, confusion and all the entailed conflicts that are thereby inherent in society. When Baudrillard[24] asks whether the iconoclasts, demanding the end of images, or iconolaters, insisting there is nothing other than images, is the wiser interpreter of modernity he fails to face the irremovable problematic just as much as Habermas who, compelled to seek some uniform clarity would, it seems, insist that we settle the matter once and for all: is that tree sacred or is it just another tree? An odd couple.

Such theoretical insights do little to ameliorate the difficulties facing social participants. Even if enlightened, an actor has the unenviable task of having to make some choice; even being fully aware of the implications, actors have to commit themselves to one position. Unpalatably, it seems we must concede that an act cannot handle a situation's metaphoricity. An act per se has to brutally simplify and distort by reducing everything to either its symbolic or its material face: it cannot be grounded on the appreciation that the two are ultimately inseparable. Once again the conceptual world is mistaken for the real.

We can briefly note an implication of this insight for a fuller appreciation of the relation of theory and practice. The dominant western belief is that these two concepts represent mutually exclusive opposites which must remain separate. A minority belief sees the necessity of collapsing the two, and insists that any worthwhile social practice must be informed by theory. The latter, though the more flexible of the two, has at times imposed its own rigidity

[24] Jean Baudrillard, *Simulations*, Semiotext (e), New York, 1983, p. 9.

by believing that the value of any theory is to be measured entirely by its direct applicability in practice. Theory in its totality has been consumed under practice. Such a position, for example, has informed so much of the current debate on Heidegger's philosophy and politics. It is also reflected in certain judgements about the writing of Derrida, which is seen as ultimately unsatisfactory as it allegedly provides no clear guidelines for practice. And so here. It is perhaps unfortunate but unavoidable that we can think about the complexities of the essential metaphoricity of social life, but that this knowledge can have only a limited impact on our behaviour. We cannot translate our thoughts, here as elsewhere, directly and identically into behaviour. Despite similarities and continuities, the two domains will continue to bear certain unbridgeable differences.

This distinction seems especially pertinent in any discussion of modernity, because, through its western heritage, it displays a strong orientation to action. Modern Man seems geared to action, an attribute of some pride. And action is a digital affair; it operates an on/off mechanism. Not unlike Freud's insistence that the unconscious cannot express negation, I insist that action cannot express both-and or neither-nor. In this sense, we can *do* only one thing at a time. But there is a profound implication of this rather banal sentiment. It is this: whereas (as we have seen) metaphoric thought to be productive has to *suppress* all other metaphoric similarities, an action to be productive may have to harm or even *destroy* all other potential actions in order to be productive.

This can best and most dramatically be exemplified by that very western notion of economics which seems to bear little relation to systems of exchange indigenous to other cultures. Western economic theory decrees the valorisation of action and *only* action. That is, according to it, there can be no economic value, and so no value, in *doing nothing*; value derives from doing something—and here is the punchline—from doing anything. Thus, to leave a forest intact has no economic value; to totally destroy it has value, which may then be doubled by attempts to restore it, whether successful or not. Likewise to dig a hole has a double value as it can subsequently be filled in again. A pure stream suitable for drinking carries no value left alone; once that stream is polluted, however, it becomes a sign of value as it indicates the presence of some polluting activity; and once again it has the added value that further action can be needed to restore the purity of the stream. Rectified pollution, therefore, is quite distinct from unaffected purity; only the former has generated value. Bottled purity could be a sound economic move to make!

We are unable to say whether this economic theory itself generated a western disposition to action or the reverse; but western man seems to wallow, unreflectively, in deeds, irrespective of their outcome, in all 'areas of activity' (as we say). Limited concern is paid to the effects of actions; one just continues acting and reacting on the consequences, no matter how deleterious, of prior actions. So much of public policy is blandly, even brazenly, geared to rectify the damage caused by the public policies of yesterday; so much medical treatment is directed at remedying the ills caused by earlier medical treatment. 'Side-effects' or 'unintended consequences' are the expressions ordained to trivialise mistakes when noticed. One tends not to judge, reflect upon, or learn from one's actions; one merely moves on, daily confronting the erstwhile 'new' as if it bore no relation to whatever action had preceded it. This is the lure and lore of the new. Modern Man is indeed present-oriented, and this way of seeing is also a way of not seeing the past and its relation to today. The actual outcomes of actions are incidental; the enactment of them everything.

Modernity is a flurry of activity: of doings and undoings and redoings. Whether private or public, the enterprise is the same: to keep on acting; never to do nothing. The essential repetitive strain. Going over old ground rather than going anywhere in particular. Not unlike an obsession. A preoccupation with occupation: 'we do, therefore we are', Modernity's Cogito.

Thinking is trimmed to match our actions. Thinking has become decision-making. Ambiguity, uncertainty, open-endedness, hypotheticalness, ambivalence are rejected for the clapper-board of digital answers. The outcome seems predetermined: just as Modern Man is unaware that he regularly misconstrues the other, so do his actions likewise fail, time after time, unwittingly, to adequately meet the occasion. One-dimensionally he is unconcerned that his production of action may be simultaneously destructive. He is adept only at juggling one ball at a time. Blindly he goes on, forward, repeating his errant ways. Perceived movement is all. Ad hocism reigns; discontinuities abound, he goes hither and thither. Modern Man is unaware that his repetitive acts contradict his faith in his own progress and development. Even in this, he seems immune to experience.

The complexity of Modernity is not a simple repetition of Babel where communication suffered from the recognised confusion of tongues. That form of public complexity has something simple about it. By contrast, the complexity of modern times rests on the innocent belief that we are all using the same language, that our positions are transparent and that our messages (univocal of course) are similar and reproducible. And this faith is in part fostered by the remarkable likeness between us all. Simulacra pervade everything: we all sound alike, look alike, act alike, but we are not the same. The veneer is false. Dissimulation reigns alongside simulation; each time we are similar but different. We thereby miss each other, and we are normally unaware of it.

'But I never said that' and 'But that is exactly what I said' are the two constant symptomatic protestations in a culture pervasive with simulacra. Through genuine misinterpretation and quite conscious deliberation we misrepresent each other, deceive the other, dissemble the other, deny the other. Who has spoken and what has been spoken are genuine concerns—not merely of a precious and obscurantist literary clique (as is so often alleged by those enamoured with the clean lines of an Occam's Razor) but by most people, no matter how unaware they may be of their concern.

The crossed communication and the displeasure, indeed anger, at allegedly being misrepresented, can be seen to characterise three strategic levels of society. We all know the frequency and the passions of these two protests in the domestic, family setting (apart from one's own experience, see the family therapy literature); in the national political setting (inter-party debate always with the public in mind is entirely based on such a strategy); and in the intellectual setting (see book reviews and author rejoinders as well as seminar discussions—the venom of misrepresentation is unparalleled). What is being highlighted here is not the frequent evil intent (which of course exists) nor the mental incapacity of certain people to understand the other (which also exists), but the ease, the structural disposition, in a complex human exchange environment, to misrepresent. What is involved in all these settings is a dialogue characterised by quoting or repeating the other. We can never repeat in some entirety or fullness the words, sentiments or deeds of another; all we can do is select and, with the passing of time and place, locate in a new context. Such quotations almost necessarily distort. The first protest is directed at what is seen as a misquotation; the second at an unacknowledged quotation, that is, a statement lacking sufficient quotation marks, dissembling, thereby, an original statement. Misrepresentation can also come about through a particular *use* of quotation marks as well. One can demean and misrepresent another by the addition of quotation marks which somehow question more than merely acknowledge. One could make reference, for example, to someone's 'scholarly' discourse.

One of the more persistent catchwords of certain post-modernist commentary is 'quotation'. With monotonous regularity we hear, for example, how post-modernist architecture incorporates some noticeable feature of an earlier style thereby ostentatiously announcing its eclecticism and its own unashamed disposition to borrow or steal. The idea is generalised: post-modernism is seen in part as an engagement with questioning (and perhaps demeaning) the notions both of authorship and of the integrity of the 'work'. The use of quotation, and its resulting collage effect, accomplishes both goals. It is for these very features, among others, that an ambivalence exists towards post-modernism in certain of today's criticism. As we have seen, modernity as an idea is characterised by a constant movement forward, by a hegemony of the new, the lineal process. Strictly speaking, one would imagine a post-modernism ought to be extending, to whatever degree possible, this innovative thrust forward, this shock of the new; but, it would seem it disconcertingly retreats from this path by apparently valoring the past? How can something new appear to be old, at least in part? A disturbing conundrum. The presence of post-modernism and the questions it raises are a constant embarrassment to Modern Man: they surreptitiously undermine a faith in the tenets of Modernity because how could *that* have borne such an offspring? As he has understood it, so certainly, it is inconceivable. Yet the two, the Modern and the Post-modern seem so mutually complicit.

Does our representative Modern Man sense, at some level or other, a resolution to this problem which would leave him abandoned? Does he sense that to the degree that a post-modernism exists it is little more than a highly self-conscious declaration of what some people have long known, but which has been suppressed by Modernity; that is, that humankind is inherently repetitive, that its new is always created from and with the old, that a 'new repetition' is not an untenable and ludicrous oxymoron but that it quite precisely denotes the necessary nature of our moves. And, if so, that the post-modern predates not follows modernity. Artists have always known the worth of quotation. The transcription, the copy, the 'work in the manner of' are merely the highly visible tip of what painters and musicians, for example, have always practised, exploited and, with varying degrees of awareness, understood as the essence of their art.

There is nothing new about quotation. What perhaps is new is the ostentatious way some self-proclaimed post-modernists frame their quotations in quotation marks. They act as if only they practised quotation, as if it were a particular style one may choose or not to pursue. On the contrary, quotation is a strategic word reminding us that we all, artists or otherwise, are necessarily and constantly engaged in it. Each move we make unconsciously, selectively carries something from the past with it. We can never rid ourselves of some form or other of repetition. Do I not repeat myself?

The forms it may take and our dispositions towards it may vary of course. Manning Clark, who recently completed his five-volume history of Australia, saw his country repeating the struggles of other places, of other times and of other humans just as much as experiencing, for the first time, a virginal battle in the New World: man against nature, man against man, man against woman, white man against aborigine, man against himself. Clark was hardly sanguine about the paradoxes and contradictions which emerged. Of course, he saw certain things geared lineally and irretrievably. Technology ensured, for example, that once and for all 'The mighty bush with iron rails/ Is tethered to the world'. But the big things repeat themselves; hope and despair return and return, always to be experienced anew. His fourth volume, ending in the centennial year, expressed an optimism and a faith despite it all appearing beyond human control once again.

> In December of 1889 huge black clouds rolled in over the parched land; the thunder clapped, the lightning shot jagged light over a lurid sky. Rain came down in torrents. *Once again* the rivers ran into the sea, yet the sea was not full. From the place whence the rivers came, thither they *returned again*. *Another* great dry was over; there was to be *another* green year in Australia. Men were *again* to believe they would find profit from all their labour under the sun. The earth abideth for ever. (my emphasis)[25]

[25] C.M.H. Clark, I quote only from his fourth volume, *A History of Australia*, Vol. 4, Melbourne University Press, Melbourne, 1978, p. 409. A fuller treatment of

To Clark, time is that of a fugue. Within it something peculiarly Australian emerges: the archetypal 'selector', Dad Rudd, a character in the book, *On Our Selection*.

> Dad was Australia's Everyman—not a Prince Hamlet, or a Mr. Pickwick, or a Sam Weller, or a Huckleberry Finn, or an Evgeny Onegin, or a Faust, but Dad Rudd, the man who slaved his guts out to win the status of a landowner, got dead drunk and was carried home from the local pub, and did his block, and shouted and raved, and sometimes bawled like a bull, but at other times was tender with man and beast. He did not know why the material reward was not commensurate with all their striving, all their suffering; he did not whine, or blame others, or shake his fist at the 'Architect of the Universe' and ask Him, Why did you do this to me? He did not cry out that he did not accept God's world, and wanted to 'hand Him back his ticket'. He had no metaphysical anguish: he was an Australian.[26]

Forms and dispositions, I have said, vary. A bitter pessimism is not uncommon among the youth of today. I have recently seen one expression of it, which is also a timely reminder that philosophy is not to be found only in textbooks. A sweat-shirt graffito, as cheeky as it is dark reads 'Same old shit, different day'.

I cannot help thinking that the social sciences have a long way to go before they manage to handle deftly the rich variations inherent and evident in the many faces of repetition: in the combinations constantly reworkable between a new and an old, a here and a there, a self and an other. I think music is so quotable: and in particular I cannot help thinking of jazz, of Bach, and of the ragas of India. And the idea of Modernity fades from my mind.

---

this volume by Manning Clark can be found in my 'Metaphor, the Writing of History and Manning Clark', *Australia 1888*, No. 3, Dec. 1979, pp. 53–65.
[26] *Ibid.*, p. 176.

Omnipotence and its Enemies | 7

> *I have in mind particularly the prevailing moral climate of our Judeo-Christian civilization that can sometimes forgive and try to redeem the man who is victim of his passions, whether they be sexual or aggressive, but that finds it very difficult to give a fair hearing to a man who presents himself as smugly superior and arrogantly self-righteous.*[1]

WHAT'S IN a quotation? Not necessarily, of course, what the person quoted actually articulated, let alone intended to articulate. To begin with, the context is changed. Not necessarily what the person quoting is actually articulating, let alone intends to articulate. A quotation just seems a good idea at the time. It may be. Besides, it is often necessary; it may even be unavoidable. But nothing is guaranteed by its use; except, perhaps, a Pandora's Box. And then a politics of the collage. *The Satanic Verses* is one sustained collage of quotations, and so, on an ordinary scale, is this commentary. It would be wrong to assume a finality in either. They merely open up the box, for good and bad; never close it.

I want to consider Rushdie's two recent and obviously well-worked essays of defence and argument: 'In Good Faith' (G.F.), published in *The Independent*, and 'Is Nothing Sacred?' (N.S.), the Herbert

---

[1] E.S. Wolf, *Treating the Self*, Guilford Press, New York, 1988, p. 8.

This chapter first appeared in *Third Text*, No. II, special issue, 1990, pp. 135–43.

Read Memorial Lecture.² It is interesting that such consciously-crafted pieces of writing should display (in my interpretation, with all the caveats that must imply) their antidotally operating parts so clearly. To highlight them is to 'redescribe' their author, and as he readily admits, that is all we can do. How much this redescription casts a new illumination on the works of fiction by that author, and on the works of friction which followed, I leave to others to decide.

Time and again he declares himself a secularist. He makes clear that religion is not for him. To Rushdie, the two categories, belief and non-belief, are unambiguous in their reference and exhaustive in their classification of human commitment. But, unlike many of the other 'disenchanted' modernists whom he admires, such as the cool pragmatist, Richard Rorty, Rushdie is fired with 'enthusiasm' (to use, anachronistically, the eighteenth century English term for a fervid passion about religious matters). He hates and fears religion. It is no matter for indifference. The religious he identifies with the 'True Believer', a position he distinguishes from someone in love, even a devoted lover, as knowing no restraint. 'The True Believer knows he is simply right, and you are wrong. He will seek to convert you, even by force, and if he cannot he will, at the very least, despise you for your unbelief' (N.S. 3). His repeated returns to the theme are significant. 'To respect the sacred is to be paralysed by it. The idea of the sacred is quite simply one of the most conservative notions in any culture, because it seeks to turn other ideas—Uncertainty, Progress, Change—into crimes.' (N.S. 3). And elsewhere he explains the likely origins of his unequivocal position: 'To be an Indian of my generation was also to be convinced of the vital importance of Jawaharlal's Nehru's vision of a secular India. Secularism, for India, is not simply a point of view; it is a question of survival' (G.F. 19).

Is Rushdie's concern about religion (his current persecution notwithstanding) which is a concern with his own secularism an over-concern? He would be reluctant to agree because, in fact, he identifies himself with the uncommitted modernist hero, with wanderers, tramps, tricksters, and devils who have displaced 'prophets and suffering saints' (N.S. 10). He even recounts the contemporary moral of *Moby Dick*, yet disconcertingly fails to recognise

² 'In Good Faith' (henceforth G.F.), *The Independent on Sunday*, 4 February 1990, pp. 18–20. Detailed references in the text. 'Is Nothing Sacred?' (henceforth N.S.), The Herbert Read Memorial Lecture, 6 February 1990, Granta. Detailed references in the text.

himself: 'Herman Melville ... offers us a very modern parable: Ahab, gripped by his possession, perishes; Ishmael, a man without strong feelings or powerful affiliations, survives. The self-interested modern man is the sole survivor; those who worship the whale—for pursuit is a form of worship—perish by the whale' (N.S. 9). Has Rushdie a blind-spot about his blind-spot? Why does he have such a polarised notion about religion and the secular? This question is not being asked because we do not expect such sharp dualities to be expressed these days—on the contrary; but it comes as a surprise from a person strongly holding certain other views. In an awkward, if not incompatible, juxtaposition, Rushdie carries with pride what could be called both 'modernist' and 'post-modernist' perspectives. The latter announces the end of foundationalism and absolute categories, and celebrates the ubiquity of metaphor. Indeed, we could say mixed-metaphor, the 'migrant's-eye view of the world', (G.F.18) as he describes it.

> *The Satanic Verses* celebrates hybridity, impurity, intermingling, the transformation that comes of new and unexpected combinations of human beings, cultures, ideas, politics, movies, songs. It rejoices in mongrelisation and fears the absolutism of the Pure. Mélange, hotch-potch, a bit of this and a bit of that is *how newness enters the world*.... *The Satanic Verses* is for change-by-fusion, change-by-conjoining. It is a love song to our mongrel selves. (original emphasis)

As he elaborates, the book is written 'from the very experience of uprooting, disjuncture and metamorphosis (slow or rapid, painful or pleasurable) that is the migrant condition, and from which, I believe, can be derived a metaphor for all humanity.' What he says here is a sound characterisation of his novels, including *The Satanic Verses*. They celebrate the hybrid; they resonate with mixed metaphors; they jumble, fuse, contradict, merge, and displace. The serious conjoins the ribald, the sacred is profaned, reality is made surreal. Rushdie's fiction is a grand projection of his own migrant experience: a collage of the old and the new, the East and the West, of faiths and disenchantments. It is his redescription of the world, his story, his perspective, and in that sense, as legitimate as any other.

But what is worth noting is his complete failure to translate these mongrel perspectives of his fiction into his discourse about the world and the world of fiction. From metaphor he suddenly turns to literality, from confusion and uncertainty to positivist dualities, from mixtures to homogeneities and clear boundaries, from a technicoloured palette to black and white, from flippant trickster to stern advocate. His discursive terrain collapses neatly into two mutually exclusive and antagonistic camps: he, his fellow secularists and the disenchanted are on the side of all that is good; the religious together with all True Believers stand for everything evil. God and the devil perversely confront each other. This reality is bereft of any shadings, complexities, ambivalences; it is, rather, a very simple, unpleasant struggle between two monoliths, and one without any obvious resolution short of some total victory. This most conventional (although it may be too dramatic to be entirely commonplace) and stark representation merely repeats itself in Rushdie's depiction of literature. Once again there are few options, no mongrel presence, little room to manoeuvre and negotiate. Literature and religion (and politics) exclude each other.

There apparently has never been, nor could there be, a religious literature or a political literature. It is inconceivable to Rushdie; his categories are exclusive, airtight, pure (that word which he otherwise finds anathema; 'apostles of purity...have wrought havoc among mere mixed-up human beings' (G.F. 18).

Despite denials and disguises, when Rushdie talks about literature, he talks in reverence of a sacred place. It demands no privileged language—true; it must be, however, he argues, in the words of Carlos Fuentes, a 'privileged arena'. And he elaborates 'By this he does not mean that it is the kind of holy space which one must put off one's shoes to enter; it is not an arena to revere; it claims no special rights except the right to be the stage upon which the great debates of society can be conducted' (N.S. 7). Its special right to be a stage, with whatever that entails, is unnegotiable.

Literature, which we would expect Rushdie in the light of his historicist perspective to appreciate as yet another historical event, is placed outside and above history, above criticism, above change. He forgets his own strictures and demands for 'questioning and deconstruction' as well as his warning that 'to respect the sacred is to be paralysed by it.' Rushdie denies to anyone the right to challenge this position. Literature is beyond debate; it may only be praised, and this is what Rushdie proceeds to do, and in doing so, forgets once again his own warning: 'the act of making sacred is in truth an event in history' and, thereby, in need of being challenged.

Rushdie exalts literature. Despite his ultimate denials, which we must neither ignore nor simply take at face value, he conceives of literature in the language of a secular religion. He sees it replacing religion and mediating between the material and spiritual worlds, and offering us something new—'something that might even be called a secular definition of transcendence' (N.S. 7). We need to note carefully the weight and value of his following words, because like his fiction, his discourse contains parentheses within parentheses, and as we will see, gestures of affirmations and denials. We need to be as nimble as he. So, bear carefully his judgement on this cosmic function of literature: 'I believe it can. I believe it must. And I believe that, at its best, it does.' The repetition and rhetorical beat cannot be ignored. The message cannot be simply cancelled at some subsequent and convenient moment.

He itemises three human needs which down the ages have been satisfied by religion, and which he sees open to literature to replace: our 'awestruck wonderment at life', the 'great questions of existence' and a 'code to live by'. Along with so many other commentators, Rushdie notes the failure of 'secular, rationalist materialism' to answer these needs. He also notes that 'the soul needs...explanations of the heart...not simply rational explanations' (N.S. 8). But he rejects 'totalized' ones, and he believes 'the peoples of Europe' do also. Indeed, he suggests that 'this rejection of totalized explanations is the modern condition.' The novel he therefore sees as admirably suited to this task for the reason 'that reality and morality are not givens but imperfect human constructs, is the point from which fiction begins.' As he says, the quest for the Grail not the Grail itself is the goal. 'The challenge of literature is to start from this point, and still find a way of fulfilling our unaltered spiritual requirements' (N.S. 9). The novel as a secular religion becomes subversive as well. While answering 'our need for wonderment and understanding' it will, at the same time, disenchant by bringing us 'harsh and unpalatable news... . It tells us there are no rules. It hands down no commandments. We have to make up our own rules as best we can, make them up as we go along' (N.S. 10). And Rushdie pursues the distinction between (his) novel and (their) religion 'And it tells us there are no answers;...If religion is an answer, if political ideology is an answer, then literature is an inquiry; great literature, by asking extraordinary questions, opens new doors in our minds' (N.S. 10). It challenges sacralised absolutes.

Nearing the end of the lecture (and we cannot ignore its title, its figurative and quotational quality, 'Is Nothing Sacred?'), Rushdie introduces a gloss, an editorial commentary on what he has already argued at length. He notes 'the slightly messianic tone' in what he has written, and decides, then and there as it were, to reject the position he has been at pains to establish.

> But now I find myself backing away from the idea of sacralizing literature with which I flirted at the beginning of this text: I cannot bear the idea of the writer as secular prophet....Literature is an interim report from the consciousness of the artist, and so it can never be 'finished' or 'perfect'....we shall just have to get along without the shield of sacralization, and a good thing, too. We must not become what we oppose. The only privilege literature deserves—and this privilege it requires in order to exist—is the privilege of being the arena of discourse, the place where the struggle of languages can be acted out. (N.S. 15)

Rushdie has succeeded in making his point, pointedly: literature deserves to be made sacred, and for very good reasons; but there is some hesitation, some ambivalence—would it not lose its moral edge over its dogmatic opponents if it were seen to bear a comparable mantle of untouchability? So, let it be; we all now know what it could be. Rushdie has not rejected his grandiose elevation of literature; if he had wished to do so he would have rewritten the lecture. Rather, he has persuaded us of the reasonableness and wisdom of his case, and having done that, he has astutely, tactically, withdrawn and denied his victory. He has cleverly won two battles, even though he may secretly feel a little uncomfortable.

Immediately following this lofty, if not sublime, evaluation of literature's worth, Rushdie introduces a humble allegory about waking up in a large, rambling house, in fairly bad condition, in which one day you discover an ' unimportant-looking little room' in which there are voices whispering just to you and talking about everything conceivable and in every conceivable manner; and then one day the talking stops and life becomes unbearable. Rushdie concludes the lecture on this note:

> Literature is the one place in any society where, within the secrecy of our own heads, we can hear voices talking about everything in

every possible way. The reason for ensuring that that privileged arena is preserved is not that writers want the absolute freedom to say and do whatever they please. It is that we, all of us, readers and writers and citizens and generals and godmen, need that little, unimportant looking room. We do not need to call it sacred, but we do need to remember that it is necessary. (N.S. 16)

Before pursuing this curious yet somewhat appealing imagery of voices in a little room we should briefly note that his denial, here, of any absolute freedom appears inconsistent with his stipulation, in 'In Good Faith', that artists must have the right to offend and challenge anything, otherwise freedom 'ceases to exist'. And he adds 'Language and the imagination cannot be imprisoned, or art dies, and with it, a little of what makes us human'(G.F. 19).

Let us now listen to his voices. There are many voices to these voices, but I am happy to read the allegory as referring to a human need (which may not be recognised of course) for what could be called 'optional necessities'; for us, in our imaginative lives, to be exposed to all possibilities of thought, appetite, feeling and disposition. That, unlike any existential social system which must foreclose our cultural and behavioural options for the most pragmatic and reasonable purposes, our speculative creations can entertain endless novelty, overturn all taboos, reassess every given value. So, this unimportant-looking room functions both as a safety-valve, a therapeutic release from the inevitable repressions of social life, and as an endless reference source with which we can redefine and revalue that which we have. It supplies material we can use to redescribe our social condition. It is, in other words, Rushdie's mode of ensuring our potential freedom. We can now appreciate something which that author leaves undeveloped. The idea of 'redescription' which he sees as our only possibility given the death of foundationalism which historicists have wisely brought about, acquires an additional value, in fact a supreme value. To be capable of redescribing is not an optional extra, it is our necessity for options. It is not that that is all we can do in the absence of absolutes; rather it is that which we must do, and continue to do forever. To fail to do so, for whatever reason, is to renounce our freedom, to announce our unfreedom. To maintain or repeat a description, no matter how admirable it may be, is to curtail ourselves, to diminish our being.

For, to Rushdie the first, final and ultimate quality of being human is our capacity to change, to be new. Freedom, the fundamental quality of being, is to him change, movement, novelty. Rushdie is merely repeating one cornerstone of modernist thought. It is, one could also suggest, his particular, unconscious manifestation of diaspora. The migrant is free and becomes the endless wanderer; there is no home, no permanent settlement, no one truth. One just moves on (psychically if not physically), detaches oneself, and constructs anew, always anew. To stay is felt a retreat, an admission of failure, an abject acceptance of some other god in the place and name of the one originally left. Some primary disenchantment, some familial severance prohibits forever a rooting, a permanent name, a proper name, a pure and constant identity. We have here a diasporic reinforcement of modernism—an over-commitment, an excess; to be his migrant is to be assertively modern. One can espouse only one cause: to be free, unfettered, autonomous, new. In this light, we can now redescribe his secular commitment, which is quite distinct from merely being secular.

Only secularism, it would seem, can allow one to change, to move on, because it not only promotes a disenchantment but a constant discontent, an insatiable one. It is, therefore, a challenge, if not an obsession, rather than a place of refuge or disinterest. A demand to be new. A calling—to be creative, endlessly. And a prohibition to remain, to repeat, to be (the) old. To be old, not to be new, means one thing to Rushdie—to be religious. Religion is everything that newness, modernness and freedom are not. It represents, totalistically and agonistically, the opposite of all he highly values. It is not only because he identifies religion with intolerance, dogmatism and obscurantism—indeed his flag-waving secularism is likewise intolerant, dogmatic and on a closer look, lacking clarity. No, he has to oppose religion because it is incompatible with his fundamental faith in a generic creativity. To him, 'religiously new' is a senseless oxymoron. Once again we discover that Rushdie perceives the mongrel and the hybrid only selectively; that he, himself, succumbs to the evil called 'purity' more than he believes; that he, himself, is an 'apostle of purity' against which he allegedly battles. He cannot conceive of religion being at all associated with modernism, change and novelty. As he identifies himself as an artist, and indeed, an avant garde artist, one constantly at the edge of creativity, he has to be secular. He feels he has to carry the flag, unequivocally, militantly.

He has no choice; he has, ironically, no freedom of manoeuvre. What may otherwise have appeared to us as a little odd is now understandable: 'My sense of god ceased to exist long ago, *and as a result* I was drawn towards the great creative possibilities offered by surrealism, modernism, and their successors' (N.S. 4, my emphasis).

Rushdie's image of art as necessarily new, as each time a step forward into a virginally untouched domain, this powerful echo of the western dominant doctrine, co-exists oddly with his ideas of metaphor and of the necessary mélange of things. His image of the new, of change, of freedom, of art, of autonomy is one of an unqualified purity. He should know there is no such thing. But it is because, at some level or other, he believes in such a pure state that he is able to give literature such a role outside social reality, such a grandiose function on its behalf of society. Words are detached, entirely sovereign to themselves; not in their materiality as certain French writers have stressed, but in their ideality, their entire sense, operation and cultural meaning.

And thus Rushdie's total incomprehension of his critics. To him it is so simple and clear; they had evidently ignored the 'fictionality of fiction' (G.F. 18); they had confused the world of imagination with that of social reality; they had thought that what is said in the novel, for example, about the fictional Mahound is somehow related to the non-fictional Prophet. Rushdie genuinely believes his critics have made 'a category mistake'. But it is Rushdie who makes a mistake about categories, by believing so devoutly that they are demarcated and bounded so sharply. He seems incapable of appreciating that literature, apart from being literature, is at the same time variously politics, culture, psychology, autobiography, social theory, and literary theory. Literature as much as anything else is a hybrid; there is nothing pure about it, either in its formation or in its consequence. And there is no pure reading of it; such an idea lacks all credibility, not unlike Rushdie's innocent expectation that the only true reading of his work is one which mirrors his intentions. Naturally he has every right to feel aggrieved, and he more than many authors, at what he believes to be grossly and dangerously misleading interpretations of his work, but he seems conceptually ill-equipped to understand his various critics. He can only propose that his readers are naive and incapable of understanding 'fiction', or are scoundrels or have been blindly led by fanatics. On the one occasion he mentions politics, he uses the term in its most narrow and obvious form. 'The controversy over *The Satanic Verses* needs to be looked at as a political event, not purely a theological one. In India, where the trouble started, the Muslim fundamentalist MP Syed Shahabuddin used my novel as a stick with which to threaten the wobbling Rajiv Gandhi government. The demand for the book's banning was powerplay to demonstrate the strength of the Muslim vote, on which Congress had traditionally relied and which it could ill afford to lose' (G.F. 20). This is all very true, but it is such a limited notion of politics to a conventionally pure form. He entirely eschews the politics of publishing, the politics of his book, the politics of such a book in the international setting of today. His discourse disallows such considerations.

That he is unable to understand his critics goes hand in hand with his ignorance of, and apparent lack of concern with, the public, any public. Hence, for example, his incredulity; 'It has been bewildering to learn that people *do not care about art*' he says in good faith (G.F. 18) (and in italics!). What expectations had he nurtured? And what degree of emotion lies behind the word 'bewildered' used by such a master of language? He is not in touch with a public because, ultimately, his real concern, literature, is something beyond human reality. All art is, and has to be—to some extent. With Rushdie it seems detached from reality in an unusual way, to an exceptional degree: thus the fertility of the imagination, the quicksilver quality of the language, the chimera of his historical characters, the utter absurdity of the situation, the deceptive quality of his similitude, the nonsense of the novel. There is no restraint, no reality principle operating on his words. His fictionality seems quite unfettered. His sole concern is for its creation; all else: its future public, its readership, its consequences seem immaterial. Not unlike certain historical gods, his sacred literature is quite irresponsible. It is autonomous, a law unto itself. Again, a form of grandiosity; and perhaps we can now suggest something further—Rushdie's attitude to literature reminds us of Freud's expression, an 'omnipotence of thoughts', in which 'things become less important than ideas of things'[3] or where there exists 'the overvaluation of mental processes as compared with reality', which Freud associated with animistic or magical thought. He notes however that, 'In only a single field of our civilization has the onmipotence of thoughts been retained, and that is in the field of

[3] S. Freud, 'Totem and Taboo', *Standard Edition*, Hogarth Press, London, Vol. 13, 1913–14, pp. 85, 87, 90.

art' and he adds 'People speak with justice of the "magic of art" and compare artists to magicians.' Rushdie sees art, in particular, his art, 'raised' to what could be called omnipotent heights, an art beyond the conventional parameters of art, an avant garde that strives to be *sui generis*, a literature clawing at the boundary of possibilities of literature (this is surely one reason why his work attracts such extreme reactions). His literature is 'a love song' to the glory of language, for the sake of language. Its representational quality is incidental. He senses the power of untrammelled words.

It was said that Rushdie was concerned to be free, new and different. And that certain other preoccupations followed. We could propose now that this compulsion to be new reaches an excessive form: Rushdie not only wants to be but (secretly?) believes himself to be unique, exceptional, a genius, heroic. Omnipotent? Treasured? He refers to his childhood love of 'cheap comics' featuring the likes of Batman, Superman, Spiderman, Aquaman; that is, of 'mutants, hybrids, freaks'. These books he 'devoured and kissed'. The lesson he learned from these 'super-heroes' had nothing to do with their crime-busting proclivities; rather,'the perhaps unintentionally radical truth that exceptionality was the greatest and most heroic of values; that those who were unlike the crowd were to be treasured the most lovingly; and that this exceptionality was a treasure so great and so easily misunderstood that it had to be concealed, in ordinary life . . . (by) a "secret identity".' And he continues:

> Now it is obviously true that those other freakish, hybrid, mutant, exceptional beings—novelists—those creatures of the most freakish, hybrid and metaphoric of forms, the novel, have frequently been obliged to hide behind secret identities, whether for reasons of gender or terror. But the most wonderful of the many wonderful truths about the novel form is that the greater the writer, the greater his or her exceptionality. The geniuses of the novel are those whose voices are fully and undisguisably their own, who, to borrow William Gass's image, *sign every word they write*. What draws us to an author is his or her 'unlikeness' . . . (N.S. 13). (Original emphasis)

Few, admirer or reviler, would deny that Rushdie has achieved such a signature. The sign is his. With apparent omnipotence, the Sign is His.

With such an understanding of literature and of his exalted standing in it, it is difficult or inconceivable for Rushdie to consider, before or after writing, questions of context, of setting, of judicious self-restraint, of response, of consequence. As it seems difficult or inconceivable for him to consider literature in any perspective other than that of its freedom, novelty and cosmic omnipotence. To tinker with this heroic image would constitute the worst of betrayals.

But if Rushdie achieves a remarkable quality of individuality in his fictions, if he has truly left his mark, the same cannot be said of his discursive writing. Here he becomes a powerful but representative voice only, and a hapless victim, of a particular tradition. I do not refer to the obvious, liberal tradition of freedom of speech, but to another, less noticed but comparably sacrosanct doctrine. It is the aesthetic glorification of art, in particular, of literature, which places it both as the supreme human achievement, the discussion of which inevitably broaches the transcendental, and an object whose place and function cannot be questioned. It is hallowed ground. Literature is perceived as something above mundane reality, as something never sullied by such concerns, and yet, paradoxically, as something essential to life's endurance and perfection. A twin godhead: literature is sacred, its virtue and purity so prized that it can only be revered, never to be touched without defiling it; and literature is omnipotent, so almighty in its power and force that, while it can move mountains, its wrath is feared. Its blazing beacon hated by the forces of darkness. Rushdie is saying little that is new, but he says it well. And he cannot help it.

He is a prisoner of this powerful tradition's righteousness. Literature in general, his fiction in particular, his polarised vision of the world is something beyond debate. Thus, his undisguised animosity towards his critics. Those who suggest his position is that of a 'secular fundamentalism' are dismissed as 'apologists of religion' (N.S. 5); those who wonder that 'he must surely have known' are herded together as 'mountebanks and bishops, fundamentalists and Mr John le Carré' (G.F. 20). His discourse allows dialogue only by the converted.

The tradition he represents is reinforced in its pure self-image by the Other it keeps in mind: in the non-literary world by the True Believer, and in the literary world by the writer answerable and subservient to a doctrine, cause or system. The obscene banalities thereby produced in the name of art this century have functioned as proof to this tradition that it holds the entire monopoly of literary virtue and wisdom. It can conceive of no other alternative. It is as if, for example, the words of Vaclav Havel that 'truth is not only what one thinks, but also under what circumstances, to whom, and how one says it' were to diminish literature.[4]

One really never knows when one starts a journey what unexpected sightings one may make on the way, what seductive detour one may encounter in sight of home, what final spin of the wheel one may impetuously make. And so now.

Freud's discussions on the 'magic of art' and on the 'omnipotence of thoughts' lead, can lead, lead me (choose one depending on taste for chance) to the question of the 'uncanny'. The English 'uncanny' is a translation of the German 'unheimlich', literally 'unhomely'. On reading this I thought of the diasporic situation, the unhomeliness of the migrant, and of Rushdie. And then of its opposite: 'heimlich', 'homely'; and of them both, the familiar and the unfamiliar; and secrecy, the hidden—in one case it being too familiar, in the other too strange. And what of the repressed, and of the forgotten? And I was intrigued to discover that the uncanny seems to be the play between all these: a familiar unexpectedly made unfamiliar, a forgotten secret suddenly revealed, a home being made disconcertingly foreign and unwelcome. The fear and anxiety of uncomforting disorientation. And then certain sentences of Freud: 'An uncanny effect is often and easily produced when the distinction between imagination and reality is effaced, as when something that we have hitherto regarded as imaginary appears before us in reality, or when a symbol takes over the full functions of the thing it symbolizes.'[5] And Freud discusses the powerful role of the uncanny in literature, in particular when an omnipotence of thoughts nimbly plays and sways between the two worlds of fantasy and reality. He reminds us that 'the story-teller has a peculiarly directive power over us; by means of the moods he can put us into, he is able to guide the current of our emotions, to dam it up in one direction and make it flow in another.' And I was taken (aback) by one likely reaction he mentions, when a writer pretends to move in the world of common reality. 'We react to his inventions as we would have reacted to real experiences; by the time we have seen through his trick it is already too late and the author has achieved his object. But

[4] Quoted in 'Political Acts', Tony Mitchell, *Editions* (Sydney), 7, 1990, p. 10.
[5] S. Freud, 'The Uncanny', *Standard Edition*, Vol. 17, pp. 244, 251.

it must be added that his success is not unalloyed. We retain a feeling of dissatisfaction, a kind of grudge against the attempted deceit.'

Could it be that *The Satanic Verses* worked an uncanny magic on a particular community, the Muslim one, here and there, whose realities it played so many ingenious and dissembling games with, whose familiarities were time and again conjured with and displaced, whose received truths were turned to home truths. The reality of unheimlich. To feel unhomely among the homely must be a disturbing experience. That and the wrath it could generate in defence and retaliation is one reading of the book and its subsequent affair which no westerner, secular or christian, could fully know or feel.

III

India
and
Occidental
Accidence

Religion, Politics and its Sacred State

8

SUDHIR KAKAR, an Indian psychoanalyst, recently raises the question of psychoanalysis and religious healing.[1] Siblings or strangers? he asks. In the classical sense of the former, the two are certainly 'wary strangers', Kakar continues, as not only did Freud consider religion to be the chief enemy of science, but his idea of cure was based on rational, conscious thought replacing and curbing unconscious drives and defences (within which the need for religion arises). However, with the innovations of Klein, Mahler, Kohut and others, emphasis is directed towards unconscious relational motivation. Instead of words being the carriers of knowledge and cure, as in classical Freudian therapy, and silence and quiescence seen as resistance, the latter gains prominence, and the 'eyes that recognise' become more crucial than the words that

---

[1] Sudhir Kakar, 'Psychoanalysis and Religious Healing, Siblings or Strangers?', *Journal of the American Academy of Religion*, LIII, 3, 1985, pp. 841–53. This chapter first appeared in an earlier form as 'Six Theses on the Question of Religion and Politics in India Today', *Economic and Political Weekly*, 25 July 1987, pp. PI–57– PE–63.

explain. The guru-healer of Indian religious traditions and this newer type of western psychoanalyst draw closer in a common quest of 'healing': 'the central expression of both in psychoanalysis and religion'. The two are 'rivals rather than enemies'.

We stay with Freud a little longer. Jacques Derrida puts the question of chance and psychoanalysis.[2] Freud, at one stage of his writing, wished to distinguish psychoanalysis, science and himself from such things as superstition, paranoia, religion and metaphysics in their common but differing orientations to chance. What they all share, he suggests, is a compulsive tendency to interpret random signs in order to reconstitute a meaning, a necessity. As he says 'not to let chance count as chance but to interpret it'. To this degree, Freud and a superstitious person are in agreement. Derrida notes 'What this means is that they both believe in chance if to believe in chance means that one believes that all chance means something and therefore that there is no chance. Thus we have the identity of non-chance and chance'. To Freud, there is one crucial difference in the two orientations. 'I believe in external (real) chance, but not in internal (psychic) accidental events. With the superstitious person it is the other way round'. That is, 'he (Freud) opposes one belief to another, a belief to a credulity', Derrida comments. It is not that Freud believes that the world 'is thrown to chance', but that he insists, here, that we must not confuse two domains nor their proper causalities: 'there is no chance in the unconscious. The apparent randomness must be placed in the service of an unavoidable necessity that in fact is never contradicted'. Derrida reminds us that these two contextual worlds, psychic/physical, internal/external, whilst being distinguishable in occidental commonsense, are not necessarily so elsewhere; and, more significantly, not elsewhere in the work of Freud where time and again there is a need to collapse such distinctions—*for psychoanalysis as a science to emerge*. His critical idea of drive, for example, he describes as 'a concept...on the frontier between the mental and the physical'. And the entire Freudian science depends so much on the ideal of projection: the throwing of one's internal world onto one's external reality. As Derrida says, such distinctions are, for the Freudian project 'simultaneously convenient and without solidity'. It needs such strategic distinctions to deny them. A

---

[2] Jacques Derrida, 'My chances/mes chances: A Rendezvous with some Epicurian Stereophonies', *Taking Chances: Derrida*, Psychoanalysis and Literature, J. Smith, W. Kerridan (eds.), The John Hopkins University Press, Baltimore, 1984, pp. 1–32.

clear and absolute distinction, however, denying any 'bastardy or hybridisation', emanates from a defensive, and therefore, dogmatic Freud. Elsewhere, when science (or himself) is not on the line, Freud willingly concedes 'we are all too ready to forget that in fact everything to do with our life is chance—chance which nevertheless has a share in the law and necessity of nature'.

So, Kakar, continuing his practice of psychoanalysis, nevertheless wants to break down certain rigid barriers so long held dear by the dominant western tradition of reason. Where does science end and religion begin? Or, are they engaged in each other? Is modern western psychotherapy so different from the practices of Indian (and other) shamans, mystics and gurus? What is special about our knowledge; about our use of words? Can silence be significant again? And Derrida, a philosopher, continuing to illustrate there is nothing privileged about philosophy, about the absolute demarcations it has established and within which western knowledge continues to operate. Where should we draw a line on chance—without at one extreme surrendering all attempts to know and understand, or at the other extreme becoming indistinguishable from the (imputed) paranoid, superstitious, credulous, religious? And, if there is nowhere to draw the line, where does that leave us?

I like to think that these two small articles are symptomatic. (Or are they just chance occurrences I came across by accident?) Symptomatic of an increasing dissatisfaction with a faith we rarely challenge—our faith in reason. Not just any 'thinking', or doing things with words; rather our unquestioned trust in certain basic assumption of western rationality which we continue, unconsciously, to apply to fit the world to make the world fit—without doubt. We may at times, for example, question the contents of our concepts; we rarely question the concept of our concepts.

Certain metaphors we coin we know as concepts. They are the natural tools that we in the West use to describe and explain the world, not just our western part of it, but its entirety. Their perceived naturalness has several facets. Our concepts, to begin with, have a wholeness, an integrity, a unity, an essence about them—in short a homogeneity, a monolithic quality—as if sculptured by a deity. Boundaries impervious. The interior pure. It is (almost) inconceivable to consider a concept characterised by unevenness, contamination, irregularity, mixture, contradiction. At least, if 'unnaturally' one were to attempt to think this, one would be forced to use unseemly language, oxymorons, or even to appear (to the unsympathetic) as ignorantly self-contradictory or foolishly mystical. To express dissatisfaction with our concepts, in other words, to highlight their metaphoricity, is to place oneself at risk—in a variety of ways. How does one, for example, continue to use the word 'science' in order to show its unscientificity—and to show that as an essential character of its science?

One of the powerful means by which a concept in the West maintains its essence is by it being paired in opposition to that which it is not. It would seem, thereby, its character were better protected; its propriety unsullied, short of, naturally, a total surrender to the opposition. It is axiomatic, for example, that nature cannot be culture, that mind cannot be matter, that self cannot be other, that cause cannot be effect, that science cannot be magic. Once again, we quickly find ourselves in a form of 'double-bind' if we explore the limits of oppositional metaphors.

And our concepts/metaphors are universally applied. For not only are they used to explain ourselves, and to some degree or other, to form ourselves (we should never assume an identity between our self-descriptions and our actuality), they are used to explain, and to some degree, form others. It is interesting to wonder whether the West has had more success in forming others according to some preordained plan than it has had in forming itself. A strong case for the affirmative could, I believe, be mounted on the grounds of power and knowledge. But we must leave that for the moment.

One of the most significant ways that the West has mapped the world and thereby carved up its territories (the Bateson sense of map/territory has many permutative outcomes) involves its transplantation of that major western dichotomy, religion/secular, beyond its own shores. The essays by Kakar and Derrida are, therefore, doubly apposite. Both challenge the established dualities. Both leave us in some doubt about the conventional understandings of what constitutes religion and how (or whether) that differs from secular sciences.

The question of religion in India (where the West has certainly left its mark) and its relation to secularism, and in particular to the idea of secular politics, has until recently always been viewed within the dominant western mould. Let us now attempt to do otherwise.

In fifth-century Ionia, Xenophania once quipped 'if the ox could paint a picture, his god would look like an ox'.³ (He apparently did not think to say that if an ox could think,...) Thus the relativity of religious faiths was proclaimed. Despite this, or is it because of this, the West has continued to refer to the plurality of religions, even to their incommensurable idiosyncracies, without questioning the continued use of the one word religion by which they are encompassed. What is this essence or 'family resemblance' to justify the global concept? Why is it not disturbing that at one stage it was the considered scholarly belief that the Australian aboriginal culture had no religion at all, and that, later, this belief was replaced by another which concluded that that culture was *entirely* religious—that nothing existed outside it?

And what of Hinduism? Is it a religion? Or is it an Indian way of life, A culture? Is it both? Or neither? What is the quality of this word we have inherited from the Arabs who coined it to describe all that which was indigenous beyond the Indus river? It may be no one thing, other than what it is not. And this in three ways. Firstly, it may be several rather than one. Romila Thapar is one of many who insists that 'It would perhaps be more correct to speak of the Hindu religions (in the plural) rather than of "Hinduism" (in the singular)...the major asset of what we call "Hinduism" was that it was not a uniform monolithic religion, but a juxtaposition of flexible religious sects. This flexibility was its strength and its distinguishing feature'.⁴ There was no original Hinduism from which, over time, sprang a variety of marginal sects, each bearing some family resemblance to each other (as with the Christian tradition). No wonder Thapar may say ' "Hindu" became a term of administrative convenience' only—beyond this act of fiat there was little in reality to justify any such singluar labelling. There is no Hindu essence or core, notwithstanding emerging sects proclaiming they were indeed expressing it—a different one each time.

It is this disparateness, this heterogeneity, which western observers, no doubt with Semitic religions somewhere in their minds, attempt to capture when they struggle to define this chimera called

---

³ See E.R. Dodds, *The Greeks and the Irrational*, University of California Press, Berkeley, 1951, p. 181.

⁴ Romila Thapar, 'Syndicated Moksha', *Seminar*, No. 313, 1985, pp. 14–22. See especially p. 19. In this chapter I am interested only in Hinduism; I do not discuss the minority religions. I am not, however, thereby equating India with Hindu India. It is, nevertheless, the dominant influence.

Hinduism. Monier-Williams, in 1877, for example, elaborates it as a set of contradictions.

> It is all tolerant, all compliant, all comprehensive, all-absorbing. It has its spiritual and its material aspect, its esoteric and exoteric, its objective and its subjective, its rational and it irrational, its pure and its impure. It may be compared to a huge polygon, or irregular multilateral figure. It has one side for the practical, another for the severely moral, another for the devotional and imaginative, another for the sensuous and sensual, and another for the philosophical and speculative. Those who rest in ceremonial observances find it all sufficient; those who deny the efficacy of works, and make faith the one requisite, need not wander from its pale; those who are addicted to sensual objects may have their tastes gratified; those who delight in meditating on the nature of God and Man, the relation of matter and spirit, the mystery of separate existence, and the origin of evil, may here indulge their love of speculation.[5]

But we should not rest contented with an image of Hinduism merely as a polymorphous pluralism of religions. It may be better understood as complex ways of life, as the entire culture by which the majority of Indians live and perceive their lives. It constitutes the amalgam of what the occidental isolates as religion *and* the secular; in India, it is the living tissue, one, whole and indivisible. Thapar constantly points to the social parameters of religious movements. What each group was in its social identity it was in its religious quality. The two spheres were enmeshed in each other. Expressions of animosity or toleration, of political competition or cooperation were as

---

[5] Quoted by Nirad Chaudhuri, *Hinduism*, Chatto & Windus, London, 1979, pp. 145–46. It seems worthwhile to comment about the word 'tolerant' in the first line of the quotation. I am not concerned with the accuracy or otherwise of each of the words the writer uses to characterize Hinduism. The quotation, *in its totality*, is an interesting illustration how one westerner attempts to capture the inclusiveness, elusiveness and contradictoriness of Hinduism. It is worth making one more observation. It is often pointed out that the idea of the tolerance of Hinduism first gained prominence in nineteenth century orientalist writings which, for one reason or another, ignored India's counter-history of conflict and violence. That may be so. However, we ought also to consider that in nineteenth century discourse, a word like tolerance may be representing current scientific, especially mechanistic, imagery, namely that a structure has the resilience, flexibility and viability to withstand certain tensions and contradictions; that it may endure despite such pressures. Monier-Williams may not be commenting on the peacefulness but on the elasticity of Hinduism.

much about social, economic and political matters as they were about religious concerns. 'The intertwining of politics and religion was obvious'⁶ that author concludes. Boundaries diffuse, evaporate. We are left floundering in search of the purely religious or the purely non-religious. What would be the non-Hindu? Can we conceive a Hindu conception of being secular?

The problematic of Hinduism presents itself at yet a third level. It is not only that it confronts us with a heterogeneity rather than an essence; nor does it merely confuse us over the question of its possible boundaries; rather, it challenges our very notion of conceptualisation. It defies our irreducible understanding about identity. Having neither a centre nor a periphery, an inner or an outer, a self or an other, it places itself beyond conception. It is a state of being with such qualities as to be without quality. Something like this open-ended all-inclusiveness, this beyond conceptualisation, is captured in Wendy O'Flaherty's summation of Hindu mythology.

> [Its] universe pulses from extreme to extreme like a pendulum. Since a perfect balance can never be reached, the pendulum can never be at rest....Hinduism is content to keep each as it is.... Indian mythology celebrates the idea that the universe is boundlessly various, that everything occurs simultaneously, that all possibilities may exist without excluding each other. The myths rejoice in all the experiences that stretch and fill the human spirit.⁷

The West, to some degree or other, has always seen Hinduism as a scandal—phallic gods conjoining the sensual and the ascetic have always seemed an improper pollution of the sacred by the profane. From a different perspective we could, for the moment, profitably see Hinduism as a *sacrilege*. Being neither a religion nor a secular way of life, it is a manifestation of something which defies western classification, especially the simple western opposition duality. Think of it, strategically, as sacrilege, which according to the OED is 'robbery, profaning of sacred buildings, outrage of consecrated person or thing, violation of what is sacred.' And what is sacred here is the western conceptions of religion and its only conceivable

---

⁶ Thapar, *op. cit.*, p. 17.

⁷ W.D. O'Flaherty, *Asceticism and Eroticism in the Mythology of Siva*, Oxford University Press, Delhi, 1973, pp. 317–18.

alternative, its exclusively separate other, secular life. Hinduism violates this world-view, establishes that it is a cultural and not the natural, universal classification to which all cultures must immutably comply. Its first violation is, therefore, an exhibitionist one; exposing, nakedly, the ethnocentric nature of our hallowed language, reason and their rites/rights. Its second violation constitutes a more insidious sacrilege. It may go beyond ethnocentrism, and undermine our faith in the applicability of the conceptual dichotomy in the West as well. It may, in other words, help convert us to a re-examination of our own 'reasonable history' (Foucault) structured as it is by homogeneous, monolithic concepts, exclusive and proper to themselves, bumping against each other as if lumps of solid matter. To begin with, we may appreciate the operation of repetition, projection, and internalisation within any society and realise the continuities between so-called religious beliefs and practices and so-called secular beliefs and practices within any one society at a particular moment of history and, further, the discontinuities between 'fellow-religionists' or between 'fellow-secularists' at different moments of history. The assumed constancy of concept has to ignore the impact and significance of psychocultural simulation, that unconscious mirroring of mirroring, anywhere and everywhere. As we live together we copy each other, we copy the copying. In certain ways we become like each other. Our identities mix.

There may be religions, as there may be secularisms. At any one moment, however, their mutual intercourse creates bastards. Homogeneity, purity, sharpness of demarcation, proper species will hardly be bred. We are left speechless; we have no name for this hybrid other than life: and that is a macula conception.

A deep concern for the question 'what am I?' is not one that has preoccupied humanity evenly throughout its history. It has been suggested that it acquired prominence in the West for the first time as late as the seventeenth and eighteenth centuries: a product of coalescing forces like the curiosity of the Enlightenment, the Cartesian *cogito*, the novelty of introspection and the role of the active state in classifying, ordering, recording and regimenting its citizenry. This is the historical moment in the West which manifested what Foucault refers to as the 'creation of the concept of man'. Consciousness of self became a *common* possibility. The idea of self was no longer a question and problem merely for the philosopher.

Late nineteenth century saw the propagation and profusion of this form of consciousness in India. We are accustomed to recognising it usually only in one form—Indian nationalism—but the broader cultural change which made that possible, which constituted it, tends to be neglected: that is, the likelihood, need, desirability, necessity of confronting the questions who exactly am I? What is my precise identity? Where in the order of things do I properly belong? The self was no longer merely a subjective, existential body acting and reacting according to changing circumstances; rather the self now became also an object of its own study. More and more Indians now observed themselves, distinguished themselves, judged themselves, labelled themselves. A new form of cultural introspection sent its roots deep. A new clarity of self-definition, a demand for some unequivocal certitude about one's being etched itself on the face of the Indian public, and, over the last 100 years, continued to leave its mark and spread its sign throughout the entire continental culture.

This is not to say that differences, their particular loyalties and their concomitant conflicts had not existed before: bloody rivalries, persecutions and conversions of faith (voluntary and enforced) have a long history. Nevertheless, during the last century, a pervasive consciousness of self qualitatively changed the normative order of things, the relations between people, the hearts and bodies of the social actors. One perhaps could say that, as never before, self-identity became a political matter in India. Power has always been (as power must, by definition, always be) a handmaiden to one's station and status in life; it now acquired a more public, national face. One's social group was now one's political affiliation—to be pursued and protected. Caste consciousness, for example, began to transform a caste system (I use that last word guardedly) in which some degree of interdependence, reciprocity and mutuality had previously conjoined with its hierarchically-ordered separateness. Now, jealousy and rivalry became highlighted; caste associations were now made possible; competition, the rebuttal of others' claims, and the conscious espousal of exclusive self-interested aims were in order.

Communalism, likewise, was born—as a concept, a question, an issue, and interest—to be defended, deplored, denied, debated. The only stance on the matter henceforth 'discouraged' was indifference. 'A constant preoccupation' with the question of who really am I or, more precisely, what do I really want to become gripped more and more Indians. Am I a Sikh or a Hindu? A Muslim or an Indian? A Brahmin or Tamil? A Bengali or a nationalist? Whatever the question was, 'it had to be put into words'. In the name of India, the leaders of the country, before and after independence, railed against 'fissiparous tendencies', be they religious, linguistic, regional or caste loyalties, which, they said, weakened the country, which divided Indian from Indian. Yet these passions expended, these frustrations suffered were, in themselves, merely part, yet another sign of the changed culture. Such pleas were, perversely, as much cause as effect of the new politics of selfness, this dominating conscious concern with identity. 'Rather than a massive censorship...what was involved was a regulated and polymorphous incitement to discourse' on all such matters.[8]

The British presence has always been credited with stimulating the growth of nationalist values in nineteenth century India. But it seems it was equally 'responsible' for the emergence of the entire spectrum of identity politics, be the 'community' one based on caste, region, religion, or later class, and much later gender. Many factors undoubtedly produced such a change, but I am concerned here with only one of these; something profound, hidden and unintentional. I refer to a changed mode of thought the British unwittingly fostered within the Indian psyche.

Ever since later classical Greek thought, the West has always shown a favoured tendency to dualistic thinking: to the consideration of exclusive opposition pairs, invariably in a hierarchical structure, that is, to an 'either-or' logic. Ever since Aristotle, certain things have always been an anathema, a non-thought, an impossibility, a non-sense: contradiction, inconsistency, a tolerance for ambiguity, ambivalence, paradox. To the West, the presence of such qualities

---

[8] This quotation and the two preceding ones in the same paragraph come from Michel Foucault's *The History of Sexuality*, Vol. 1, An Introduction, Allen Lane, London, 1979, pp. 27, 32, 34. It would be interesting to pursue an argument that there is a structural isomorphism between sexuality in Europe and communalism in India since the nineteenth century. In each case, something considered undesirable and illegitimate (except by the practitioners) and something thought worthy of being repressed, on the contrary explodes into a dominant new discourse and practice.

As this book was about to go to press, I discovered a recent work which appears to support, in one way or another, my general contention that communal consciousness was a creation of nineteenth century British India. See G. Pandey, *The Construction of Communalism in Colonial North India*, Oxford University Press, Delhi, 1990.

represent the denial of rational thought, the other of what is reasonable. The Indian traditions, on the other hand, seem not to have been dominated by any one form of thought being considered the correct one. Monism, dualism and non-dualism, for example, have all been influential without any one acquiring a hegemonic role. There has, therefore, been no one overall continuous tradition of Indian thought of what is 'proper' to it. In other words, 'both-and' and 'neither-nor' have co-existed with an 'either-or'. This should not surprise us; without such a fluid state of affairs it would be difficult to understand how Hinduism can be characterised as I have proposed, as sustained contraries. The failure of dualities to acquire a privileged position in Indian thought as it did in the West shows itself in many ways. In discussing the common western allegation of Indian inconsistency, for example, Kakar says:

> For a Westerner the consistency or inconsistency relates to some immutably absolute values; for example justice. Something is either just or unjust. To an Indian mind values are contextual. In different situations a particular thing may or may not be right....It is the judgement of a content which determines the action rather than the absolute nature of the action itself.[9]

The influence of the British in nineteenth century India affected this state of affairs. By their education, legislation, administration, judicial codes and procedures, and even by that apparently simple operation of 'objective' classification, the census, the British, unwittingly, imposed dualistic 'either-or' oppositions as the 'natural' normative order of thought. In a multitude of ways, Indians learned that one is either this or that; that one cannot be both or neither or indifferent. They now perceived the world and their place in it as composed of clearly divided, bounded, exclusive entities. The significance of identity thus became a new, paramount concern. A cultural revolution occurred: in its specific manifestation it absorbed the thoughts, language, actions and commitments of so many; in its general cultural change it spread unnoticed: an orthodoxy of being was gradually replacing a heterodoxy of beings.

It is neither possible nor necessary here to suggest what proportion of Indians, by the late twentieth century, have been moved, and

[9] Quoted by A. George in *Social Ferment in India*, The Athlone Press, London, 1986, pp. 22–23.

to what degree, by such a cultural change. It, perhaps, affects only a minority still; but without doubt, because of its strategic role that is a significant minority. Nevertheless, it is the cultural *possibility*, even likelihood, of becoming conscious of some identity or other, of thereby creating an oppositional other, and of acting, with full intention, with commitment (that is, with some *consistency*!) in pursuit of conscious interests, that characterises the profound change in India over the last 100 years. The quality and quantity of politics that this has produced, or rather, that this is, is new to India.

It is within this specific historical and cultural setting that we need to reassess, to identify, the contemporary phenomenon known as 'religious conflict', in particular, the so-called militant Hindu revivalism. It is a new phenomenon: as recent as any of the conflicts using region, caste, language, class or gender, which sponsors a group identity, loyalty and commitment, which proclaims its other as its exclusive opposition, and which pursues these divisions intentionally and politically. It is the triumph of a sustained consciousness over a being fluctuating between indifference and anger, union and separation, action and reaction. 'Religious conflict' in twentieth century India is not therefore to be confused, despite our paucity of language, with religious conflict in centuries gone by.

But nothing is wholly new. It (as everything) carries traces of the past necessarily, and it intentionally constructs an image of the past as well as takes its symbols from the past. It attempts to create and live a mythic reality—of homogeneity and purity over place and time. In one sense, whether to refer to this phenomenon as 'Hindu' or even 'religious' is an academic question; an answer would tell us little. Hinduism's traditional lack of any essence has always allowed (and must conceptually permit) diverse specific mutations to emerge. Gandhianism is just one of many in recent times. Hinduism propagates Hinduisms. The question whether it is religious or not reminds us of our earlier appeal for inclusiveness. We do not have to answer in those terms. Today, a vigorous proselytising mission dominates its character. This may remind us of certain other religions, but certainly not 'Hinduism'. As Nandy says: 'To use the term Hindu to self-define is to flout the traditional self-definition of the Hindu; and to assert aggressively one's Hinduism is to very nearly deny one's Hinduism'.[10] It may, therefore remind us as well of

---

[10] Ashis Nandy, *The Intimate Enemy*, Oxford University Press, Delhi, 1983, p. 103. See also Nandy's 'An Anti-Secularist Manifesto', in *Seminar*, October 1985.

movements, other than religious, which place so much emphasis on conversion. It is political as much as, if not more than, anything else. As it is for political reasons, rather than for purposes of 'objective truth', that it is labelled, and it labels itself, Hindu and religious. Expressions like revivalist and fundamentalist are without any historical or epistemological grounding at all. Once again, their use serves contemporary political purposes only. And it is useful for more than one side.

To persist exclusively with language like Hindu revivalism, Sikh religious extremism or Muslim fundamentalism or with the general rubric 'communalism', ultimately highlights a distorted 'contents' of certain conflicts, while suppressing the 'form' which they bear in common with all the other confrontations based on oppositional dualities of exclusive identity consciousness. What Dumont has said about religion and communalism applies equally to the structure of politicised caste, region and language in India today. There is, he says 'a change in the nature or place of communalism; religion becomes here a mere appearance; people are not really concerned with the substance of religion, religion having become a sign of their being *distinct*'[11] (my emphasis). Any form of consciousness is a question about boundaries, about the creation and maintenance of an inside and an outside. In any situation of heightened self-consciousness the world is redrawn, realigned and recentred around sets of similarities and differences, each being born through the other, and each referring to the self and to the other. The politics of proselytisation is a complex one, involving the manipulation of incentives, as rewards and punishments, of symbols and even of the identity and quality of the other. The process is as 'pragmatic' as it is 'principled'. Form coalesces as content: time and again it is difference and similarity that counts rather than a particular who or what. *It is difference that makes the difference.* An exclusive consciousness becomes an end in itself; at the same time, it becomes the means of maintaining that end.

Tolerance is immediately conjured up as word-magic whenever so-called religious conflict is mentioned. It has acquired an aura of the obvious, the only commonsense, the sole panacea. It has become dogma, theology—never to be questioned, only besought. But, as

---

[11] Quoted by R. Lannoy in *The Speaking Tree*, Oxford University Press, London, 1974, p. 246.

presented, it seems an unconsidered solution, whether it is made to rest on an enlightened equality of respect (demanding a new Moral Man), or an enlightened equality of disinterest (demanding a new Rational Man), or an enlightened concern for only one interest, that of the state (demanding a new Indian Man). Each solution is a totalistic one; each rests on an absolute conversion, an entire eradication of the old and its replacement, without trace, by a new. And it is monolithic.

But tolerance may be the result of less grand postures. It may, for example, be the other face of an indifference for difference. Such a lack of consciousness for communal distinctions may well be the basis of what social harmony continues to survive in rural India. It is worthwhile to be reminded by precedents elsewhere that desirable outcomes (in any concerns) are not necessarily the product of noble intentions. Redwood, for example, concludes his study of the Enlightenment in England by suggesting that 'toleration was correctly (*sic*) resisted for many decades, but its eventual victory in many ways represented a triumph for apathy and pragmatism'.[12] A banal process not unlike that of the decline of influence of religion and the church during the same period which that author argues was brought about more by ridicule, wit and irony—by laughter—than by the rational arguments of reasonable men.

Toleration can wear so many entirely other faces. It may be confusion, uncertainty, doubt; it may be fear, deference, weakness, compliance; it may be self-confidence, assurance, mastery; it may be paternalism, even derision; it may be neglect; it may be preordained to bear. Each manifestation will produce a different scenario, form of accommodation, style of social relation and political conflict. It is obvious that not all forms of conflict will cease, nor ought that to be desired. When we consider the entire breadth of contemporary group consciousness, it is clear that intolerance rather than a stoic tolerance of things is often desirable—not least against the many forms of patriarchy and exploitation. A passion for justice, for example, is different from a state of being driven by unsensed forces of fear and hatred which transform themselves, it would seem inexorably, into an obsession with self-supremacy and an uncontrollable urge to destroy the other. Violence in India today is not caused by religion or caste or nationality; these are merely some of the settings

---

[12] John Redwood, *Reason, Ridicule and Religion: The Age of Enlightenment in England 1660–1750*, Thames & Hudson, London, 1976, p. 198.

(the household being another) where violence erupts. Can its increasing eruption be seen as the absurdist extension of an either-or logic in an historical setting in which separatist consciousness asserts itself, when what has been previously bonded is being fractured, when some form of inclusiveness is being ruptured into exclusive dualities and oppositions?

Against this we may want to insist that ultimately tolerance is not a position at all, not yet one more moral or psychological disposition to be urged. It may preferably be seen as the outcome of an absence (social and psychic) of a need for any one final position. Final positions incite final solutions.

> All religious movements in India are political.... The people have not yet learned to sever religious faith from civil government.
> Senior British Official, 1863[13]

A typical British and western sentiment expressing their firm belief in the unequivocal separation of domains and in the attributes proper to each. A belief inherited and regularly reiterated by spokesmen for the Indian state since independence. But why this insistence of a separation between religion and politics? Obviously, this significant problem is beyond the scope of this paper; however, perhaps we can create one lesson from the English experience of the Restoration period, its Age of Enlightenment, or in Redwood's apt phrase, 'the age of enthusiasts against enthusiasm'.[14] Having experienced regicide, the Civil War and the commonwealth, *enthusiasm* was accredited in the popular mind 'with all the ills of the period as sole or prime cause'. What was this thing seen (suddenly) as anathema? The word's associations were broad but they all began within religion: possession by a god, supernatural inspiration, prophetic or poetic ecstasy, fancied inspiration, ill-regulated religious emotion or speculation (and, eventually, still early eighteenth century) rapturous intensity of feeling, passionate eagerness. Enthusiasm was seen to be fanned by demagogy; in contrast, more people began to see the role of the state limited to purposes of tax, regulation, order and liberty and not to 'fulfil the aims of the godly on earth' or as 'the rule of the

---

[13] Quoted by R.A. Kapur, *Sikh Separatism: The Politics of Faith*, Allen & Unwin, London, 1986, p. 36. That author does not necessarily judge the statement by the British official in the way I do.

[14] Redwood, *op. cit.*, p. 16.

saints'. Such enthusiastic concerns would lead only to 'dissension, lunacy and social disorder', it was devoutly believed.[15]

It was this kind of religion (or politics or thought or expectation), this conveyor of enthusiasm, which was cast out of public life in England at that time (at the same time creating the particular separation of 'public' from 'private' we, in the west, have inherited). In the name of a quiet life, enthusiasm was exorcised from the body politic. Or rather, could we say, the state acquired a monopoly not only of the legitimate use of coercion, as we all know, but of the sole franchise for the production, sale and distribution of passionate beliefs. Enthusiasm for nationalism, for example, has always been a legitimate cause. Other morally and emotionally charged concerns, if emanating from society, constitute interference, are a threat to the state's ordained role of ordering and orchestrating a nation's fate. Enthusiasm must never be encouraged to enter the public marketplace, as it may displace the order of things as proclaimed by the state. In this sense, society is always a concern for the state; it has the potential of being carried away with its own enthusiasms. The state secretly confides in itself, surely, that it could do a better job of governing were it not for the ubiquitous presence of society with its divisions, interests and faiths!

Indian society has always been a problem for the Indian state—British or Congress. Congress government leaders, Jawaharlal Nehru in particular, have consistently, though unwittingly, expressed such a statist sentiment. It is not merely that they have voiced alarm at the 'fissiparous tendencies' of religious, regional, linguistic and caste conflicts but that, indirectly and directly, they see all group loyalties, all sectional interests, all conflicts, all ideals—all politics—as illegitimate. That between the Indian masses and the Indian state (a Congresss state of course) there was to be a void; but a space filled, joined by all acquiring and expressing one interest, one loyalty, one enthusiasm—to be 'Indian'. The state and society conjoin in one homogenised, mythic union, India—the end of conflict; apocalypse; a mystagogic state where the state may finally do its will—in the name of reason and science.[16]

While Congress has been the voice articulating most loudly such

[15] *Ibid.*, pp. 183, 198.
[16] I attempt to illustrate this tendency in ' "This Great Organisation of Ours": The Generations of Congress Discourse', in *Struggling and Ruling: The Indian National Congress, 1885–1985*, J. Masselos (ed.), Sterling Publ., Delhi, 1987, pp. 141–53.

a sentiment, it has no monopoly on it. There is a dominant discourse in India today—a particular corporatist one—propagated by many political parties and 'informed opinion': Indians must espouse, enthusiastically, one legitimate consciousness only—to be 'Indian'. This unquestioned and inspired revelation is its only path to salvation! It is a demand for nothing short of a loyal following of whoever, whatever, becomes the Grand Articulator of the national interest. It is a moral blackmail against anyone—women, untouchables, Biharis, poets—who wish to articulate some particular interest. It is a denial of Indian society. It is the reification of politics as matters of state, as things entirely divorced from their social setting.

But the actuality is that the Indian state cannot avoid, now or in the future, being enmeshed with the very fabric of Indian society; and this means with the religions, castes, languages, classes and genders that constitute that culture. And we must appreciate that passion or quietude can emanate equally from all and any area of Indian life. Enthusiasm or its lack has no one proper place of origin. Reason and reasonableness (an interesting lexical association) are likewise nomadic in their attachments.

To consider the possibility of the state in India being secular—as being either not involved in religion or as being equally distant from each religion—is a sham. This is not a question of what is desirable; rather it pertains to what is *conceivable*. It is as if the state *could* be autonomous from Indian society: an assumption fusing the idea of the Platonic philosopher-king and the three brass monkeys. It is as if the state's desire to be even-handed or neutral were sufficient to maintain its integrity as secular. Whereas, the actions and non-actions of the state are necessarily political: whatever they are, they will have, and must have, political consequences. And the most significant consequence is its unavoidably *differential* impact on the different segments of society. This, of course, is so everywhere; but because of the heterogeneity of Indian society, the impact of the state there has to be even more uneven. One banal point is too much ignored: the state, whatever its intentions and desires, is indubitably a *political* machine. *It* creates divisions, conflicts, interests, alliances, expectations, frustrations and heightened consciousness just as much as society does. No legislation, or lack of, can constitute neutrality, uniformity, even-handedness. How can we believe in the possibility of 'uniform legislation' unless we are content to read the bill literally, formalistically, and think of its language as belonging in limbo, there isolated from the responses of society. As if a flat rate of tax, for example, was uniform legislation!

The secular state mystique ultimately lets the state off the hook, as it encourages it to blame the (unfortunate) affairs of things entirely on society and *not to take responsibility for its own deeds and nondeeds.*

Perhaps we should reword the sentiment expressed by the senior British official in 1863: 'All governments in India (as elsewhere) are political. They have not yet learned that they cannot sever society from civil government.'

Each metaphor we use to get a grip on reality throws some light on what engages us, but at the same time casts a shadow. It hides from our view (and thereby removes from our practice) all the differences suppressed, as well as all the other potential metaphoric classifications that could be made but are unthought of in our preoccupation with one metaphor. The particular metaphor we choose, or inherit, *engages us*, in *its* world. Certain language, questions and values *obviously* follow, others, equally obviously do not. To begin with describing some conflict in India today as 'communal' for example, sets one particular train of discourse into operation—and it illuminates along that perspective—but its parameters necessarily inhibit other questions, other perspectives. How we set and label a problem determines, to some large degree, what we foresee as its resolution. The 'communal problem' is a paradigm example of this in India at the moment. Change the characterisation of the problem and we confront new dilemmas, new social forces, new operations, new solutions to be sought. With such a change we also become aware, perhaps for the first time, of political interests heavily invested in the continued pursuit of the problem as earlier labelled. All reformulations are by nature as much political as intellectual. This is not a problem of jargon, journalese, or of emotive, subjective language which can allegedly be set right by a scrupulous use of scientific objectivity. It is inherent in the way we have to think about anything. Rather, its danger lies in the belief, pervasive in western thought, that such language, the concepts we rigorously apply, are actually scientific and true. They are taken as literal: as the innocent, transparent, accurate bearers in print of The Real. This belief in our language; this idea that with greater definitional clarity, with lack of ambiguity, with univalent reference, we draw closer, as map to

- 26 (middle) gd exmp of implications of naming

- 38, fn 9 - ck ref (over →)

- pp 67-94: very gd disc. of language - Dwight debate, espec. role of metaphor

- pp 108-118: shortcomings of the extensively language-based approach to understanding social policy

- 132 - Complexity & modernism (compare with Mulgan)

- p 162, etc - Oppositional thinking & the notion of boundaries (eg public/private p235 — ck article Rorty

(**) pp 258-9   H10
"politics of irresolution
and the role of
public/private dualism"

(Ro)
(***)   Role of metaphor
         in social policy

terrain, to the real contours embedded in reality—this, which we take as the apogee of our rational heritage, is the nadir of our culture, our symptomatic delusion.

Literalness breeds essences, breeds 'analytic' distinctions, clear boundaries, and the separateness of others. Everything can then be, must be, classified as only one thing or another. The 'proper' is born. Each phenomenon, read each concept, can own only one meaning, one set of associations, can belong in one family or species, and can be contrasted with only one opposite, its negation. Literalness begets dogma.

Such a dogma permeates much of the debate about religion in India today. It is automatically linked with obscurantism, divisiveness and intolerance. It has only one opposite—the secular—characterised by the modern, the rational, the fair-minded and the future good of the Indian nation. Nothing can exist, nothing is conceivable, outside this duality. And nothing can properly belong to both sides of the opposition. Even the arts of India have been analysed to determine whether they are to be classed as either essentially religious and devotional or cultural and aesthetic. They literally cannot be both. May or may not the state use its funds to restore ancient temples? Is the television serialisation of the *Ramayana* political or not? Too many Indians (and probably westerners) believe there are simple, absolute answers, based on unchallengeable criteria, to such questions. There are not. They will need to be answered without a moral guarantee, without the political consequences being certain.

And has not the Hindu temple, for example, always been the location of so many things, such as devotion, culture, leisure, sociability, business, politics, feuds, healing, entertainment and personal advancement? What is improper to it? Perhaps the same can be said of the mosque and the *gurudwara*. I do not know.

If I refuse, as I do, to entertain the conventional idea of the 'secular state' in India, this does not force me to opt for 'the opposite' (the western opposite), that is for some form of theocracy. I am just refusing to accept that dualistic metaphor as my frame of reference. We can entertain others. The same strategy applies to the fundamental opposition of religion and the secular. I will not accept the double-bind; I no longer have faith in that reasonable distinction.

What is this state that is neither secular nor theocratic? As if some single word or concept would conjure up, as with a magician, the ideal object or state to be sought! I have no word. Any third label at this moment would generate negative consequences. Debate would concentrate on the precision of the concept proposed, on the abstracted qualities attributed to it (with concern for all the 'traces' of the word's history as it resonates in this, its latest historical setting), and on the imperviousness or otherwise of its boundaries alongside those of the secular and the theocratic. In other words, debate could so easily repeat the wayward quest for some 'proper' qualities marking it off unequivocally from that which it must not be. A new word (which may, of course, emerge in time) is not, therefore, a solution; rather it is an invitation for yet another repetition of that element of the western tradition I am attempting to break.

A new and immediate agenda is, nevertheless, called for. The Indian state, for example, is up for judgement, for persistent critical evaluation now—but no longer in terms of whether its actions (and non-actions) fit the template of being secular or not. Rather, what is demanded is judgement of a more imprecise, more complex and difficult, yet nevertheless, rigorous form. 'God may be dead', there may no longer be any absolute benchmarks for judging politics, or art, or science, but that absence does not open the floodgates to total indiscrimination or callous nihilism. Anything does not go. We can begin at once an intricate, qualitative scrutiny: is the state performing with firmness rather than with weakness and venality; with flexibility rather than with dogma; with due concern for both short- and long-term consequences; with informed intelligence rather than with rashness, impetuosity and arbitrary whim; with consideration for particular traditions yet with an appreciation that change has always occurred and will continue to occur; with respect for the rich diversity of the Indian peoples; with imagination even flair; with sympathy even compassion? Nothing suggested here implies a ready solution or even the likelihood of a consensual judgement. Both change and success will be uneven. But a new political discourse, no longer dependent on simple dualities, can begin at once.

So, this is not the time for answers, for final solutions. It is rather the moment to wrestle with our habits of thought, with the tyranny of our particular conceptualised pasts, with the fetters of our received dichotomies, with the ease of formulae by which we have learned to know, instantly and only too well, the good from the bad.

This may be the time, however, for a new social myth, for an imagery about a future, ideal Indianness. Being an 'Indian' must not be understood as an alternative, as a replacement, of being a Hindu, a Muslim, a Gujarati or a Chamar. That is, it must not be seen, once again, as an either-or choice between only two positions (and one being morally superior). Rather, being an Indian should entail being, *as well*, all those other identities of family, kin, caste, region, language, religion, class and gender. It should mean the ability and right to move between and across multiple loyalties, multiple interests. To be, that is, open to constant re-positioning, to be inconstant with one's commitments (to be 'inconsistent' if one wishes), to be the prisoner of none. There is no harm being at times 'communal-oriented'; danger exists when being communal (or being anything) absorbs all one's strength, dictates the only one possible perspective on the world, creates one's True Faith and its devil, its constant other.

A consciousness of being Indian does not achieve this mode of Indianness: the preferred model is beyond-consciousness, it is a certain indifference to any labelling, it is immune to any monopoly, it is a refusal to be assumed, taken for granted, numbered. This form of Indianness is an unconscious denial of any totality, an ease with being multiple, a contentment with being, over time, ambivalent[17] in one's loves and hates, with being somehow, both and neither. It is, at the one extreme not being torn asunder with doubt and indecision and, at the other extreme, not being rigid, full of certitude and un-moving. It is being both complex and flexible and being at ease with that state of affairs—one which ultimately eludes our power to describe with any linguistic precision. Perhaps fortunately.

The West has gone a long way in forming a new India, in its own image as it were. An image, of course, that India was destined never to live up to. The West can afford to shake its head in disappointment even disgust because, even now, it lacks the sensitivity to wonder whether its own image was ever relevant. It continues to blame the round hole for the ill-fit of the square peg.

The western metaphoric opposition of religion/secular has done enormous damage to India. Whether that country can rescue itself

---

[17] I would like to promote the notion of 'ambivalence'. Firstly, I would like to use this word in all the richness that Freud's insight could allow us, and like him, stress its ubiquitous presence in all of us. However, while I appreciate its pathological dimensions, I wish to stress its potential positive virtues and thus rescue the term from its commonly unfavourable associations. Unlike Freud, I would want to say 'let's aim at ambivalence'!

in the future is an open question; recent history cannot be rewritten here as anywhere. Certainly there are now voices in that continent telling us (and their fellow Indians) that the western model is wrong for them.

As we have already seen, Hinduism and the Indian situation generally can operate subversively, as an outrage, thereby displaying the western image for just what it is: not a universal concept, but one 'ethnic' perspective having no privileged position (other than its contingent global power) beyond its own shores. In this regard, the scales are being tipped ever so slightly in the opposite direction: We, in the West, have learned something about ourselves through the influence of India. It may even encourage us in the near future to reassess the decisions we made during our Enlightenment era, in particular to reconsider the costs and benefits of our specific separation of the 'public' from the 'private'.

But maybe we can go further in readjusting global debts. I end by describing an Ideal Indian, a mythic figure for the future. Having expressed that, I now realise that, in fact, this image is what I also desire for the Ideal Westerner (to talk in gross stereotypes for the moment's convenience). I can now see more clearly as well how the contemporary westerner falls short of this ideal.

In particular, I would like the West to nurture the value of a healthy ambivalence in one's identities, loyalties and commitments, an 'ease with being multiple', an indifference to labelling of either one's self or of others. But, as we know, we depend so much on firm boundaries; we tend to label and judge in black and white, and with certitude. Our consciousness, our identities, our knowledge are all digitally geared. Even for those who try hard to break from such a vice.

'I am Thou'   9

IN 1910 Freud published his work, *Leonardo da Vinci and a Memory of his Childhood*. Nine years later, Marcel Duchamp accomplished his work on Leonardo, his Readymade *LHOOQ*, the Mona Lisa with a beard. We can safely presume that Freud would not have appreciated this latter contribution to da Vinciana.

There is a point to this apparently random association; indeed it could be read as inscribing the chapter which follows.

It begins with Freud's book.[1] It is not concerned, as most commentaries are, with an analysis of Freud's analysis. This is not to be yet another plucking of feathers from a particular bird's tail/tale. It is interested only in the beginning and end of that study: in the case for the case, not the case-work itself; in the 'problem' called Leonardo da Vinci. Why was that person a worthy case for analysis?

Leonardo da Vinci (1452–1519) was admired even by his contemporaries as one of the greatest men of the Italian Renaissance;

[1] S. Freud, *Leonardo da Vinci: A Study in Psychosexuality*, authorised translation by A.A. Brill, Vintage Books, New York, 1947. All page references will be included in the text. A slightly different version of this chapter appeared as '"I am Thou": towards a psychoanalytic language of respect' in *Meanjin*, 47, 4, Summer 1988, pp. 769–84.

still, even then he appeared as mysterious to them as he now appears to us. An all-sided genius. Although he left masterpieces of the art of painting,—the investigator in him has never quite left the artist. Often it has severely injured the artist and in the end it has suppressed the artist altogether. (p. 4)

Why was he a mystery to his contemporaries, Freud asks? Certainly not because he was 'many-sided in his capacities and knowledge...manifold talents in the same person was not unusual in the time'(p. 5); nor because of his social demeanour: he was tall, strong, 'of consummate beauty', 'jovial and affectionate' and enjoyed music and company (pp. 5–6). So what made him mysterious, even then?

The turning of his interest from his art to science, which increased with age, must also have been responsible for widening the gap between himself and his contemporaries. All his efforts with which, according to their opinion, he wasted his time instead of diligently filling orders and becoming rich—seemed to his contemporaries as capricious playing, or even caused them to suspect him of being in the service of the 'black art'. (p. 7)

Expressing this another way: his art suffered. As Freud says:

The effect that this had on his paintings was that he disliked to handle the brush; he painted less and, what was more often the case, the things he began were mostly left unfinished; he cared less and less for the future fate of his works. It was this mode of working that was held up to him by his contemporaries, to whom his attitude towards his art remained a riddle. (p. 8)

And this remains the riddle for Freud to solve. 'The painful struggle with the work, the final flight from it and the indifference to its future fate may be seen in many other artists, but this behaviour is shown in Leonardo to the highest degree'(p. 9) It is these qualities of Leonardo which Freud now elaborates. The slowness of his work, evident from the beginning, he sees as a 'symptom of his inhibition, a forerunner of his turning away from painting' later in his life. This slowness encouraged him to forego fresco painting, demanding speed, for oil colours, allowing a more leisurely execution. This favoured method, however, was responsible for the gradual destruction of some of his most important work, as the oils eventually separated from their brick-wall background (p. 12). As Freud comments 'It seems here as if a peculiar interest, that of the experimenter, at first reinforced the artistic, only later to damage the art production' (13). This slowness is no isolated phenomenon.

> Leonardo evinces still some other unusual traits and apparent contradictions. Thus a certain inactivity and indifference seemed very evident in him. At a time when every individual sought to gain the widest latitude for his activity, which could not take place without the development of energetic aggression towards others, he surprised everyone by his quiet peacefulness, his shunning of all competition and controversies. He was mild and kind to all. (p. 13)

And Freud illustrates: rejecting a meat diet, releasing caged birds, condemning war and designating man 'as the worst of the wild beasts'. But there are contradictions. 'This effeminate delicacy of feeling', Freud notes, did not prevent him from attending executions to sketch the fear-ridden features of the condemned; nor from inventing cruel offensive weapons, nor from being chief military engineer to Cesare Borgia in his campaign against Romagna. 'Often, Freud adds, he seemed to be indifferent to good and evil' (p. 14).

> Moreover, Leonardo presented an example of cool sexual rejection which one would not expect in an artist and a portrayer of feminine beauty.... His posthumous works, which not only treat of the greatest scientific problems but also comprise the most guileless objects which to us do not seem worthy of so great a mind (an allegorical natural history, animal fables, witticisms, prophecies) are chaste to a degree—one might say abstinent... They evade everything sexual (p. 15).

Freud thinks it is likely that Leonardo never had a sexual or a spiritual relationship with a woman, and that he probably had no sexual relations with any of the handsome young men he took as pupils. It was not that he was 'dispassionate...he only transmuted his passion into inquisitiveness.... His affects were controlled and subjected to the investigation impulse He neither loved nor hated, but questioned....' (p. 20).

Such an interpretation is given weight by Leonardo's own words—'great love springs from great knowledge of the beloved object, and if you little know it, you will be able to love it only little or not at all'(p. 19), and elsewhere, 'one has no right to love or to hate anything if one has not acquired a thorough knowledge of its nature'(p. 18). The consequences of such an approach are serious, according to Freud. 'Not to love before one gains full knowledge of the thing loved presupposes a delay which is harmful. When one finally reaches cognition, he neither loves nor hates properly; one remains beyond love and hatred. One has investigated instead of having loved' (p. 22). And thus the unusual career path of Leonardo:

> Investigations may have started with his art, with his urge to investigate the attributes and laws of light, of colour, of shades and of perspective. He wished to be...master in the imitation of nature. ... He was driven further and further to investigate the objects of the art... their interior structure and biological functions.... And, finally, he was pulled along by this overwhelming desire until the connection was torn from the demands of his art. He was no longer able to limit his demands, to isolate the work of art... The artist had at once taken into his service the investigator to assist him; now the servant was stronger and suppressed his master. (pp. 23–25)

Leonardo was turned away from his art, as well, by his wasting his time in playful trivialities.

> Leonardo remained infantile in some ways throughout his whole life.... As a grown-up he still continued playing, which sometimes made him appear strange and incomprehensible to his contemporaries. When he constructed the most artistic mechanical toys for court festivities and receptions, we were displeased by it, because we disliked to see the master waste his power on such petty stuff...(these) fantastic productions of the youthful artist which he created for his own amusement (p. 106).

Freud sums up the case why Leonardo was a worthy subject for analysis.

His infantile past had gained control over him. The investigation, however, which now took the place of his artistic production, seems to have borne certain traits which betrayed the activity of unconscious impulses; this was seen in his insatiability, his regardless obstinacy, and in his lack of ability to adjust himself to actual conditions. (p. 115)

It has been said that a signature is always signed, ultimately, by others. There is no Nietzsche, no Marx, no Freud—there are only others' Nietzsches, Marxs, Freuds. So with problems. There are no problems given, unequivocal, present; only problems set, named, bounded. The problem called Leonardo is the problem created by others. He is a mystery to, by, for his contemporaries, Freud, and undoubtedly, many others. The base of this problem is that Leonardo is labelled, is known as, is signed 'artist', more precisely 'painter'. Change that signature and the problem (called Leonardo) changes, perhaps dissipates. If he were known as the great scientist, we would at most wonder that such Renaissance figures could still find time for painting as well. It would not constitute a problem which we would feel obliged to solve.

Freud's Leonardo, however, has apparently an obligation to remain at his easel. This is his proper place, his one legitimate role. Freud's text is splattered with the expression '*his* art' (my emphasis). The propriety of this relationship is 'unquestionable'. Thus Freud, with consistency, refers to other activities as a movement away from. Departures from, returns to—his own home. Engineering, science are detours, moments of deviance—and thus a mystery. Despite Freud's frequent statements of admiration for Leonardo's science, it and all other activities of the man are placed conceptually and dualistically, as the other, as the inferior other, as a fall from grace. The analytic problem being posed is 'how come such a great artist did not stick to his art?'. It is this inconstancy that allegedly demands an explanation.

This enigma of a moving away from and then returning to one's proper place (Leonardo's 'fort/da'?) is exacerbated by Freud's particular notion of what constitutes proper art. Marcel Duchamp re-enters the scene. Freud is untouched by modernist or twentieth century western paradigms of art. The new paradigms challenge, wittily or savagely, established dualities between art and non-art, high art and popular art, the product and the process, form and content, the means/tools/instruments and the end/the work, the artifice and the reality, the original and the copy, the serious and the playful, chance and necessity, sincerity and deception. It problematizes authorship, creativity, uniqueness. It questions totality, coherence, endurance and permanence. In place of homogeneity it praises heterogeneity; ambivalence, ambiguity and paradox replace univalence, clarity and unequivocal representation. The artist is no longer distinct from the art; struggle is made superior to resolution: 'to succeed is to fail', the words of Jean Cocteau, underpin so much of the modernist ethos. The frame, the framework of art as previously conceived is destroyed; its setting is upset; its very phenomenality is fractured, dissipated. Where is it, what is it, is placed on the agenda. Art as a playful activity encapsulates its most serious mission. Profundity is allied to the apparently trivial; pretentiousness is outcast as the only impiety. The profane becomes the sacred.

So what Freud dismisses as the unfortunate, infantile, trivial waste of time with playful entertainments and fantastic toys may be reinterpreted as Leonardo's unwillingness to comply with conventional ideas of 'genre', of exclusive boundaries to the thing called art. Consider two examples of 'such petty stuff' Freud quotes from Vasari. 'He made a doughy mass out of wax, and when it softened he formed thereof very delicate animals filled with air; when he blew into them they flew into the air, and when the air was exhausted they fell to the ground' (p. 104). And another: 'He had often cleaned the intestines of a sheep so well that one could hold them in the hollow of the hand; he then brought them into a big room, and attached them to a blacksmith's bellows which he kept in an adjacent room; he then blew them up until they filled up the whole room so that everybody had to crowd into a corner' (p. 105). One does not have to resort to the Dadaist friends of Duchamp in Zurich to appreciate the family-resemblance of all such 'Happenings'. All we can say is that Leonardo engaged in art—in a variety of its forms. Leonardo becomes a problem, in part, because of Freud's restrictive frame around art.

Leonardo also becomes a problem because of other boundaries constructed by Freud (and others). It is time now to consider the turning away from his art to science, or, more precisely, to investigate 'investigation . . . which took the place of his artistic production'. This investigation is invested, by Freud, with the attributes of theft. It steals time, as it steals the man, away from his prime cause.

It appropriates illicitly. And, as with theft, it merely reallocates something; it is never productive. Thus Freud refers to the productivity, the creativity, the bringing-into-being of Leonardo's art—but never of his science. That brings forth nothing, it is non-procreative, a negation of life. Investigation is merely looking, a passive voyeurism. It was also theft with violence. It 'severely injured the artist and in the end it suppressed the artist altogether.' It left him maimed: 'Its effect... was that he disliked to handle the brush—(and presumably dispirited), he cared less and less for the future fate of his works' (note 'works' of art, never 'works' of science).

This productive, artistic component of Leonardo was his masculine self, was his father. When 'he' was dominant, his art flourished. 'As he took his father as a model... he passed through a period of manly creative power and artistic production in Milan, where favoured by fate he found a substitute for his father in Duke Ludovico Sforza' (p. 114). Freud maintains this gender imagery even when it sits most uncomfortably. 'Whoever works as an artist', Freud says, 'feels as a *father* to his works' (p. 94; my emphasis). The productive, the procreative, the giving-birth, the creation of a new and whole canvas/child bearing his name is the only legitimate work—and it is the work of man.

On the other hand, science, as investigation, Freud associates with non-work, non-creation, with hesitation, delay, detour, inactivity, indifference, effeminate delicacy and lack of any real passionate affect. As we have seen: 'he neither loved nor hated, but questioned...he transmuted his passion into inquisitiveness ...he has investigated instead of having loved.'

Thus the problem set by Freud, a problem worthy of analysis: Leonardo's masculine self, full of passion and capable of producing great art works struggles against and finally succumbs to his feminine self, a cool, passionless, indifferent, endless pursuit of investigation. An insatiable inquisitiveness which absorbs him totally; an insatiability without end, without product. A means becomes the end in itself; the servant, the investigator, suppresses the master, becomes the master.

There is no need to labour our surprise at Freud's quixotic gendering. He is merely registering, once again, a traditional western association.[2] At least, we could concede, to identify art with

---

[2] Regarding the 'very old philosopheme of *production*', see Derrida's brief discussion in *Spurs: Nietzsche's Styles*, University of Chicago Press, Chicago, 1978: 'Production, just as much for Nietzsche as for all of tradition, is masculine', pp. 75–79.

masculinity and science and engineering with femininity is a novel breach of convention. Of greater concern, here, is Freud's conception of passion. This seems the linchpin in his setting of the problem, and, therefore, with his subsequent analysis of the case called Leonardo.

Why does Freud see passion only in the art and not in the other activities? Or, to use the words Freud once employs, why does he see his passion 'transmuted into inquisitiveness?' Freud places a lot of weight on Leonardo's own words: 'the utterances (which follow) furnish the key to his character' he says (p. 18). One sentence is translated by Freud as 'One has no right to love or to hate anything if one has not acquired a thorough knowledge of its nature' (p. 18). Freud assertively rejects such notions:

> There is no psychological value in these utterances of Leonardo. What they maintain is obviously false, and Leonardo must have known this as well as we do. It is not true that people refrain from loving and hating until they have studied and become familiar with the nature of the object to whom they wish to give these affects. On the contrary they love impulsively; they are guided by emotional motives which have nothing to do with cognition; and their consequences are rather weakened by thought and reflection. Leonardo could have meant only that the love practised by people is not the proper and unobjectionable kind, one should so love as to hold back the affect, and subject it to mental elaboration, and only after it has stood the test of the intellect should free play be given to it. (p. 19)

It is evident from the language Freud employs here that he invests heavily in this double-gesture: the psychological falseness of Leonardo's propositions, and their significance in revealing Leonardo's character. Indeed, Freud must have felt so strongly on this issue that he *mistranslates* Leonardo, and 'he must have known this as well as we do'! The first statement is included in the text in Italian. It reads 'Nessuna cosa si puo amare ne odiare, se prima no si ha cognition di quella', which cannot be translated as 'one has no *right* to...' but 'no-one is *able* to...' Leonardo is clearly not saying that 'one *should* so love as to hold back the affect...' nor is he denying that people can love impulsively. No such censorious dictates are being moralised. What Leonardo seems to be suggesting is that one should not, as it possibly was in Renaissance Italy and as it certainly was at that moment in 1910 Vienna,—one should not so sharply separate passion from knowledge, affect from cognition, the mind from the body. This is not a question about deferment or constraint; it is an attempt to distinguish the different quantities and qualities of emotion (both love and hate are referred to) and to indicate how these are affected by the nature of one's knowledge. Multivalence, not a crude literalness, is at stake. A non-duality, not a violently divisive dualism is being grappled with. To love, to know—each resonates here allusively, elusively, mutually. Each is a condition of the other; each is within the other; the two are inseparable; they are signs of the other. The pursuit of one is not at the sacrifice of the other. Leonardo is, at the same time, explaining and justifying himself: he values profundity. To him, a casual acquaintance is a superficial reward.

Freud's apparent refusal to appreciate this cohabitation, this mutual procreation of knowing and feeling, determines his case against Leonardo, determines Leonardo as a case. It is, therefore, inconceivable for him to see Leonardo's science and engineering, his investigations, his inquisitiveness, as passionate. They are, at the very best, transmutations, sublimations—inferior translations of his passionate self. Cerebral matters only. Cold, calculating calculus. Disembowelled. Indifferent. Producing 'neither love nor hate'. Thus Freud coolly enumerates Leonardo's scientific discoveries up to the point where Leonardo 'could enter in his book...the cognition: ...The sun does not move.' And, instantly passing this by, Freud notes 'His investigations were thus extended over all realms of natural science....' Freud, so often the master of nuance, of understatement, of overstatement, slides past, without comment, that monumentally dramatic entry: 'The sun does not move'. He even notes, without noting, the original Italian 'Il sole non si move'. Without noting the power, the powerful brevity, the triumphant glory of such an exclamation, climax, ejaculation. And Leonardo marks all this in capital letters!—a sign which once again Freud specifies without signifying. Is the unconscious Freud challenging the conscious Freud? What need Leonardo have added to express his passion, his ecstasy more dramatically? Can 'cognition' in coitus with affect be expressed in words more graphically?

From the evidence Freud provides, Leonardo seemed indifferent to physical sexuality—certainly with women, and, perhaps with effort, with any of the handsome, young men he constantly surrounded himself with. Does Freud, ultimately, rest his case, rest the case to be entitled Leonardo, artist, on some isomorphic deduction: Leonardo is without sexual passion; he is, therefore, without passion in his sublimated activity, his investigations, his cool and insatiable inquisitiveness? Freud seems to admit some such simple translation between the man's life and his work, when, near the end of the book, he concludes: 'The object of our work was to explain the inhibitions in Leonardo's sexual life *and* in his artistic activity' (my emphasis) (p. 111). His art is to be seen as a simple, transparent mirror of his life. A facile one-to-oneness. I am reminded of Michel Foucault being questioned on the writing style of Raymond Roussel.[3]

> When Cocteau wrote his works, people said 'It's not surprising that he flaunts his sexuality and his sexual preferences with such ostentation since he is a homosexual.' Then Proust, about Proust they said, 'It's not surprising that he hides and reveals his sexuality, that he lets it appear clearly while also hiding it in his work, since he is a homosexual.' And it also could be said about Roussel, 'It's not surprising that he hides it completely since he is a homosexual.' In other words, of the three possible modes of behaviour— hiding it entirely, hiding it while revealing it, or flaunting it—all can appear as a result of sexuality.

To Freud, Leonardo's inhibitions in one quarter reproduce inhibitions in another. Why could not the situation be redescribed as inhibitions in one producing *jouissance* in the other? Even restricting oneself to the Freudian material, a reader is struck by the exuberance, the over-plenitude, the extravagance of the 'works' of Leonardo!

But perhaps the problem is even more complex. Once again, Freud's Leonardo is presented within dualistic categories: we have, on the one hand, the person, and on the other, the works of that person. What becomes of the case if we were to jettison that dichotomy? Once again, we return to Foucault and his response to the problem.

[3] Michel Foucault, *Death and the Labyrinth*, New York, 1968, Postscript, 'An Interview with M. Foucault', by Charles Ruas, p. 183.

> I believe it is better to try to understand that someone who is a writer is not simply doing his work in his books, in what he publishes, but that his major work is, in the end, himself in the process of writing his books. The private life of an individual, his sexual preference, and his work are interrelated not because his work translates his sexual life, but because the work includes the whole life as well as the text. The work is more than the work: the subject who is writing is part of the work. (p. 184)

There are other Leonardos lurking in the text of Freud's Leonardo.

Let us reinvestigate love—a central motif, in its presence and absence, of Freud's portrait of Leonardo. Freud is struck by Leonardo's 'insatiability, his regardless obstinacy, and in his lack of ability to adjust himself to actual conditions' (p. 115). *Could this not be a telling depiction of being in love?*—never being sated, ever demanding more, a refusal to forego the pursuit, unwilling and unable to consider other contingencies, others' conventions. What Leonardo was in love with is immaterial, ultimately indeterminable: we may say, however, life, his life, his inquisitive and creative life, the entire cosmos, he and the cosmic order. The condition of love is, paradigmatically, the time one ignores all boundaries, proprieties, positions; one just does, one just is. One is beside oneself, beyond oneself—neither body nor mind, neither self nor other, neither past nor future. One is lost; one loses oneself—both active and passive, subject and object, free and determined. The coitus of love is the union of chance and necessity. One perhaps could redirect and revalue Freud's own words: one 'readily forgets one's own insignificant self...and one becomes truly humble' in such a state of love; in fact, one has gone beyond humility as well as hubris. One is touched with the sublime; one has gone beyond consciousness and self-consciousness. Such love will lead you anywhere, everywhere. You neither linger nor complete. You are inconstant; love, in this sense, is always unfaithful love. You are, in a way, in love with love. And love knows no authority. Once again Freud points in the right direction, but with his boundaries, restricts his insight. Leonardo, the sublime lover, rejects not only the authority of the church but also that of his elders, his peers, society, his future judges. Their opinions, prescriptions, proscriptions count for nothing. He is free of all constraints—other than that of his own need to love. 'The need for a support of some authority is so imperative (for most human beings) that their world becomes shaky when their authority is menaced, Leonardo alone was able to exist without such support' (p. 97). Leonardo was complete, full, unto himself: his experience of love, of life, of its myriad passionate satisfactions was his only benchmark—regardless of others. He was, in this sense, as they say 'obsessed'—a quality distinct in kind and value from Freud's judgement that he was of the 'obsessive type', with the 'reasoning mania' and inhibiting 'abulias' of the neurotic type.

Models vary. Let us now investigate another. We turn to one moment of Hindu literature, and pay regard to what another psychoanalyst, Sudhir Kakar, has written recently about the love of Krishna, the blue-god, and his consort, Radha.[4] But why love? What does it mean? What does it represent? Kakar soon reminds us: 'Love is not *about* something: it *is*' (original emphasis, p. 81) and that is why it 'can be reproduced in music with greater fidelity than in words since there is a direct rather than signified correspondence between musical forms and the forms of emotional life' (p. 81). Could it be significant that music is the one art form that Freud admits having little appreciation for?

Kakar concentrates on Jayadeva, who wrote, and composed in music, his love poems of Krishna and Radha in the twelfth century. Boundaries are breached immediately: Radha is a simple cowherd in love with, loved by, a god. She is, moreover, another man's wife. Their love is adulterous. In this, as with her passionate cravings and desperate sufferings, she is the 'personification of *mahabhava*, a "great feeling" that is heedless of social proprieties and unbounded by conventions' (p. 82).

> Jayadeva *knows* (original emphasis) that the enrichment of the heart and the arousal of the senses belong together.... This coincidence of knowledge and feeling is intimately tied to an illusion, or at least a crossing-over, of genders. ...Radha's passionate love for Krishna...is not an allegory for religious passion but *is* religious passion. Jayadeva thus does not need to make a

---

[4] Sudhir Kakar, 'The Cloistered Passion of Radha and Krishna', in *Tales of Love, Sex and Danger*, S. Kakar and J. Ross, Oxford University Press, Delhi, 1986. Page references will be included in the text.

distinction or choose between the religious and the erotic... Radha incarnates a state of permanent amorous tension, a here-and-now of desire.... She personifies an enduring arousal that does not seek orgasmic resolution.... Hers is an effort to reach the very essence of eroticism. (p. 88, original emphasis)

Such poetry, Kakar has already reminded us, is 'pre-eminently feminine in its orientation, and the erotic love for Krishna is envisioned entirely from the woman's viewpoint.'

(It entails) the fantasy—of unending and sustained sexual excitement. The absence of *kama* (lust) does not mean an absence of desire, but simply of orgasm.... Krishna's eroticism has no ulterior purpose of consequence, such as a birth. It exists for itself, in itself (pp. 88–89). Separateness and union are not different categories of love...but are merely different phases of the cycle of love, both intimately connected through the workings of desire. (p. 91)

Sexual excitement is stimulated by fantasies, in particular those which oscillate between an anticipation of danger and the expectation of its replacement by pleasure. With the love of Radha and Krishna, fantasies are coloured by the theme of the 'forbidden crossing of boundaries', a theme resonating on several levels. Their adultery 'crosses the boundaries set by social mores and norms (p. 91)...In counterpoint to the damnation heaped upon her in religious and legal texts, the adulteress was assured of the poet's admiration' (p. 93). Indeed, to some poets, 'the adulterous was symbolic of the sacred, the overwhelming moment that denies world and society, transcending the profanity of everyday convention, as it forges an unconditional (and unruly) relationship with god as the lover' (p. 94).

The crossing of sexual boundaries provides an other major source—and becomes another major effect—of their sexual excitement. 'We grow up in an established social milieu which affixes to gender sex roles that seem to emanate from our bodies. Can all this be changed, should it—when it is the distinctions of sex that impel and permit man and woman to come together? To these questions the Indian love poetry and art respond with a resounding yes' (p. 97). So at times the lovers are depicted as one androgynous entity at others, dressed in each other's clothes. Frequently they 'invert' sexual roles. At one moment we may experience Radha's excitement:

> She bristles with pain, sucks in breath
> Cries, shudders, gasps,
> Broods deep, reels, stammers,
> Falls, raises herself, then faints.
> When fevers of passion rage so high,
> A frail girl may live by your charm(p. 90)

At another moment, with Radha taking the active role we hear Krishna cry out:

> Punish me, lovely fool!
> Bite me with your cruel teeth!
> Chain me with your creeper arms!
> Crush me with your hard breasts!
> Angry goddess, don't weaken with joy!
> Let Love's despised arrows
> Pierce me to sap my life's power! (p. 97)

Kakar adds, 'It was only under the influence of nineteenth century western phallocentricity, one of the dubious intellectual blessings of British colonial rule, that many educated Indians would become uneasy with this accentuation of femininity in a culture hero.' He mentions, for example, the Bengali writer, B.C. Chatterji, proponent of a virile nationalism, who says of Jayadeva's poems: 'From the beginning to the end, it does not contain a single expression of manly feelings—of womanly feelings there is a great deal—or a single elevated sentiment—I do not deny his high poetical merits—but that does not make him less the poet of an effeminate and sensual race' (p. 98).

Kakar insists that 'the wish to be a woman is not a later distortion of phallic strivings but rather another legacy.... [There is] a primal yearning of men—to yield their heroic trappings and delight in womanliness, woman's and their own' (p. 99). And he concludes 'Krishna's erotic homage to Radha conveys something of the aching quality of the man's fantasy of surrender at the height of sexual excitement... The thrusting penis, man realises once again, can never take or hold the woman.... The "secret of men" gods included... is that they want to be that which they cannot have: Woman' (p. 100).

And we supplement Kakar with moments from another recent writing, from Ramchandra Gandhi's[5] volume subtitled *Meditations on the Truth of India*, which we could further subtitle *Explorations in Advaita*, that is, non-duality. (p. 4)

Hindu advaitin orthodoxy is the extremest salvational heterodoxy, for if at the heart of heterodoxy is a rejection of constraining otherness, advaita—is the most radical repudiation of otherness and its shackles that can be conceived of. Hinduism is the orthodoxy of heterodoxy, of the heterodoxy of orthodoxy (p. 29).

There is in truth only unlikeness, no otherness at all. (44) The so-called others are not others at all but oneself elsewhere-situated. (p. 48)

Samyoga, (juxtaposition) is sanctified surrealism.... The heights of our spiritual history are not all those synthesis and absorption and assimilation, they are also the achievements of non-violent contacting and co-existence;...unintercoursing juxtaposition dramatise the Vedic vision of oneness in diversity.... Yet perhaps Indian uniqueness is not co-existence as such but the co-existence of co-existence and synthesis. (pp. 59–60)

We must not even speak of the one *and* (orig emph.) the other, only of the timeless alternation of the two, not of Radha and Krishna but Radha-Krishna.

Brahmacarya (celibacy) is not sexual deprivation, nor is sexual love spiritual misery (p. 116). Brahmacarya demands...its acceptance and celebration as the language of silence of spiritual biology, just as sexual love calls for acceptance and celebration as speech or speaking, the other side of the self-same language; all language being defined equally by its areas of speech and its zones of silence (p. 168). Brahma (is) a faring unto vastness, not a prudish joyless insistence on littleness. Hypocrisy and cruelty abound in the moralist camp of Brahmacarya, as they do in the moralist camp of sexual love.... 'I am a body-mind-ego etc.' is utterly false as a final description of the structure of ourselves, the very paradigm of falsehood,... self-consciousness can only describe itself as 'I-am-that-I-am.... Self-consciousness is

---

[5] Ramchandra Gandhi, *I am Thou: Meditations on the Truth of India*, Indian Philosophical Quarterly Publ., Pune, 1984. Page references will be included in the text.

without any form—Reflective human communication—is the mystery of being addressed—being identified without in the slightest way being described, classified, placed (pp. 170–72).

Human beings are capable of an intensity of Cartesian self-consciousness which almost confers upon them a status of non-corporeality, but they are equally capable of a degree of *Carvaka* (materialist) self-forgetfulness which makes of them throbbing masses of flesh and blood. The former capacity is a foundation of brahamacarya, and the latter of sexual love (p. 183).

Sri Krishna and Sri Radha are lovers, not spouses. In this bold image sacred myth draws our attention to the oneness of divine reality. Divine consciousness and its *sakti* (spiritual energy or force) are one like lovers, not two like spouses (p. 189).

(The) utilitarianism of the one-man-one-life variety will reduce all relationships of man to man and to himself to devouring: to cannibalism, incest, murder, suicide. (p. 204)

Philosophical analysts, logical purists, would at this point probably vehemently assert that whether or not advaita violates psychoanalysis, whether or not it is a regressive infantilism, it patently violates that purest norm of thought, the conscience of reason, the law of logic that everything is what it is and not another thing, that everyone is what he or she is, and not someone else: the law of identity. It is not so much our science or politics or ethics or aesthetics that have let us down, it is rather the very pride of our rationalist self-image, our logic, that has abandoned us (p. 210–12).

Matching brahmacarya and sexual and moral and political passion,—a discovery of playfulness and seriousness in one another.... (p. 293).

Gandhi's (the grandfather) distinctive contribution to modernity...is a philosophy of walking,...the spiritual truth of nomadism...(against) the motorised...one-track, delinquent modern civilization's deep fear and hatred of the all-directioned-ness of meandering, looking, loving, challenging, be-ing. Monadism's fear of nomadism. ...Gandhi is a line taken for a walk by God, in the manner of Klee's great painting (p. 203).

'I am Thou', in quotation marks, forms the title of this chapter. The quotation marks here serve their double purpose: to mark its derivation from elsewhere—it is the title of Ramchandra Gandhi's book; it is also to remark it, to raise it, strategically, as a means of loosening Freud's creation of the problem called Leonardo.

Freud has always been appreciated, among other things, for his collapsing of distinctions generally held sacredly apart by western thought. In the present work he explicitly notes, for example, that 'We no longer believe that health and disease, normal and nervous, are sharply distinguished from each other' (p. 11). Here, as elsewhere, he constantly undermines the surety behind so many of the dualities entrenched in our language: mental/physical, inner/outer, past/present, self/others, chance/necessity, to name a few. Indeed, he *had* to, in order to create a psychoanalysis. And yet! The problem he sees Leonardo to be, his very construction of the case, begins and ends by sharp bifurcation. His thought is from complexity to simple duality, not the other way. His final depiction of Leonardo is by art *versus* science, masculinity versus femininity, work versus passive observation, passion versus indifference and inactivity, completion versus delay, decisiveness versus infantile impulse, sexual versus chaste, love versus control, social adjustment versus obstinacy. Furthermore, these sharp dualities are hierarchically structured, and without doubt. Freud unequivocally approves, psychologically and ethically, one side only of the split. We are presented with a struggle between good and evil; and with regrets, a narrative of a satanic victory. Despite Freud's disavowals, the very structure of his language prevents him from respecting Leonardo; he appreciates only one part of that Renaissance character—those elements which allegedly constitute his painterliness. This dualism prevents him from respecting (to observe carefully, take into account, pay attention to, treat with consideration, to regard with some esteem) so much of the man and his works. He disregards certain elements; they are the other to be dismissed as deviations, falls, gaps, misfortunes: only they, and never the positive, masculine qualities of painterliness, are regressive, infantile sublimations. Only under their spell is Leonardo 'pulled along', 'driven further and further', responding to 'unconscious impulses'. It is as if all that which constitutes the other is foreign to Freud; things that once labelled, classed as such, are no longer subjects, only objects to be handled.

A respectful language (of psychoanalysis) would constantly question the homogeneity of its concepts, the exclusiveness of its dualities, the literalness of its labels. It would persist in seeing and appreciating the heterogeneity, the contradictoriness, the impurity of reality, and attempt in its translations into language to regard/respect such diversity. Analysis of any type demands distinctions which violate but those based on a narrowness of outlook, a certitude of position, a faith in some Proper, a need for constant boundaries, violate most. It is as antidote to such tightly constrained analytic language that Kakar and Gandhi are inserted. They take notice of complexity; it is considered regardable (worthy of being regarded); it is not an inchoate state to be violently dissected into simple component parts; it is not to be resolved, dismissed, digitalised into an 'either-or' confrontation. It is to be explored, minutely, like a labyrinth; which, at the end (without finality) still remains a labyrinth, but one now appreciated—in value—because it is understood better. As with the quality of a good translation, it adds something.

It is not only because love, passion and sexuality are central to the question called Leonardo that I chose the particular tracts of Kakar and Gandhi. It is because the 'language of these words' is so pertinent. These words resonate, of necessity, with breached boundaries: they are, in this sense, the irreducible mystery and paradox of human life. The more they are regarded, the more one knows that any one thing is never simply itself: what is masculine is also feminine, what is self is also other, what is body is also mind, what is present is also absent, what is now is also deferred, what is internal is also external. Yet, the moment this is conceded, we face a further paradox. These words can no longer mean what they meant before we began. We are now saying more than what we are saying. We are struggling against language, and there is nothing that can be done to rectify the dilemma—at least in words. We now have to appreciate, and exploit, the necessity and desirability of the allusiveness of language. We need, as it were, to place all our language in the questioning-frame of quotation marks, warning ourselves and others to regard, to respect carefully, what is being said. We can then appreciate that each similarity hides a difference, that each difference carries a similarity. Constancy of viewpoint and hierarchical ordering dissolve. We face the absolutely unavoidable metaphoricity of both language and reality. It has been said that 'we live our own metaphors'; but it is even more complex: 'we live between and across our mixed-metaphors'. Language can only allude, inadequately, to this rich elusiveness. It is not only Leonardo, but love, passion and sexuality, and therefore the humblest of us who are, in the end, a mystery, ineffable: each to be delineated in part, but parts dissolving as quickly as they appear, never to be classified, closed off, made whole, terminated. We are all worthy of analysis—but respectfully so.

'I am Thou' exemplifies this inevitable complexity of human reality. The expression must be appreciated in its entire metaphoricity; its apparent simplicity must not be misconstrued as a matter-of-fact, absurd literality: not only do the 'I' and 'Thou' stand for each and every conceptual component conceivable, but the 'am' is also elliptical—it is *and* it is not. Each facet, each moment, each element, is the same yet different: none can ever be reduced to a wholeness unto itself. In addition, 'thou' rather than 'you' conjures up the intimacy of all such relatedness: it is not only in love that we are incestuously bonded with and by our others; we are always within and beside ourselves. Contradiction is no longer a prohibition of thought or life.

While certain individuals, even entire cultures, may, in some way or other, 'know' this, others certainly do not and deny it. Rape is not love; B.C. Chatterji is repelled by 'effeminate' sentiments; we know the pervasiveness of 'monadism's fear of nomadism'. All manifest a demand to keep things separate, classified, in place, in their proper place. A fear of impurity, a deep faith in the naturalness and righteousness of the 'autonomy' of all properties. The strength of dualistic thinking in the West is nothing but the epistemological manifestation of this cultural belief.

Within his critique of western rationality, Freud had to combat this predilection to keep apart. He often succeeded but he also often succumbed. His understanding of Leonardo, his construction of the case, remained too much within the dominant western perspective. This was especially inappropriate, because, even from the information provided by Freud, Leonardo seemed willing and happy (and driven?) to breach so many boundaries, conventional now as then. His creativity refused to separate art, science, engineering and ephemeral entertainments. His passionate embrace with life, his life, required little need to distinguish between men and women, physical sexuality and brahmacarya. He was unconcerned to distinguish between the process and the product; 'be-ing' was his preoccupation, his life was a 'line taken for a walk'. This required no bowing to commercial success for its rewards and satisfactions.

He would brook no authority. He knew the intercourse of mind and body, the thrill, perhaps the *mahabhava* in revealing yet another body of knowledge.

It is this man, who refused to abide by most western proprieties and demarcations, whom Freud constructs on the unequivocalness of binary opposites. Yet it is odd that Freud fails to entertain one particular thought. There is one area in which Leonardo could well be said to have succumbed to western proprieties, indeed the very paradigm of western propriety. It could be said that Leonardo divided his life between what we commonly call the 'private' and the 'public'. In a certain way, he was too autonomous, complete unto himself. Certain things were not for others' eyes and ears. His diary, written with his left hand, was a coded one. It is possible that he felt that certain thoughts, desires, fantasies, and activities were private, 'properly' so. Just as Radha and Krishna used the darkness of the forest night to increase the excitation of their love to keep it hidden from the eyes of others (and perhaps from their own as well), so, maybe, did Leonardo attempt to keep some things secret. He remained silent on sex. This we do know. All we can do is regard that silence, and wonder what it may mean. This we may never know.

In the manner of an epilogue, we could raise the question why Freud withdrew from the full potential of his analytic language in his portrait of Leonardo. Why did this give him pleasure?—or what pain did he thereby avoid? One possible explanation suggests itself; rather, is suggested by the deliberate presence of Kakar and Gandhi, of a 'Hindu thought' which the British usually found a mystery, an anathema. To breach the boundaries of dualism forces us, as we have seen, to struggle against language, to battle with the canons of rationality and science. One can easily end by sounding bewitched, enchanted, occultist, mystical, uttering mumbo-jumbo. Was this the danger Freud faced throughout his career? He frequently expressed a determination to distinguish his work, his science, from the credulity and foolishness of certain others: the superstitious, the religious, the primitive. The one duality he would never concede breaching was that between the realm of the supernatural and that of the natural. To him, anything hovering close to the transcendental belongs exclusively to the 'symptomatic', an object of psychoanalysis, never its property. His famed clarity of expression could be read, as it were, as his living proof—to others and perhaps to himself—that what psychoanalysis had to say was sayable within the parameters of established western scientific rationality. (Even so, what he said is still rejected as irrational sorcery by so many.) Perhaps we have too often underestimated the constraints within which he felt he had to work: forcing, one moment, a drawing-back from the flames of mystical nonsense; at the next, stretching the limits of rationality in an effort to do justice to all that which is so apparently non-rational and mysterious. His guiding principle was unequivocal: his science must not be confounded with non-science, his quest must be distinguished from those labelled mystical. In whatever guise they may appear, he knew the latter belonged to the 'primitive'. In his later life he may have risked his identity more than ever (his thoughts now encompassing such inexplicable ideas as the life and death instincts), but in 1910, in *Leonardo*, his thoughts remained on firmer ground. Demarcations were sharp and they stayed in place. But perhaps an anxiety in Freud shows itself in his text.

Apart from the surprising mistranslation we have already noted, there are other moments which betray a symptomatic quality. From the beginning he appears to need to legitimise his dualistic characterisation of Leonardo by referring to opinion in Italy at the time. To do this a few times seems quite appropriate; to refer 'to his (Leonardo's) contemporaries' and similar expressions the number of times that he does, seems to manifest another quality altogether. As if he needed to distance himself from the very observations he is in the process of making his own. He is, after all, attempting a psychoanalytic interpretation independent of time and place, not an historico-sociological study explaining why Leonardo was considered a mystery in his time. Consider Freud's reference to Leonardo's 'mild and kind' disposition: '*At a time* (my emphasis) when every individual sought to gain the widest latitude for his activity, which could not take place without the development of energetic aggression towards others, he surprised everyone by his quiet peacefulness, his shunning of all competition and controversies' (p. 13). We know that *at that time* has nothing to do with it; Freud believes, *now*, that Leonardo should have been more aggressive.

He is also in a hurry to build up the case called Leonardo under the signatures of his Florentine contemporaries. In a writer as fastidious as he, it is surely significant that he failed to correct, no matter how many times he may have rearranged his material, a trivial error. Early in the work he says of Leonardo: 'The turning of his interest from his art to science... must *also* have been responsible for widening the gap between himself and his contemporaries' (p. 7, my emphasis). Note 'also'. Yet this is the *very first* reason he provides to show how Leonardo was a mystery 'to his contemporaries'.

And what is the nature of the anxiety that apparently impels Freud, at one instance, to remind his readers that for all his great scientific discoveries Leonardo was not Freud? Immediately after his strangely inadequate reference to the 'cognition', 'the sun does not move', he lavishes on Leonardo his strongest praise as a scientist 'over almost all realms of natural science, in every one of which he was a discoverer or at least a prophet and pathfinder' (we must forego discussion on these last two descriptions—more akin to religion than to science!). Freud then continues: 'However, his curiosity continued to be directed to the outer world; something kept him away from the investigation of the psychic life of men; there was little room for psychology in the "Academia Vinciana", for which he drew very artistic and complicated emblems' (p. 24).

Did Freud need to keep his distance from Leonardo? And, by alienating himself, alienate that creative person from himself as well? We know how Freud feared things Italian: a culture impregnated with religiosity; and Leonardo, typical of the Renaissance in which 'humanism' and 'religion', the sacred and profane, were enmeshed with each other; and an art which likewise refused to be facilely classified as either one or the other. Freud confronting the ineffable. If he were to surrender, to lower the rigid boundaries between all the compartmentalised components of psychic and cultural life, did he know, at some level or other, that he would have eventually to question his fundamental faith in western rationality and science, and concede that there may be no unequivocal border between them and the so-called mystical thought of primitives. That there are many modes of rationality. That not one of them is absolutely privileged. That any line delineating one from the other is ultimately arbitrary. That Leonardo's art was no more humanist and secular than it was religious and spiritual. Ultimately Freud turned his back on Leonardo and on a richer, 'mystic-impregnated' language of respect, in favour of a culturally determined myth: that the ideal, the benchmark, the real is encapsulated by the thought and work of modern western, secular man. He could not face the music.

Freud did not learn from Leonardo. Nor have many others; he has merely been appropriated and classified.

A Maha-raga or a Lesson in the West

10

'No, no', he said, gently but emphatically. 'If you go to bed, you should sleep. If you are reading, you should read. If you are eating, you should eat. And if you are thinking, then you should think. Never mix the different activities. No good ever comes of it, and what's more, you can't enjoy—neither can you profit from—any of them.'[1]

THIS, THE somewhat dramatic sermon experienced by Gayatri Devi, the future Maharani of Jaipur, when as a young girl she says good-night to her grandfather, the Maharaja of Baroda, adding, as an aside, that she was too excited with the affairs of the day to go to sleep immediately. As she notes, her grandfather's reply 'lives clearly in my memory'.

There will be more than one reaction to this utterance. But, could we hazard that most readers will be struck, to some degree or other, by the uncommon and, let's admit it, the slightly bizarre quality of the admonition. But in what way bizarre? Bizzare—to whom? Coming from whom?

[1] *A Princess Remembers: the Memoirs of the Maharani of Jaipur*, Gayatri Devi (and Santha Rama Rau), Tarang Paperbacks, Delhi, 1976, pp. 23–24. This chapter was first published in slightly different form in *Chai: Criticism, Heresy and Interpretation*, 1, 1, 1988, pp. 89–103.

It cannot be, surely, that we, say western readers (please bear with this and other stereotypes for the moment), find it odd because it somehow conjures up non-western, and to be precise, Indian thinking? There is nothing characteristically Indian about it—at least not as we have been taught to characterise that. We would as quickly dispel the next obvious move; it is not characteristically western. Without doubt. By now, if not sooner, a suspicion crystallises. Could it be a caricature of western thought?

Of course. An Indian, learning English, learning western as it were, got it wrong; this time not so much the actual words of an expression (which we know is common, and which is now seen to constitute a new category of language—Indian English), no, this time it is a very thought itself, a way of looking at the world, a western approach to ordering one's life and affairs. It is even understandable how the particular Indian could have got it wrong. He was well known and admired for being modern, for having cultivated a western outlook on things; as a ruler, he advanced the cause of change, of progress. He had learnt his lessons well and was exemplary. One could imagine, without really knowing anything precisely about his life, his acquiring this new set of principles. He was told, repeatedly, by British officials, and he just indirectly absorbed certain lessons on how to behave, publicly and privately. In particular, he understood that certain things were to be kept separate, rather were to be separated, because up until then, he and his fellow Indians had not done so. He now realised what a serious mistake this was, this mixing things together, and how entrenched a habit, a bad habit, this was in Indian culture. At some or other level of consciousness, this leader of men grasped what he saw to be the essence of western success and he knew what he had to do, and not do, to emulate it. Eventually, he internalised a new set of commandments. In actuality, there was only one commandment; so what was vital was to appreciate its many, varied exemplary applications, its synecdochic parts, its symbolic elements, its symptomatic traits. Its basic move was elementary. It was so obvious, once one had begun to think differently about things—all things, from the humblest, most personal habits to the most profoundly significant public affairs. Once one has grasped the dictum, which we could repeat here, excusably but tellingly in an anachronistic, Christian guise 'Thou shall not mix genres', the degree of one's seriousness and fervour would depend solely on the breath of one's imagination. To start with, it was imperative to keep politics and religion apart. They must be understood, no matter how difficult this would be for an Indian, as two entirely distinct spheres of human behaviour. Now, this Maharaja may have been aware that the British officials whom he so carefully observed were quite commonly, in his day, a bit anti-religious. You could put it this way. They would say that things that are religious do not belong in politics, that if they were to become entangled politics would suffer. The Maharaja may or may not have realised that they rarely said that if the two were mixed, then religion would suffer. No, they wouldn't say that, perhaps because they did not want to get involved in religion; they didn't want to mix in that area (see what I mean? you have to keep certain things apart). What they were properly concerned with, and with only that, was the public realm, with state matters. They were concerned to protect its propriety, its integrity, its essence from anything (not just religion) which didn't belong. That meant, also, that one had to keep apart matters of state, say economic concerns, from the realm of family, kinship and caste. Now, in many ways this initially seemed difficult for the Maharaja, his rule being essentially a dynastic one; but he quickly learned to distinguish when he was talking and acting in the name of the state, and when, on the other hand, he was engaged in merely personal, family matters. For his subjects this task would be easier; they would have no need to discriminate finely between kinship and kingship. The problem wouldn't arise. This exemplary prince did not take long to appreciate how the most intimate of matters were, or rather ought to be affected, by this radically new consciousness of things. He may even have acquired a new, secret admiration for some particular family member and ex-ruler of the State of Baroda who was well-known for having preached the wisdom of never allowing one's emotions to interfere with one's judgements of state; that, for example, in temper, one may leap to decisions one may live to regret. And, realising the sagacity of his heir he became, at the same time, doubly appreciative of the wisdom of the entire western tradition because had it not seen, early in its history, the importance of reason being kept pure from the fires of passion, and was not this just one more example of the West's general approach to life: separate that which does not belong, and maintain constant vigil. It was likely that this Maharaja had the insight to articulate all this in a variety of ways. He was, after all, educated and had acquired an analytical way of thinking. He saw distinctions; he made them. He saw that another way of expressing this was to talk of clarity of purpose, of specific goal-oriented activity (again excuse the anachronism), of functional differentiation, of the division of labour, not in the social sense, for, after all, India had operated a mode of this long before it was adopted (in a more democratic way) by the West. No, I mean an internal division of labour: with application, one could learn, and one certainly should do so, to do one thing at a time, and thereby, axiomatically, do it well. It makes sense that being fully engaged in one role, one function, with one purpose in mind at any one time, greatly enhances the probability of it being executed best. This result is overdetermined. Not only is a goal no longer compromised, diluted, made ambiguous by the presence of another; not only does one learn to understand and appreciate in its fine, detailed self the unblemished essence of any one activity; one also becomes expert in handling whatever is at hand. Everything—subject, object and their relations—become concentrated. An internalised specialization: a mental, emotional, psychological, cognitive compartmentalisation. Everything is to belong in its own, proper place.

The Maharaja began to make distinctions that he and his Indian peers were unaccustomed to do. He now comprehended the difference between the public and the private and how, of course (and the number of times he pondered that 'of course' and remarked to himself how odd it was that certain things had never previously been so obvious) this separation benefited both those spheres; it protected the public generally because no longer would matters of state be contaminated by the intrusion of personal affairs; it protected the individual because it was now clear that certain things were, and ought to remain, personal and private, and that the state had no right to interfere in such matters. He now saw clearly the propriety of different matters. He may at times (who knows?) have felt himself to be a man of quality simply because he was so adept at picking the quality of all things. He somehow knew where each thing belonged. Confident and maybe a little self-satisfied he now, in all ways, had a position to maintain regarding all matters.

This need to isolate individual activities demanded a new precision in thought and language. To enable sharp delineation of realms one could no longer be equivocal in the use of language. Things had to be clearly represented by particular words; one could no longer tolerate ambiguity in expression, polysemy in definition nor, most of all, variety in the ways one classified the world. Henceforth things were to be understood in one way only, and language was to be trimmed and fitted to accommodate this cognitive stencil. The ideal was evident: a one-to-one correspondence between word and reference. Language must be literal, and truth enthroned in its only possible form: the literal truth, the identity of word and thing. One tests, quite objectively, measure by measure: do words comply with reality? Truth reigns; it is clear—and absolute. Not unlike the Christian God.

Yes indeed, the Maharaja of Baroda was pleased that he had used the occasion so fittingly to teach his granddaughter a lesson; the lesson which, were she to follow throughout her life, would mould her as a modern person; and would help her lead India towards progress, towards a less obscurantist future because, ultimately, it had certainly become clearer to him that the strength of the West (of which England was merely an example) lay not solely in its military power and technical innovativeness (these, perhaps, had been over-emphasised) nor in what he saw as their natural assertiveness (which could certainly become aggressive), but on their habits of thought, which he now understood as shaping everything they did—their science, their education, their logic, their administration of people and things, their discipline, self-discipline, their rule. And by this he meant more than anything their analytic predilection, their ability, maybe even a cultural compulsion, to divide, separate, distinguish, and, by so doing, maintain the essential quality of each thing, ensuring its operation immune from the impact of other, external domains. It was because of this fundamental, cultural orientation, he realised, that westerners were able to be so objective (sometimes the maharaja wrestled with the dilemma whether this objectivity was either cause or effect of this separation compulsion). They were objective because they separated themselves, as it were, from whatever they were handling. They could treat matters or problems for just what they were, without confusing things, without getting involved. They remained reasonable because they kept their distance. This was the element common to their science, scholarship and political administration. Whatever it may be, each item was treated objectively, as a thing outside. And continuity followed: generations may pass, scientists or officials may die, but the same procedure, the same knowledge is automatically carried on. He fully understood the British role in places like India; the decisions they knew they had to take: no matter how unpleasant, even harsh, they executed them, objectively. There was nothing cruel in what they did; the British officials were merely acting as neutral or independent transmitters, instruments would be a good word, of policy. And that's what he admired so much in the officials with whom he had dealings: they may be aloof, even distant, but they were reliable. If they said something, they meant it; their word was as good as their deed. They were always on time, in place, so proper, correct. Punctual. Orderly.

The Maharaja of Baroda would have smiled 'gently but emphatically' with approval had he known that at about the same time that he seized the occasion to give a timely lesson to his granddaughter, in distant Paris, an expatriate American woman wrote 'A rose is a rose is a rose is a rose.' He would have understood.

Let us now return. It was suggested that this piece of advice sounded odd because it was by an Indian attempting to adopt a western viewpoint but not getting it wholly right. And when one misses a cultural nuance one slips drastically and appears quite off-beam. But what exactly did he get wrong? Was it something like the Maharaja unconsciously showed his non-westernness in the very process of being consciously western, as he attempted to teach a western lesson to his granddaughter! Thus the odd character of his utterance.

It is commonly believed that traditionally Indian children are reared, socialised, brought up (no word seems quite satisfactory) differently from the way children are in western cultures. The latter utilises verbal-based instructions expressing universal, absolute values; the former does not, depending rather on the efficacy of emulation of adult behaviour, thereby avoiding verbal instruction and any articulation of universals. It is in this sense that the maharaja, possibly without awareness, adopts a western mode of child-rearing: language formulating a universal rule. He apparently did not feel confident that his young granddaughter would have learned adequately from observing and internalising the norms of his daily practice (and we are told how regular he was in all such matters). He may have been over-concerned. He was, however, apparently too concerned to be western for he generalised where preferably he should not have, or he formulated a law of a culture which would have preferred it to remain as it always had been: as implicit commonsense. (The most fundamental assumptions of any culture, its pre-knowledge, its commonsense, are understandably the most difficult to reveal and articulate. One imagines that it is the outsider who is best placed to sense this commonality. Within the culture itself such assumptions may receive conscious articulation only in the form of particular historical exemplars not in their most sweeping, trans-historical, and therefore universal, transcendental form.) The maharaja's error was an ironic one: believing that he was dealing with something the West considered absolute (and he had good reason for such a belief) he generalised, and applied it in areas the West would consider trivial, beneath consideration—such as sleeping and eating; he then added an absurd element by associating these petty things with thinking and reading. The Maharaja had in a way contradicted himself: by grouping together those four activities he had broken his own rule never to mix disparate things. The Maharaja displaced the value of the tradition; by the illustrations he chose to accompany the absolute dictum he destroyed its value. He made it appear absurd by applying it as he did—which possibly was inevitable once one redirects adult, worldly affairs into matters appropriate to children. Once again he had destroyed the spirit of the law/lore by failing to separate significant affairs from childish minutiae. It proves, in a way, that one cannot really mix certain things, like cultures and people. Nothing but bowdlerisation and bastardy result.

But, having said that, we now have to concede that we are presented with an oddity of a different quality. Western universals may not be as absolute as we all commonly assume them to be. The desirability, necessity, even compulsion to analyse, separate and keep distinct is contextual after all. Change the setting and it changes its value, meaning, sense, relevance. Has the West deceived itself? It is that whenever a dictum is relevant it speaks and acts as though it were universal, natural, true; but whenever that dictum is irrelevant, it receives no mention, in particular its irrelevance receives no mention? It appears appropriate every time we are made to think of it—only. Each way we are encouraged to ignore the context. How bizarre. How cunning. So, is the oddity of the maharaja's lesson ultimately a western construction; the dissonance created and felt being within a western context?

Let us reread and re-site the maharaja; suddenly an Indian perspective appears. This would in no way be an artifice because the lesson, still ostensibly modern and western, nevertheless contains an Indian graft—or root. Whether the maharaja was aware or not of this is indeterminable and immaterial.

Once again it is commonly believed that a significant difference between western and Indian culture centres around the problem of means/ends. The former, it is assumed, operates behaviour as means to other ends; it plans, thinks ahead and orchestrates in the expectation that the actions chosen will be the most appropriate to achieve certain future goals. This means-rationality, it is said, has become our dominant institutionalised mode of thinking at least during the last two or three centuries. Its dominance has been celebrated, since Max Weber, as our most characteristic virtue and as our finest gift to the world. How something is valued depends on its success in the future; its worth is delayed as its gratification is postponed. Contrariwise, Indian culture is understood to celebrate the value of the moment, the worth of the experience itself, the significance of anything as an end in itself. There is scant concern for planning, for having an eye on the future, the result, the consequence. Stereotypically it is said that Indians find westerners manipulative who, in turn, find Indians irresponsible.

Has the Maharaja of Baroda grafted western separativeness with Indian instantaneousness? The analytic unit merging with delight in the moment. The exhortation 'not to mix genres' is laced (mixed!) with the plea to enjoy the moment, to enjoy whatever one is doing at any particular time. What is being said is that one cannot fully appreciate any experience if one uses it instrumentally, as an occasion to achieve something else as well. 'Killing two birds with one stone' is quite reprehensible. Rather, one ought to milk the moment. Life becomes living in the moment; being tied neither to the passions of the past nor to the utilitarianisms of an engineered future. Irrespective of consequence, one should learn to 'enjoy' and 'profit' from life as it occurs. This is a philosophy of presence as distinct from a western philosophy of absence, of constant deferral. The western analytic of separateness proclaims the autonomy of the activities and disciplines of life, the Indian perspective announces the autonomy of the occasion. No experience need be insignificant; each moment of activity (high or low, good or bad—terms which now said lose their worth) has worth—if each is treated with full regard. In the first case, the autonomy refers to something innate, objectively so, in the domain of activity, be that science, economics, art, politics, warfare. People are merely exhorted to respect these qualities which are independent of human agency. In the second case, activities as such remain undifferentiated in value; it is the participant who manifests autonomy by a total engagement with whatever is present; an engagement not weakened by ulterior motivation, by distraction, by calculation.

A different distance is highlighted in each case. In the former, separateness forges a space between each and every activity, each belongs to its own proper place; at the same time, space is maintained between these objects and the human subject engaged in their performance. Detached, one executes each paradigmatic activity. A surgeon a symbol. In the latter, full engagement in the moment opens a space between the present and its past and future. Such a particular distance is created that time loses its dimensions; there is always nothing but presence. Yet this presence carries its own distancing quality. Its engagement demands a separation by the participant from all which presently surrounds it. The individual becomes the sole concern, the entire question of worth; the dot of engagement removed totally from time and place but restored fully to its potential self: free and full. So, remark the prince's 'you can't enjoy—neither can you profit from': the maharani and ourselves are not told exactly how or why, but we certainly are not being encouraged to act in order to become, for example, wealthier, or to benefit society, or even in order to subsequently feel good about it. No, engagement constitutes its own reward, and this benefit will be immediately experienced, lived, in mind and body. We will know it, be it. This is not conjuring up brilliant jubilation, spectacular triumphs; rather, it exalts the otherwise humble, it shows euphoria emanating from simplicity. Nothing could be further removed from the alternative image of the western individual; engaged as a neutral implementer, disengaged as a human subject. 'Enjoyment', of course, entirely inappropriate, irrelevant.

The Indian graft is there with close scrutiny, rather, with a different scrutiny; one which withdraws from a dominant western view only within which the maharaja inevitably appears a bit odd. Nor do accusations of triviality monopolise one's response. What the maharaja is saying now appears profound not childish. The childlike examples— eat, sleep, read—increase rather than decrease the profundity. To the western ear, if there is still, or again, discomfort, it is because while it has always welcomed considerations of practical matters and things pertaining to reason, it still is uneasy about things psychological let alone spiritual. The maharaja's sentiments, cut in an Indian cloth, can appear both these. There is, undoubtedly, a tradition of spirituality, simplicity and renunciation which to the modern westerner is associated with our feudal past or with India and the non-western world. But with only a slight adjustment of perspective and language are we not witnessing also modern western psychological notions of cure: a similar message constitutes the core of every therapeutic practice back to Fromm and Maslow, back again to Jung and Freud, and yet again back to Nietzsche—whom we know was impressed with Indian thought—and beyond. To all of these, the psychically healthy person is one freed from the past, unanxious for the future, engaged with but uncontrolled by the present. The maharani is being told about the Nietzschean Overman, Jungian individuation, the autonomous person, liberation, about being!

The modal westerner feels a bit uncomfortable with these things. Such talk is to be avoided; it is disconcerting, out of place. A western voice prefers to project the conventional image of itself: engaged in the rational pursuit of means calculated to achieve in the future the desired and planned ends. For this purpose, analytic distinctions and objectivity are maintained while our cognitive and organisational skills are appropriately deployed. But there is a problem here. Some critics could insist that this image of the West has always been misleading; or, at least, that it is becoming less accurate a picture of contemporary western reality. They would argue that immediate gratification is now the dominant orientation; that people live for the moment. The age of deferral and distance is gone; at best it is an ideal of a certain professional middle class. There is, according to this critique, now no proper place for anything, no distinction between public and private, no separation of object from subject, no neutral calculation of performance—nothing but exploitation of the moment and the gratification of personal interests. So, we are presented with a further unexpected dilemma. What is the difference between the maharaja's advice (and the model of the western therapeutic cure) and this mode of immediate gratification? The one appearing so ideal; the other seen as base, crass consumerism—yet so apparently similar? The confusion is aggravated: the same cultural criticism is being made in India today about the increasing prevalence of short-term, selfish, materialist behaviour. Are we dealing with a universalism? Or is it a latest manifestation of cross-cultural emulation?

From where does the maharaja's voice come? Let us begin to unravel this by questioning the language we have been using. Do we know what means and ends mean, other than what they sound like when we express them in tautological definition: a means is the means to some end; the one a process the other a goal; the one immediate in time, the other distant, thereby the one always preceding the other? But how do we tell one from the other when faced with one—or the other? When pressed for clear distinctions, one becomes confused: in a way, means becomes little (or big as we will suggest) ends in themselves; ends become means to other, more elusive ends. And, having reached that level of clarification, could we not then concede that there are really no absolute distinctions between the two: that whatever one chooses to consider is, in fact, both; or, at least, never solely one or the other? I mention big. Is it not the case that much that once started out, innocently and temporarily, as a handy means to some significant goal, after a time becomes the displaced goal in itself? And a goal that, no matter how much denied, becomes a cancer on the original ends? In its name, at its service, it forfeits this end or permanently defers it, imposing on the subjects miserable or draconian or life-denying ordinances which for some time are tolerated only because they are said to be unfortunately necessary for the time being, or under the existing circumstances, or because surely we all really want to obtain the goals we say we do; until the time arrives that such rationlisations become less and less frequent, less and less necessary, because the temporary state of affairs is now seen as permanent, as natural, as just the way things are ordained: and those people who periodically remind us of the original ends are dismissed as impractical idealists, irrelevant nuisances, as cranks, deviants, criminals. Do we recognise it all? Is this not a picture of our society? I say 'of our society'—modern or not, western or Indian. Is this not a picture of the daily operation, and constant legitimation, of power, authority, discipline, education, the law, the economic system, fiscal policy, welfare policy, non-welfare policy, the pursuit of security, peace, war, deterrence, diplomacy, intelligence, counter-intelligence, the pursuit of happiness, of wealth, of truth, of god, of life, of death. Have we missed anything? Do you see the picture? Perhaps I got carried away. Could we say, at least, that an element of deception, and self-deception, enter our consciousness of things? Means come wrapped as ends, and ends come as means. Simulation reigns. And, as whenever that occurs, we have difficulty in distinguishing its presence from the effects of dissimulation. So, if we say that we believe in separating means and ends, what are we saying? Are we doing anything more than confirming an habitual language usage, upholding a cultural ideology, projecting a preferred self-image and (or) expressing an aspiration? What we are not doing is providing some unequivocal description of our actual state of affairs—even if for no other reason than that any such account could so easily be denied and reread as its opposite. Means and ends are eminently rereadable. And so is the maharaja.

The West (or its representative voice) certainly prides itself on the idea that it distinguishes means from ends, and would insist that the basic rationality of its social formations and the fundamental cause of its pre-eminent successes is its valuation of means over ends, its instrumental postponement of gratification. In the fullest sense of the terms one could epitomise this western imagery as responsible government (as divide and rule!). As reaction to this, two countervailing traditions urge an alternative strategy of life. One, a popular culture, and non-ascetic one, manifests immediacy as the essential human orientation. One consumes at, and for, the moment. There is no need here to reiterate the endless faces of consumerism—its guises are manifold—in a market, bazaar, disposable, vendible, touting, punting culture, in our free-wheeling way of life. But it may be worth reminding ourselves of its operations elsewhere. Consider the political forum and its representation of the public interest. What weight is given future ecological health compared to the immediate needs of the extractive industries and the daily comforts and convenience of the general citizenry? And of education policies geared to relevance and current trade statistics? And of immigration and welfare policies which seem to dare the future (not) to pay retribution upon us? Need we continue? The scales, each time, favour the short-term, the momentary advantage, the instant reward, immediate satisfaction.

The other, a minority culture, redressing the strictures of abstinence and deferral by espousing a triumph of the therapeutic. Mental health, stretching from its least ascetic form of sensual liberation to its most ascetic manifestations in the restrained euphoria of an analytic cure or a spiritual renunciation, emphasise the present. One learns to cope with it or to enjoy it. (Interestingly, in the West at least, one has to be educated for this quality of here-and-nowness, being able to beness; yet no such teaching is apparently required for the former mode of immediacy.) What is the difference despite the similarity? How facile would it be to see a distinction in terms of that grandest of classical western (Greek) dualities, that of mind and body? Immediacy (a convenient label for the popular culture) appealing to the material, bodily satisfactions and, henceforth (to some), to the baser things in life. On the other hand, spontaneity (to label the other), satisfying the psyche, the (to some) higher things in life. Note the paradox: it is the culture of the minority which has established the hierarchy: things pertaining to the senses, passions are deemed lower value than things pertaining to the mind or spirit. Or is it only an apparent paradox—whatever is *more* valued cannot be attributed to a majority, without destroying its superior worth? Or are we unwarrantedly universalising? Perhaps all we have done is describe the particular western tradition in which the mind seems to have maintained a hegemonic edge irrespective of numbers. When we grossly consume we secretly know we are betraying a moral norm.

Which makes us think that the maharaja's voice was an Indian one after all. A western voice surely would have chosen *either* mental *or* bodily illustrations for its lesson. He chose both. He also declined priority to either; with an emphatic lack of distinction he goes from sleeping to reading to eating to thinking. The alternations are so definite that one is momentarily tempted to suggest the maharaja was giving the West and not his granddaughter a lesson. A lesson that things of the flesh are of equal value with things of the spirit; and that indeed, there is limited value in distinguishing the two. As in so many things, the West separates that which the Indian tradition hesitates to do. When the Maharaja insists 'never mix the different activities' he is not, undoubtedly, whatever else he may be saying, speaking in favour of either spiritual or material matters. They go together; they mix. The not-mixing he is advocating is ungraded, general and inclusive, but different.

Because in a way, a particular Indian consciousness of separation can be seen also at work here. I refer to Hindu notions of purity and pollution. It is believed that attributes of purity (unblemished perfection), its opposite impurity, and all degrees between, are inherently present in everything. Humans constantly confront all qualities, and in that sense, pollutions are unavoidable. All one can do, and a Hindu is obliged to, is to diminish the polluting effects of impurity either by insulating oneself from its practice or by isolating oneself from those more pure (the two aspects of the caste division of labour) or by purifying oneself if unavoidably polluted. While all things are thereby hierarchically valued in terms of purity, they are, at the same time, considered equally necessary. What is unavoidable must be, in a way, respected; each is a complement of the other.

So, Hindu belief about purity is an engagement with the questions of separation and togetherness, of exclusiveness within inclusiveness, of coping with the inevitable, avoiding the unavoidable, achieving the unachievable. Its struggle exemplifies the cosmic tension of purity and impurity: the necessity to challenge necessity; the outcome being neither success nor failure, purity nor impurity.

Can we not see some confrontation of this dilemma in the maharaja's lesson? It is often noted that nothing presents more constant anxiety to Indians in their daily lives than questions of pollution. Categoric responses (such as punitive treatments of lower castes) are often the product of anxiety, an over-sensitivity to situations interpreted as tending too much another way. The question we need to raise here, is why the maharaja felt obliged to answer his granddaughter as he did. Why did he react so strongly? She had said she was retiring to bed, but not to sleep, rather to excitedly relive all the wonderful things that had occurred that day. In a non-Hindu setting we could consider his reaction quite uncalled for, its meaning as part of a particular dialogue quite incomprehensible. Within a Hindu setting, it becomes more explicable, it appears less extreme. That is, we can imagine how it may have happened: the Maharaja saw in the girl's excitement an extreme, that of mixing, the pollutions of the undifferentiated. His reaction was to stress the opposite: the importance of maintaining the purity of all things, the separateness of functions, the unreal and unattainable faultlessness of all things. The maharaja was not being odd or bizarre or meaningless, only extremely anxious— as a Hindu. He may, we cannot know, have been responding at some level to more than just his granddaughter.

Questions of pollution, however, are not restricted to cultures like India. But whereas the Hindu notion of purity is an idealised state of stainlessness attributable to inanimate and animate beings, a western notion of purity refers to domains freed from the polluting interference of other domains. Where the Indian model expects constant struggle and compromise, the West insists on the need to cut free, to liberate a domain from an historically-determined, overarching control; and once free, vigilance to maintain this independence, this purity. Where the Indian is faced with a constant ethical dilemma, and hence anxiety, the westerner is engaged in a simple struggle of good versus evil. Evil representing past history, dependence, interference and lack of sovereignty; good being the new, the free, the independent—no longer hobbled or restrained by the interests of the other. It is the state versus the church, the secular over the religious, science over philosophy, art over ideology, contract over status, economics over politics, reason over passion, the literal over the figurative. Its presence ubiquitous.

It is this demand to keep apart, this separation compulsion, with which we began this chapter (and this book) with which the maharaja's lesson was compared as a faulty and bizarre caricature that we are now returning to. It is a western matter of propriety, an assumption never doubted, that the various domains of practical concerns possess essential qualities distinguishing one from the other; that the rational, efficient operation of each can be attained only when allowed to unfold within its own laws; and that our knowledge of such innate processes can be acquired only by specialists of each domain. The western legitimacy of disciplines. Impurity enters whenever boundaries are breached—when generalists express opinions about which, by definition, they are not qualified to do, or when experts pass beyond their proper domains of expertise. The very means (and ends) of production are put in jeopardy when a domain's essence is polluted by the intrusive interests of another—when art is marred by ideology; an economic system tinkered with by politics, scientific progress held back by ethical questions, when a very logic itself is blurred by rhetoric. The purist scourges such mongrel behaviour and classes its practitioners as untouchable. Battles may ensue, but authority rests, by necessity (otherwise the setting would not be western), within each domain not across them. This is so institutionally and in the language of legitimacy; authority can speak only for purity and for the separation of domains; that which questions the wisdom of separate development, that which practises adulteration, is placed, conceptually and institutionally, outside, as illegitimate, as soiled, as ultimately non-western. Not unlike the Hindu, however, the westerner also experiences an anxiety, which helps to explain the over-zealous commitment to its belief. It concerns a repressed doubt about its self-identity. A persistent and strongly held self-image of the West is that of its unique freedom. This is the quality which gives it its greatest pride and which is seen most positively to explain its successes. To the degree it holds an historical dimension to its self-image it is one which portrays an evolution to more and more freedom; wresting its own, personal autonomy from churches, absolute rulers, the sway of superstition, any form of transcendental determination, the encroachment of other. The crystalline, pure entity left as residue of all such liberations is the self, the individual, free, pure, responsible only to itself, in charge of its own destiny. Is there some deep western anxiety that this may not be the truth after all; or that its hegemony is a fragile one, that the free self could, without due care, slip back into a state of subjection otherwise so assiduously avoided? The cultural fear of dependence, of determinations beyond oneself, of values beyond one's own hallowed reason, of the ineffable, of not being 'modern'. We are committed to know that we, and only we, modern westerners are really free; and, as we wish to separate ourselves, distinguish ourselves, form all other, less-free people, so do we need to withdraw from tendencies within our own self which could threaten our collective image. Ultimately, the guardians of our myths remind us of our classical origins and how, ever since, our integrity has rested on the maintenance of fundamental separations: that our reason must not be polluted by our passions and that the law of contradictions tells us that things cannot simultaneously belong in two places. Our basic logic insists that things be separated: they are either this or that—never both. The end of freedom and the tyranny of obscurantism await the neglect of such wisdom. The reason of the western psyche is a pure one, unsullied by boundary transgressions, and determined to maintain its freedom.

The West sustains this imagery and strategy without atrophying into timeless and rigid categories because of its periodic co-optation of certain critics and the concomitant, welcome creation of new domains of legitimate activity and enquiry. What is seen and fought in one epoch of time as transgressive impurity is accommodated in the next as a new arena proper to itself. This is mysteriously accomplished without the myth of purity being sullied or questioned. Once again, we secretly treat our universals as contextual, we keep that from ourselves.

Eventually we have to end the quest to pin down, in some definitive form, the many voices of the Maharaja of Baroda. Certain things have become clearer. We can no longer doubt, I am sure, that the maharaja spoke in diverse tongues. To label them, however, is a more difficult task. For, once again, it is hard to overcome the dazzle of simulacra: what looks, at one moment, to be Indian then appears western, which re-emerges as a new Indian; what seem alluringly similar can suddenly appear alarmingly different; but, then again, is it? Even so, we have simplified: for convenience we have acted as if Indian and western comprised only two, homogeneous traditions. We know, of course, they do not. In the end we may decline altogether the temptation to label, and the very labels themselves. Yet they served their purpose. They were useful, even as they are shown to be, ultimately, of dubious use.

Kairos, the youngest son of Zeus, personifies opportunity, chance, the right time, the psychological moment, the auspicious moment. As one would approach his altar of opportunity near the stadium entrance at Olympia one could respond fully to the momentary confrontation and seize him by his prominent forelock. A moment later he would be passed; it was now too late, he would be beyond you and no longer could he be clasped as he was otherwise bald. The timing, using the unique moment, was everything.

The maharaja knew not to miss the opportunity that evening. He seized the occasion, and his granddaughter's memory confirms how well he used it. In how many languages does Kairos speak? How many translations, how many unrecognisable transformations exist?

Certain scholars recently suggest that notions of auspiciousness and inauspiciousness are far more significant for an understanding of Indian culture than previously granted. Similar to ideas of purity, auspiciousness—connoting sentiments of well-being—can be attributed to objects, places, events and people, even to life itself; the quality being an outcome of a conjunction of forces such as time, place, performance and purpose. As such, it may best be understood as a quality of time itself, a specific moment of time. We could call it timing; the coincidence, synchronisation of forces, requiring a meeting together at one moment of time for effect. Not just any timing but the right timing, being timely: something which appears just at the right time. The timeliness of the auspicious is caught by such words as opportune and propitious, as well as those suggesting the uncanny, like providential, heaven-sent, lucky. There is a touch of the fortuitous in all this. It is, in a sense, by chance that things suddenly come together to form a propitious moment; there to be seized or not depending on the sensitivity of some witness. It is an event, singular and unplannable.

Another form of auspiciousness has routinised its timing. We know, well ahead, the propitious occasion because its occurrence is structured. It is a ritual to be repeated: an anniversary, an almanac recording, a seasonal greeting, a routine precaution. Swiftness, as the use of time, as seizing the occasion is no longer at a premium; nor is the question of what or how to do something; rather, it is knowing when one ought or not do something quite standardised in performance: a householder to begin a journey, a *devadasi* (temple dancer) to perform a particular ritual, a girl to marry. And we are dealing with extended periods of timeliness even though certain auspicious rituals may have to be performed with a strict eye on the calendar.

Not unlike ideas of purity, auspiciousness has an elusive quality. In a way it is never present, only referred to, desired, aimed at, celebrated, or attained indirectly in the avoidance of inauspiciousness. The propitious moment, the right time observed, announces auspiciousness symbolically, the idea of it, the promise of it, the value of it, perhaps, the guarantee of it.

We cannot know whether the Maharaja was disguising his Indianness (for the sake of a western propriety) or celebrating it (for what he saw as its universal value) when he seized the auspicious moment to wish his granddaughter an auspicious life. For that is what he did when he urged her to '*enjoy*' and '*profit from*' the various activities. It is recognised by Hindus that auspiciousness, temporal well-being, derives from fulfilling two realms: that of *artha*, the idea of profit and power, and that of *kama*, the enjoyment and satisfaction of bodily desires. We cannot doubt that the maharaja was not totally conversant with this traditional belief—for, as a maharaja, he would know that he, as a prince, a maharaja, a king, symbolised, according to that tradition, more than anything and anyone else, Auspiciousness!

It would be generally assumed, I imagine, that the western world no longer operates within orientations of the auspicious. It is simply not part of our post-Enlightenment (if not post-Christian) culture. The word, indeed, is anachronistic—tolerable only in ribbon-cutting. Bicentennial oratory. And yet!

Could I suggest that, ironically, it is our western statesmen today (our counterpart to the King) who best epitomise the value of a certain auspiciousness? Its timeliness has acquired a particular twist and a new legitimacy. Its label has of course been changed; with a modern air it is called pragmatism and realism, upon which all reasonable men, not just our statesmen, have conferred the highest honour. And those who do not pay due deference to these icons are deemed foolish, unreal, irresponsible, out of touch with reality, ideologues, lacking any sense.

The altar of Kairos is dislocated. One does not seize the occasion, the special moment to achieve something valued. No. One appraises each and every moment in order to ascertain what may or may not be achieved. What is possible, impossible. What one does, as well as what one does not, is explained in terms of The Time. Expedience becomes all. The time is not right for...the time is past when we could...it is inopportune now to...it is not the appropriate time to consider.... That is, what is considered auspicious is a notion of proper, of fit, that which 'goes' with the times; it is accordingly, auspicious, to fit in with this fit. Timely now implies congenial, sympathetic, in step, in accordance with, suitable. The appreciation of this is the trademark of the realist, of just being sensible, practical, pragmatic. The very fitness to rule is exemplified thereby; it is not fitting to label this, as its critics have, opportunist! The auspicious is, ultimately, being politic. Western politics is about auspiciousness. A means/ends in itself: being politic means survival means the ability and need to be politic again and again. Timing is all. The proper fit its symbol. A lesson in harmony. Nothing may be odd. Nothing remarkable. Nothing out of place, out of time. Fancy all this being told to a mere girl! Did she learn her lesson? Which tune did she hear, I wonder?

If the Maharaja of Baroda spoke in several voices, so have I. If he enjoyed himself, so have I. If profit from his lesson, so have I; I seized the occasion. My writing has ulterior motives. I am conscious of using words for ends to be deferred; for other people, for one or another reason. But I also write for writing. The gratification is immediate. Yet I suspect, I speak a broken western. Let's admit it, it's a bit bizarre. But that seems fitting. It is a lesson to be learned.[2]

---

[2] 'There is always more than one language in language' Derrida says in 'The Retrait of Metaphor', *Enclitic*, 2, 2, 1978, p. 31.

IV

Here and There

The Politics of Irresolution | 11 |

IT WOULD be understandable—but wrong—for readers to conclude at this stage that 'anything goes', that as everything is metaphor (including that very statement), and that as nothing exists independently to evaluate one metaphor against another, then intellectual activity, political commitment and moral judgement rest on nothing more than arbitrary whim. An ultimate irresponsibility is sheeted home, as it has time and again against so-called post-structuralists, aesthetes, pragmatists and whimsical dilettantes. To concede, which I do, that my position presents problems, that no simple, neat response is available to answer critics (which is inevitable otherwise one would have discovered a benchmark), is not a sign of failure but a reminder that handling social reality has to be a messier activity once the comfort and security of absolute criteria are jettisoned. That, of course, should have read 'assumed comfort and security' because appeals to god, reason or science have never in fact produced comforting solutions; these have been deferred by constant debate over exactly what judgement god, reason or science dictates us to follow. To accept my predicament, therefore, merely entails relinquishing some past myth of comfort which lingers on despite experience.

What is not a solution is some retreat into empiricism. As if anyone could be equipped to interpret and evaluate anything in isolation from everything else. That everything is unique is certainly so, and we ought never forget it; but things are similar, in a variety of ways, as well. Both these general propositions must be grappled with. It is as if empiricists were cowed by the enormity of the task or by the realisation that all theories are in fact wrong—which is, of course, again a half-truth: all theories, that is all metaphors, are both true and false, useful and dangerous, in some way or other.[1]

Empiricism has to be rejected for more fundamental reasons as well. It is self-deceptive, it dissembles an innocence it does not possess. Empiricism, in other words, is an impossibility. All enquiry, no matter how curtailed or cautious, is actually comparative analysis. That is not something that can be left to later or to others in some self-consciously articulated way. It is rather something that imposes itself upon us all the time we think about anything. Our first metaphor, our first theory is implicitly expressed with our first simple classification or association. It is unavoidable. Empiricism suffers from all the dangers of the self-unaware. This does not prevent a work from being remarkably revealing; but in such a case, that is not the result of empiricism but of unconscious and denied theory. One could say, with caution, that empiricists do not think; rather they are thought as theorists. That all metaphoric insight will miss in some way or other does not, therefore, demand a further aggrandisement of empiricism, of further compartmentalisation of shallow and insular expertise. On the contrary it demands more theories, more metaphors, even though we know, to begin with, that they will all fail.

No one strategy automatically follows from a realisation that nothing is guaranteed. The potential range of response is well illustrated by the conflicting scenarios created by two of the most influential Anglo-American exponents of what is loosely and incorrectly known as 'relativism', Richard Rorty and Paul Feyerabend. Apparently in the name of freedom, all our options would be kept open by the latter, while they would be severely curtailed by the former.

As we consider these authors, we quickly notice how knowledge and politics are inextricably enmeshed. This is so, even though each writer resorts to politics seemingly strategically. One resorts, as we say, as a measure. Out of desperation one searches and finds a value and a benchmark in an unlikely place. One could ask: what has politics and the wider community got to do with science and knowledge?

[1] My strong opposition to the metaphors of growth, development and progress does not mean that I believe them to be totally 'wrong' or useless.

Everything, these authors answer. They insist that society has priority: knowledge is to serve it, not it knowledge.

Feyerabend has long argued[2] that to the degree that science exists (and as he understands it, it does), it exists as a complex range of related activities, not as any one thing which possesses a method, about which one may develop a theory, or about which one may establish procedures of proof, truth or veracity. Indeed, the imposition of a theory or method would be counter-productive, and the very search for better ones pointless, he argues. As they proceed, scientists both create and apply the appropriate standards. Such a state of affairs, far from being the chaotic and free-and-easy carnival his critics conjure up, is in fact its opposite, being rigorous and demanding: the scientist, no longer simply applying some proven method, must probe and judge each step of the way; some 'rules of thumb' may be helpful, but they also may not. Nothing is guaranteed, including, of course, the understanding and approval of radically innovative work by conventional establishments. 'Anything goes' can operate as much against as for innovative thought; it can be used to resist change as much as to promote it.

In such a 'relativist' world, Feyerabend urges two causes, each being attacks on any notion of 'authority', and procedures to further ensure our freedoms. The first is educational, one is tempted to call it politico-educational. The present situation he characterises as doctrinaire, ideological, destructive of curiosity and creativity and difficult to distinguish from propaganda. It is the inculcation of deference to authority. His solution he places in italics: *'the best education consists in immunizing people against systematic attempts at education.'*[3] This is not the time to elaborate this critical mode of education; I support it in principle. It seems doomed, however, to remain a dissident and minority project.

Closely related to this sustained openness is his insistence that we must tolerate any evil, for not only are we unable to *prove* by any reasonable means that it is inherently evil—as distinct from being not pleasing to oneself, but who knows, Feyerabend continues, what good may emerge from the most unpropitious source. Even a fascism, he says, should be allowed to survive.

He is right in insisting that we cannot prove a case and we cannot know outcomes, but his conclusions are unacceptable. He knows,

---

[2] *Against Method*, New Left Books, London, 1975.
[3] *Farewell to Reason*, Verso, London, 1987, p. 316.

and time and again he illustrates it, that judgements are made and positions defended in the absence of unassailable criteria and a guaranteed success. Listen to him on Galileo.

> Galileo, for example, did not just complain, he tried to convince his opponents with the best means at his disposal. These means frequently differed from standard professional procedures, they even conflicted with common sense..; but they had a reason of their own...and they were occasionally successful.[4]

Why should Feyerabend allow fascism to survive when he is ready to utilise his many talents, no matter how inadequate they may turn out to be, to combat the evils of our present education system? That reason is limited, that our knowledge relative, that our insights are nothing other than metaphoric associations—none of these do or should prevent our defending what we believe in and opposing what we disapprove of.

But Feyerabend nurtures another argument in favour of complete toleration, even of evils like fascism: we never know, he says, 'how much good it [evil] still contains and to what extent the existence of even the most insignificant good thing is tied up with the most atrocious crimes.'[5] This approach is even more plausible, he believes, once one concedes that 'Evil is part of Life': one does not welcome it one merely delimits it, 'one lets it persist in its domain'. This is an impressive case, proposing sound pragmatic reasons for espousing a transcendental value like toleration. However, it seems a metaphysical misconception of the social predicament.

Being human, privately or socially, entails the necessity of making constant choices. Feyerabend's case appears to envisage a boundless cultural environment in which we have the right to exclude nothing—because, perfectly reasonably, we cannot foretell the outcome of anything. But his implicit imagery is unreal: we cannot survive with a surfeit of anything; whether we like it or not, we cannot sustain some total plenitude. We have to be selective. Our lives are necessarily preferential, and because they are, we would be indeed perverse to choose the worse to survive rather than the better. Something has continuously to go in favour of something else. A

[4] *Ibid.*, p. 285.
[5] *Ibid.*, p. 314.

strategy of keeping our options open must not totalise the situation; it must co-exist with our periodic necessary foreclosures.

Feyerabend proposes a second strategy. It aims to curtail the power of scientific experts, and in that sense, of science as a form of knowledge. A countervailing power must be given to the non-expert. Politics, society is to be given precedence. Scientists are to be our servants not our masters.

We can readily agree with him that 'scientists may *contribute* to culture, but they cannot provide its *foundation*'[6] (original emphasis). Science, Feyerabend says, cannot be a basis of love or friendship, or of a quality and meaning of life. It cannot legislate for life, if for no other reason that it talks in universals; it cannot handle different traditions and what is suitable for one people is not for another. 'Historical traditions cannot be understood from afar' he insists. Decisions must be local, and by the people. Science must be answerable to politics. 'Now politics, as I understand it, is in many ways related to love. It respects people, considers their personal wishes .... In a word: *politics, rightly understood, is firmly "subjective"*' (original emphasis).[7]

And as further support he distinguishes a hierarchy of interests, a broadening of domains of concern. The higher and broader must have greater power over the lower and narrower.

> There exists no enterprise that is not self-correcting to some extent and that cannot be changed by the actions of even a few determined individuals. But science is part of a larger unit; it is part of a city, a region, of entire nations.... In a democracy the self-correction of the larger units includes all their parts, which means that democratic self-correction overrules the temporary results of scientific self-correction.[8]

Feyerabend writes this at a period of western history which witnesses increasing demands to supervise, if not rigorously curtail the activities of science, especially ecologically and medically sensitive areas of research. His ideas initially appeal; it would be a pity therefore if his case were misconstrued because of his insistence that the churches, being a paradigm representative of broader human interests, should once

[6] *Ibid.*, p. 305.
[7] *Ibid.*, p. 306.
[8] *Ibid.*, pp. 261–62.

more reassert themselves and express their criticisms when necessary against science. In an impressive and persuasive way Feyerabend reinterprets his own earlier work on Galileo, and wonders whether we ought not reverse our cultural tradition about whom was the hero, Galileo or Roberto Bellarmino, his church critic. Let us re-see that struggle between 'good' and 'evil' with new eyes, ones by which Galileo now becomes merely science's 'own pushy Patron Saint':

> Scientific knowledge is too specialised and connected with too narrow a vision of the world to be taken over by society without further ado. It must be examined, it must be judged from a wider point of view that includes human concerns and the values flowing therefrom, and its claims to reality must be modified so that they agree with these values.[9]

Bellarmino becomes the spokesman for the broader and more humane public good against the idea that 'society must adapt to knowledge in the shape presented by the scientists.' Feyerabend is concerned to nominate a major role to representative spokesmen for the human condition; the church he takes as symbolic and representative of this larger concern.

This second strategy highlights a dilemma symptomatic of a time of highly specialised knowledges. The danger to a society constantly obliged to adjust to the authoritatively expressed dicta of experts is aggravated once one appreciates the inevitable partiality and inadequacy of their knowledge. To comply with the truth of others is one thing; to have to bow to their narrow prejudices and cavalier solutions is quite another. But, to become disillusioned with science (or is it scientists?) does not at all justify Feyerabend's transfer of loyalty, of faith, to the people, to democracy. Nothing that he says, or nothing that I know, shows that politics could be a panacea. How could it be? Why should it be? Reason and thought the author has found wanting; in their place he has discovered those magical and powerful words to so many: consensus, action, participation. 'The consensus of those addressed, not my arguments, finally decides the matter.... All these things can be decided only if everyone is permitted to participate in the debate and encouraged to give her or his views on the

---

[9] *Ibid.*, pp. 258–59.

The Politics of Irresolution

matter.... Citizens do not just think, they decide ...'[10] Feyerabend does not believe citizens have more wisdom or finer ethics than experts (nor are they less equipped in such matters), so a basis for his new enthusiasm is not obvious.

I suspect, however, that Feyerabend's new faith rests on his notion of hierarchy, of the greater authority going to the broader or higher domain of concern. Thus, I imagine (the illustrations are mine) he would consider the general physician 'worthier' to rule than the heart specialist, holistic medicine than mainstream western medicine, a federal government over a state government, people over individuals, long-term over short-term, and, we do know, a churchman over a scientist.

The idea has an immediate appeal which soon dissipates, and it does so for two reasons: in certain ways the distinction between the generalist and the specialist is a false opposition; and, to the degree that it is not misleading, the distinction presents an irresolvable dilemma.

The opposition between what could be called the generalist and the specialist is receiving more careful scrutiny these days. It is intimately related to the problem of the part and the whole, the above and below, the inside and the outside. It concerns the question of distance, of standing back from, detached from, of not being too closely involved, of being above it all. It seems therefore, an entrenched trace of some very old oracular and theological imagery: god, up there, above, sees all, knows all and can judge best. The West has a long history in the visual and spatial metaphors of knowledge. But is this tradition of hierarchy, of an assumed superiority of outlook given to the distant over the close, a sound one? I think not. What we have is a *difference* of outlook; to be intimate or distant allows a change in perspective, ensures an alternative emphasis, concerns differing relations, is informed by competing values—but with no obvious superiority inherent in either. Each will benefit from some advantage specific to it, and will suffer from some internal disadvantage. Different and worthwhile knowledge and judgements will ensue from either; and we can be informed in yet a further way (without necessarily assuming it 'better') by considering both. They may complement each other; they may not fit each other well as all; but one does

---

[10] *Ibid.*, pp. 307–09.

not 'overrule' (Feyerabend's word) the other—nothing is solved by introducing a second, or a third, view; a point we emphasised in an earlier discussion on social policy.

And so, the view of the expert or scientist, for example, ought be countered (always? at times?) by the view of some generalist; but if a conflict of views emerges there is no reason to award preference to the generalist; it is not inherently privileged. Likewise if we substitute the public or democracy for the generalist. We are back to the most classical of political debates: rule of expert versus rule of the people. Contrary to Feyerabend I find no solace in either solution. I insist on combining a trust and a distrust towards both—one moment retreating from the authority of the expert into the hands of some broader, more general interest; the next moment a reverse withdrawal. The resolution must be the maintenance of the dilemma; we cannot risk ending the paradox. The answer, and it should be seen as a positive not a negative one, is that we must accept neither alternative as a permanent, total solution. We must positively cultivate flexible strategies.

Feyerabend implies that the alternative to narrow expertise is its conceptual opposite, the broad. In reality, however, this putative broad may be yet another narrow, or a collection of narrow viewpoints. In his or her diagnosis a general physician, for example, may need to operate on some quite specific notion of the body's organic interdependencies which may be no broader than the operative viewpoint of a cardiac or cancer specialist. A conceptual 'broad' is easily confused with a physical or concrete 'broad'. To oppose unproblematically the collective voice to that of an individual identifies the two as equally singular before it proposes the former to be a more comprehensive, and thereby more worthy, voice. Its oneness is, however, a dubious quality; the collective is, surely, more a plurality, a heterogeneity of voices. It, thereby, loses its conceptual, oppositional privilege. It has nothing other than numbers on its side—an entirely different argument.

Why does Feyerabend need some solution? After all, he did have the strength to show that science has no one method, no one truth, and constitutes no one identifiable phenomenon, and yet, at the same time, to insist that we can live with this state of affairs, with this disillusion. Why did he need to name the unnameable; to identify the method of our human and social salvation? A farewell to utopias did not accompany his 'farewell to reason'.

And yet his inclination to politics has value. To him, it (politics) must take over because of the failure of science. By this perspective he brings knowledge and politics close; we should not have one without the other, he warns us. But, surely, we cannot have one without the other—whether we like it or not. Any choice of metaphor, in discourse or social action, is a political decision as it determines the likely inclusions and exclusions of subsequent behaviour. Metaphors are a force—to create and to repress. All science, as all art, is, in this sense, politics. To impose some democratic or public supervision on science (or art) as Feyerabend proposes is not to introduce politics into other domains but merely to extend and formalise its presence more publicly.

But a politics of knowledge is ensured for further reasons, in fact, for the very characterisation of science that Feyerabend provides. Politics, in its competition for power, is a measure of conflicting values. Crudely, more disagreement more politics. If our knowledge were reached by some consensual method and its truths verifiable by some recognised, universal criteria then more items on the human agenda would be settled, finalised once and for all; they would be beyond dispute, beyond politics. Politics will always be pervasive and ubiquitous, however, not simply because of the inevitability of conflicting interests but because a situation of plenitude, saturation, completeness, fulfilment, identity, equivalence, truth and worth (our language is inadequate; at best it can allude) can never be reached, is inconceivable. We face a situation of ever-changing but lasting irresolution. We resort to politics, as it were, because we are always faced with the incomplete, the unequal, the falling short. It is as if we were constantly faced with the problem of settling a just price, and we experience, time after time, that no exchange can be based on some equal value. Any content constitutes a discontent. We politicise, apart from anything else, because we face the ubiquitous need to rectify some lack. The dilemma of the human system and its restless quality derive from the necessary irresolution of its many paradoxes. For this there cannot be a solution, a utopia. Feyerabend's innocent answer in politics as overview at best unintentionally highlights just one exemplary mode of irresolution. We will, for very good reasons, not perversity nor whim, soon need to withdraw from the rule of the generalist for some more informed opinion of the specialist; and, not before long, return once again to the generalist. We need them both and neither; they are our medicine and our poison. The best means of our survival must be found, somehow, within such awkward parameters.

It is for such reasons, I imagine, that so many, today, are attracted to pragmatism, especially as it has such a forceful advocate as Richard Rorty. One senses that only it may provide a mode of accommodation, a flexibility unfettered by needless and unworkable principles.

The search for universal justifications for our knowledge, our institutions or our behaviour, is to Rorty a pointless one. Most of western philosophy therefore has been a waste of time. In its place Rorty insists on two basic principles which are beyond negotiation. Like Feyerabend, he unequivocally places society first; and, if this were to be questioned, he would defend it, as would Rawls, by insisting that justice is and must be the first virtue of a society and everything else is predicated on this. Knowledge, in all its forms, follows from this; it is to serve society. More pointedly, as it is to assist in the constant procurement of justice, it must be geared to action. Social engineering is the expression Rorty constantly valorises. Rorty is merely being faithful to Dewey and his pragmatism. As he says, in contrast to people like Husserl, whose hero is the scientist, and Heidegger, whose hero is the poet, 'pragmatists such as Dewey turn away from the theoretical scientist to the engineers and the social workers—the people who are trying to make people more comfortable and secure, and to use science and philosophy as tools for that purpose.'[11] Rorty's succinct description of Dewey could readily, and willingly, be applied to himself—'Dewey was essentially a social democrat. His thought has no point when detached from social democratic politics.'[12]

With this as goal, he is obliged, overdeterminedly as it were, to make it work. The entailments he develops are the means to ensure its success; are its necessities from which he does not flinch. Together they constitute a systematic framework for the successful, sustained operation of a western/European liberal democracy. Rorty readily concedes that this is ethnocentric, but he believes there is no alternative. Unlike a traditional philosopher who may try, pointlessly, to defend that position by grounding, and equating, the European with the universal, Rorty dispenses with such cant and insists the

---

[11] 'Philosophy as Science, as Metaphor, and as Politics', *The Institution of Philosophy: A Discipline in Crisis?*, A. Cohen, M. Dascal (eds.), Open Court, La Salle., Ill., (hereafter, P.S.M.P.), p. 13.

[12] *Ibid.*, p. 23.

only, but adequate answer, is '*we* are in a privileged situation simply by being *us*'. Instead of reaching for transcendental principles, 'the pragmatist must remain ethnocentric and offer examples' and if still pressed to indicate what was special about Europe he would finally retort 'Do you have anything non-European to suggest which meets our European purposes better?'[13] For, once absolutes are rejected and discredited, one cannot go beyond one's own history, here as with anything; as, for example, when he quotes Rawls's justification of a conception of justice '*given our history and the traditions embedded in our public life*, it is the most reasonable doctrine *for us*'[14] (original emphasis).

Such a liberal democracy is not held together by some profound philosophic consensus. Its citizens may disagree on such irrelevant matters, just as they can and do on religious matters. A philosophical tolerance should supplement a religious tolerance. Rorty objects to left-wing intellectuals' insistence on common purity in such matters. All one needs is a civic virtue, a meta-ethic,[15] of tolerance (and thus each individual's right to seek its own perfection) and pity (and thus a keenness to reform and extend justice to all). For this to work, a society must operate a rigorous distinction between the private and public spheres. So, despite the presence of more profound disagreements, everyone should be able to cooperate in political projects—'we are all working for a utopia...of equal access to a free press, a free judiciary, and free universities.'[16] At most we would need agreement on 'empirical issues' like the workability of the democratic system. Rorty's ideal is the practical engagement of intellectuals in American reformist politics between 1920 and 1960: a brief and respectful nod in Dewey's direction, 'and then [they] got down to the details of reform and re-education.'[17] But since then, Rorty regrets, the intellectual left has become 'overtheoretical and over philosophical', more concerned with the work of Althusser or

---

[13] *Consequences of Pragmatism*, University of Minnesota Press, Minneapolis, 1982, pp. 173–74.

[14] 'The Priority of Democracy to Philosophy', *The Virginia Statute for Religious Freedom*, M.D. Peterson, R.C. Vaughan (eds.), Cambridge, Cambridge University Press, 1988, p. 265 (hereafter P.D.P.).

[15] 'Thugs and Terrorists: A Reply to Bernstein', *Political Theory*, 15, 4, November 1987, (hereafter T.T.), p. 579.

[16] *Ibid.*, p. 573.

[17] *Ibid.*, p. 570.

Habermas, for example, than with domestic reform. Practical politics requires little more than commonsense, specialist expertise and modern technology. And one more ingredient, which he regularly regrets is absent from so many French intellectuals: an enthusiasm for social engineering; they lack hope, as well as any desire for consensus and communication; they remain detached, an avant garde.[18] Rorty's utopia needs 'social scientists', we could say applied social scientists, not intellectuals or philosophers. While Feyerabend keeps on moving out and up in his quest for freedom, Rorty keeps focusing in, down and narrower in a similar quest. He constantly draws our attention to his irreducible base, 'the priority of democracy to philosophy'—an expression we could imagine Feyerabend endorsing; but what an alarming difference these identical words hide.

It is not just that the traditional activity of philosophers and intellectuals is inessential to democracy; it is harmful. Thus the fundamental role the separation of private and public domains plays in Rorty's scheme. Like religion and other 'matters of ultimate importance', philosophy and its paradigm questions about the meaning of life, truth, beauty and the like are to be pursued solely in the private domain. Accordingly, while Rorty sees the work of Foucault and Derrida, for example, as quite irrelevant to politics, 'they cannot be used for the purposes for which the left would like to use them', they serve the private purpose of 'giving us intellectuals a more coherent self-image, and a more coherent cultural utopia....' Their greatest utility, Rorty continues, lies in helping us decide 'what to do with our aloneness',[19] the expression, he explains in a footnote, being a paraphrase of Whitehead's definition of religion.

Philosophical toleration precludes the use of legal coercion (at least, as we will see, normally) against any such religious/philosophical thinking; but it will also aim at 'disengaging' discussions on such matters from the arena of social policy. Coercion is to be used against individuals whose conscience leads them to act 'so as to threaten democratic institutions.'[20] Democracy must act against such 'fanatics' because they threaten freedom and justice. Again and again, Rorty insists that the maintenance of the system, liberal democracy, takes

---

[18] 'Habermas and Lyotard on Postmodernity', *Habermas and Modernity*, R. Bernstein (ed.), Polity Press, Cambridge, 1985 (hereafter H.L.), p. 174.

[19] *T.T.*, op. cit., p. 572.

[20] *P.D.P.*, op. cit., p. 263.

priority over all else; and this is so simply because 'it is the most reasonable doctrine for us', no matter how ethnocentric and relativist that may appear. Thus, 'there is no place for the questions that Nietzsche and Loyola would raise', for example, and this is so because they are anti-democratic.

> We heirs of the Enlightenment think of enemies of liberal democracy like Nietzsche and Loyola as, to use Rawls's term, 'mad'. We do so because there is no way to see them as fellow citizens of our constitutional democracy, people whose life plans might, given ingenuity and good will, be fitted in with those of other citizens. They are not crazy because they have mistaken the ahistorical nature of human beings. They are crazy because the limits of sanity are set by what *we* can take seriously. This, in turn, is determined by our upbringing, our historical situation. (original emphasis)[21]

Rorty knows that this 'seems shockingly ethnocentric' so he spends time elaborating the case. The trouble, as he sees it, is that the 'philosophical tradition' has unfortunately led us to believe that the human self has a centre called reason and that 'argumentation will, given time and patience, penetrate to this centre.' But this is not so. Likewise if one were asked to defend the claim that 'human beings ought to be liberals rather than fanatics', we cannot allow ourselves to be 'driven back on a theory of human nature.' So, despite 'the spirit of accommodation and tolerance' we must admit that every question need not be met in the language presented, or that there may not be 'enough overlap' between vocabularies for agreement to be reached. This may lead us 'to simply *drop* questions' (original emphasis). But we try. 'We do not conclude that Nietzsche and Loyola are crazy because they hold unusual views on certain "fundamental" topics; rather, we conclude this only after extensive attempts at an exchange of political views have made us realize that we are not going to get anywhere.'[22]

Generally a liberal state can ignore the moral and religious differences of its diverse citizens, and they in turn, for pragmatic if not moral reasons, may be 'ruefully grateful' to be its citizens and thereby

---
[21] *Ibid.*, pp. 266–67.
[22] *Ibid.*, pp. 267–69.

free to pursue in private the many 'ways in which they deal with their aloneness'.

Rorty appreciates, as did Dewey and Weber, that all this entails a public disenchantment. But they all agree that the price has been worth it. So, ultimately, Rorty's light-hearted treatment of all traditional philosophical questions has a point, a pragmatic point; he wishes to promote this disenchantment, this positive good as 'it helps make the world's inhabitants more pragmatic, more tolerant, more liberal, more receptive to the appeal of instrumental rationality.' Indeed, he would see any effort to re-enchant the world as a danger 'for it is hard to be both enchanted with one version of the world and tolerant of all the others.' And, if one were to ask by what right does Rorty give priority of place as he does, rather than as others do, he would disarmingly reply: 'everyone is just insisting that the beliefs and desires they hold most dear should come first in the order of discussion. This is not arbitrariness, but sincerity.'[23]

No one could doubt Rorty's sincerity, I am sure. But it does create problems, for him, for us and for the many dissenting voices otherwise willing to share his utopian democracy. Because Rorty insists, sincerely, that it all be done on his terms only; that although he cannot adequately justify, explain or prove his case—all such moves being impossible—nevertheless he wants us to agree with him. As a pragmatist he cannot do better than report himself; than present, accurately and sincerely, his own, real heritage (his built-in convictions, not just mere preferences he once points out).[24] Time and again he openly confesses this limit, which he sees appearing embarrassingly ethnocentric. I perfectly understand this position—but now comes the problem. Rorty wants everyone else to agree with *him*, to abandon any 'pragmatist' proclivity to assert ourselves, and to succumb to his, one of many, sincere positions. Why should we? Would we not be foolish to accept? Is he treating us as fools? Should we have sniffed the danger when he did not hesitate, when he did not admit the dilemma that what is good enough for him is good enough for every other position as well. As Feyerabend did. At this stage should we have just tossed a coin? A contingent solution!

Rorty could reply that his case really rests on the effects of going along with him. And the reward is freedom to pursue one's own interests provided they curtail no other person's pursuit; and, of

[23] *Ibid.*, pp. 271–73.
[24] *Ibid.*, pp. 266, 279–80.

course, the rewards for those of commonsense and technical expertise as they pursue justice for all in the public arena. It seems worth it—provided you are one of the elect, a fellow pragmatist. If you are not; if you show limited sympathy for social engineering or if you believe certain of your values ought to impinge on public policy but you are unable to convince others of this cause, then the exchange loses its value. And you lose your freedom.

I said that Rorty's sincerity created problems for him as well. It is, I believe, that his deep, personal faith in a particular pragmatism and an equally particular liberal democracy (or its mythic representation) has made him too concerned for their combined success. He will, it seems, brook no presence which could mar it; he appears willing to go to any extreme to accomplish its unqualified success. To him, no sacrifice will be too much for others to bear. We should remember that it is not only 'unreasonable' people like Nietzsche and Loyola who are going to be sacrificed for this 'experiment in cooperation';[25] it is everyone who cannot be converted by Rorty. All practising non-pragmatists found in the public arena are to be condemned as 'fanatics', 'mad' and 'crazy'. We would be foolish to pass over these words too lightly, to dismiss them as casual rhetoric, as innocent quotation ('mad' derives from Rawls). It is a language of vehemence, exclusion and unqualified intolerance. When Rorty refers to the difficulty of the enchanted remaining tolerant of others, its status as empirical description is uncertain, but as an accurate projection of the author it is telling indeed.

We need to look more carefully at Rorty's idea of tolerance. Despite the occasional acknowledgement that questions about, for example, 'the meaning of human existence' are beneficial for our personal salvation, the general temper of remarks is antipathetic. It seems more of an anxiety than a mere indifference which isolates, not fosters, such activities within the private domain; and there never to transgress. This toleration of philosophy and religion[26] is not a benign gesture of goodwill; it is the *only* possible move in defence of the public realm short of banning them, an impossible proposal. But then, who knows? We are not told what is to be done

---

[25] *Ibid.*, p. 274.

[26] See the quotation in note 19. Here, as so often, Rorty comes very close to equating religion and philosophy and rejecting both. He explains in a footnote that the expression originally comes from Whitehead's definition of religion, but he is giving a paraphrase of it. His casualness further demeans the two.

with people once they have been declared fanatics, mad or crazy. We must not assume that some physical exclusion (incarceration? expulsion?) automatically accompanies such linguistic victimisation. But, if not, has not Rorty left his liberal democracy an invidious problem? It will have to handle a public element doubly alienated. Can a democracy manage such a disenfranchised and demoralised minority (perhaps majority) within its midst? The burden for both seems awesome. This dilemma, however, can serve a useful purpose for us. It must remove a misapprehension commonly held about pragmatism that its strength, if not virtue, lies in its expedient even opportune manner of coping with the ups and downs of reality. That, not constrained by unnecessary calls to first principles, it manages with competence and flexibility to survive. On the contrary, Rorty's republic lives dangerously, and very much on principle, confrontationally. The notion of tolerance normally has a casual, laissez-faire atmosphere about it; but that type of language seems inappropriate to Rorty's utopia. A useful reminder lies behind all this. Rorty's ideal citizen is disenchanted, cool; enthusiasm is disparaged as its source in heady ideas is enclosed and insulated. But passion may arise from other than disputations on religion and philosophy; it can be bred by the treatment of one person by another. The sincerity, yet anxiety, of Rorty's cool pragmatist citizens could too easily and understandably generate passion in those fellow citizens they deem mad, dangerous and an inferior and unwanted Other.

This seems even more likely given the unreality behind Rorty's attempt to separate the public from the private. It is not only his anathema called ideas, theory, philosophy, religion that necessitated the separation of domains; it was also his misconception of politics that permitted the division to proceed. On one occasion Rorty refers to the sheer political ignorance of Nietzsche and Heidegger, about which I cannot comment; but his own, mythic ideas alarm. I use that word with deliberation because his image of political activity is that narrow, instrumentalist, 'value-free', expert decision-making which understandably disturbs Feyerabend so much, and which propels that writer to seek the civilising supervision by people with ideas.

And if there is no 'soul', there is also no nitty-gritty in Rorty's politics; no struggle for power, no deception, no challenge of new ideas, no dirt, no passion. It is consensual management, efficient, detached, unproblematic, in one orderly and progressive direction.

Planning, social engineering, by meritocratic committees. Its unreality is matched only by its unpleasantness. There is something about it we faintly recognise: is it not the common wish, in fiction and fact, of authoritarian, utopian regimes, and an identity dissolving the conventional distinction of right and left? It is the glorious but horrendous dream of politics without dissension, of perfect consensus, of politics above politics, of a perfectibility in the name of our general good—whether we want it or not.

Rorty can envisage a public separate from a private because he appears to have little difficulty, unlike certain other contemporary thinkers, in distinguishing thinking from acting, theory from practice, the political from the non-political. Being a pragmatist permits him to eschew definitional distinctions for the use of illustrations which allow an easy scoring of points: it is as if he dares us to suggest that thinking about the meaning of life is on a par with building a bridge. Time and again he repeats that theory has nothing to contribute to public affairs, and that we have mostly become 'overtheoretical, over-philosophical'. Yet in one insignificant footnote he introduces an exception which surely qualifies his entire case. In it, he suggests that feminism is 'the one useful spin-off from this leftist philosophy fetishism...where people are actually having some new ideas, actually unmasking something...[and who] have been able to develop some fresh dialectical space.'[27] (It does not even read like Rorty!) So, theory per se is not at fault; he is only fed up (and he is not alone here) with the unimaginative, arid and doctrinaire material which clog the eyeways. Rorty ignores the moral of his exemplary illustration: it is that we need more and more fresh theories, not fewer and fewer. But to have admitted that would have destroyed his entire pragmatist campaign. He would have been forced, futhermore, to concede that this feminist theorising is highly relevant in the political pursuit of justice. And that, indeed, in considering some such legislative amelioration of women we are hard-pressed to distinguish its 'theoretical' from its 'empirical' elements. Somehow, they are both and neither. But with that conclusion, Rorty's total pragmatist endeavour would evaporate.

His effort in keeping theory safely encased in the private world of consenting adults, furthermore, freezes the political agenda until the end of time. All the public arena can do is to continue to implement

---

[27] *T.T., op. cit.*, p. 577.

policies consistent with current goals; no new ideals, directions may be conceived there and none are allowed to enter from the private domain. At times Rorty introduces a hint of flexibility: a privateer may perhaps enter the public waters armed with new ideas, keen and ready to proselytise—and test his luck. But! For example, let us say it is the 1950s and the first ecologists emerge to preach their warnings and the masses are not impressed by such apocalyptic thoughts. That would be the end of the ecological movement in Rorty's utopia. He makes this perfectly clear in his endorsement of Jefferson.

> They (citizens) must abandon or modify opinions on matters of ultimate importance, the opinions that may hitherto have given sense and point to their lives, if these opinions entail public actions that cannot be justified to most of their fellow citizens.[28]

This must not be misconstrued to mean little more than what happens in any democratic system; that is, that any party normally needs to convince the people before implementing a change. In Rorty's system there is no second chance; goals are to be set, once and for all, and then frozen. Such self-confidence, such fixity of mind. So Rorty extends his ethnocentrism into the temporal dimension. We need a word for such presentcentrism. Of course, with largesse, he may give six months, even two years for new thoughts to be accepted before its initiators are sentenced henceforth to permanent public silence!

To accuse Rorty of forever freezing the future political agenda in no way would offend that author. He makes it obvious time and again that not only is he fed-up with 'theory' but that its loss from public life is nothing to regret. This sentiment is no momentary rhetorical flourish; nothing could be made more explicit: 'My hunch is that Western social and political thought may have had the last *conceptual* revolution it needs. J.S. Mill's suggestion that governments devote themselves to optimizing the balance between leaving people's private lives alone and preventing suffering seems to me pretty much the last word[29] (original emphasis).

[28] *P.D.P.*, op. cit., p. 257.
[29] *Contigency, Irony and Solidarity*, Cambridge University Press, Cambridge, 1989 (hereafter C.I.S.), p. 63.

'Dewey thought of himself as freeing us up for practice, not as providing theoretical foundations for practice'[30] Rorty once says in a footnote, but that thought is deeply etched in his mind. We would fail to understand him if we neglected its import. The mantle he is especially proud to wear is that of a man of action. His work can be read as a textbook for the inculcation of efficient practice. He has little time for persons of reflection because the questions they raise are not only wrong but time-wasting. They displace action. So, following our discussion on modernity, we can see Rorty as a hero of our times. A man of action always appears to know what to do next; he is rarely beset with doubt. We are not surprised to hear, therefore, that Rorty's political quest for justice is a straightforward matter: mere commonsense with the assistance of social science. To say he has 'hope' for the future is inappropriate: his confidence is so entrenched, so matter-of-fact that that word is too self-conscious, hinting at overcoming some doubt. The future for knowledge is just as blandly assured:

> We are all working for a utopia in which equal access to a free press, a free judiciary, and free universities will permit questions about, for example, negative liberty-versus-civic republicanism or privatism-versus-community or ethnocentrism-versus-universality (the issues that Bernstein rightly says I gloss over with my use of 'we') to get peacefully and gradually worked out through new, ever-richer, syntheses of theory and practice.[31]

His self-assurance dissolves complexities and installs simplicities, shunning any trace of difficulty or subtlety. It is his 'natural' assumption that in his utopia we will 'gradually' solve all outstanding problems through 'ever-richer' knowledge (in which, so it seems, theory plays a role!). Nothing is beyond our ability to master once we have replaced our bad habits by constructive practices. The undecidable as well as the ineffable remain inconceivable to the man of action. What always appeals to this type of person is a quality of 'cutting through the bullshit'—it could be called reductionism. Accordingly, Rorty is impressed with Orwell's description of British Conservatives

[30] *T.T.*, *op. cit.*, p. 577.
[31] *Ibid.*, p. 573.

and Stalinists 'as just two different gangs of thugs', a description which he says explains why Orwell 'is so unpopular among the radicals (because it shows that) philosophy is less relevant to politics than radical intellectuals would like it to be.!'[32]

Rorty's action-oriented pragmatism is, in many ways, a chance affair, and this is not by chance. In recent years the idea of contingency plays more and more a central role in his work. He 'commends the picture of the self as a centreless and contingent web' and, elsewhere in his effort to 'dissolve the metaphysical self' he proposes that we 'treat the self as having no centre, no essence, but *merely* as a concatenation of beliefs and desires' (original emphasis).[33] Nothing, including our language, is quasi-divine or possesses an intrinsic nature; everything is 'a product of time and chance'.[34] Rorty sees Freud as contributing to an historical process of de-divination when he showed that the origins of our conscience lie 'in the contingency of our upbringing'.[35] Likewise at the macroscopic level: he is 'impressed by the sheer contingency of history', by the way things 'just happened to be' or 'of the fate of democracy and of socialism as largely a matter of who shoots whom first, or whose agents co-opt which revolution first' (TT, p. 569).[36] And, as he very correctly says, when you see things this way, 'one's sense of the importance of the theorist in politics diminishes.' Rorty is being uncharacteristically restrained here. What he should have said is that, with this perspective, the importance of the theorist—in politics, in history, in psychology, in anthropology, in the human sciences in toto—is, not diminished, but simply eradicated. We could go further. When chance and nothing but chance rules (ah, there's the rub—we need a theory to explain why things are determined only by chance!) we can say nothing at all, absolutely nothing. We would then have the end of all sciences, knowledge and, let us not forget, the most mundane, human thinking, in the kitchen or on the way to the office. Perhaps Rorty's restraint was not by chance; this really is a case of throwing the baby out with the bath water. For a moment only I thought that Rorty may have salvaged something with a significant qualification: I pondered his expression... 'a concatenation of

[32] *Ibid.*, p. 569.
[33] P.D.P., *op. cit.*, pp. 270, 278.
[34] C.I.S., *op. cit.*, p. 22.
[35] *Ibid.*, p. 30.
[36] T.T., *op. cit.*, p. 569.

beliefs and desires', because that could imply that there is something systematic about the links and bonds between all our many beliefs and desires. There is, after all, some pattern, structure, determination to be investigated, described and even explained. There is to be a place for theory. And what a subtle, paradoxical point Rorty was making, I thought: to propose some determination of chances. How very French! But there is nothing in his texts to suggest that he meant anything like this. I was quite wrong; he was clearly using concatenation in some other, casual sense.

To allow the discussion to continue, let us assume that Rorty meant to say something like practically everything comes about by chance; so, and this is really what he wants to say, there is no need for theorists, only pragmatists. But even with this moderate, and may I say, charitable interpretation of Rorty, he has created problems for himself. If history is sheer contingency, how does he explain certain patterns he has 'found' in it—such as the traditional belief that the self has an essence, and one susceptible to reason? How can there be a tradition at all for him to uphold or rebel against? A contingent past has to be made of more heterogeneous elements than that. And if the past had been thrown together so haphazardly should he have not warned us that the future he proposed was indeed quite revolutionary as so much was to be done to eliminate chance and to ensure a smooth, peaceful, gradual growth of justice and knowledge— a far cry from the randomness of the past? And turning to the individual; if he were to reflect on his 'self', this centreless and contingent web, how would he begin to explain certain of his distinctive personal attributes, such as his unwavering confidence in the future, his faith in progress (hardly a random process), even his very fulsome espousal of pragmatism and Jeffersonian liberal democracy? Is all this a matter of chance? Is there another bunch of contradictory beliefs and desires, a counter-Rorty, he is hiding from us?

In a certain way, Rorty could be described as pre-Freudian, despite his citing Freud as a culture-hero.[37] Any notion of what could be called an unconscious is alien to him. Rorty has apparently deliberately turned his back on one of the most pervasive characteristics of twentieth century thought: that to understand human behaviour we have to look beyond mainifest, conscious phenomena. It seems that this is one thing Rorty refuses to do.

[37] C.I.S., op. cit., esp. pp. 30–39.

So much of what has been said already could now be rephrased to illustrate this, but I will restrict myself to one observation: how does he allow himself to describe the self as a centreless and contingent web, presumably be that self an Italian or a Korean, and yet to reveal his own self as future-oriented, optimistic, confident, a devout believer in pragmatism and liberal democracy and social engineering—without being perturbed? Because surely he must face the problem that no matter how centreless they may all be in one way, all selves are *not* the same, and that *one* likely explanation of this is that people internalise their immediate surroundings, and that, unconsciously, things like national dispositions develop and are manifest in the orientations of their citizens. In other words, Rorty thinks like an American and this is not by accident. There is no need to spell out what I am not saying here. This observation in no way weakens, or affects at all, the nature of his argument; nor is this to be taken as some complete explanation of his case—otherwise all Americans and only they would think like this. But this omission by Rorty illustrates a total lack of acknowledgement that hidden determinants exist in human affairs. That there are patterns in our lives, despite the contingencies. If he were to confront this, his utopia would require a radical recasting.

But he always remains close to the surface of things. He is loath to look behind or below; and the repercussions of this on his understanding of both theory and politics, on his determined separation of the private and the public are both profound and disturbing. One illustration will suffice. As part of his passionate justification for the exclusion of theorists from the public realm he explains how Rawls' and his theory of the self is a satisfactory one if one were *wanted*. But, he continues, one is not *needed* in the public sphere. As he says 'For purposes of liberal social theory, one can do without such a model. One can get along with common sense and social science, areas of discourse in which the term "the self" rarely occurs.'[38] I am sure Rorty is right: the term rarely occurs. But what a revealingly, trivial observation to make. As if the lack of conscious articulation of the word, of it not being recorded, as it were, as an agenda item, of it not being the specific topic of debate, means its absence and irrelevance. Does Rorty need tangible sense-data before he is willing

---

[38] *P.D.P.*, op. cit., p. 270.

to admit some presence? Surely this is taking the idea of the pre-eminence of conscious behaviour to ludicrous extremes; as if social science or commonsense were expressing nothing more than the literal words it records in its report or announces to the assembly. Does not each operate, by necessity, on the basis of quite complex yet implicit assumptions. Could the simplest of thoughts begin without some unstated and usually unconscious 'givens' on an entire range of things, including, of course, a notion of the self? Part of Rorty's problem here, and it sits uncomfortably with his pragmatism, is that he apparently believes (along with most of the traditionalists he wants to reject) that there is something, in the singular, called commonsense, which is basic, universal and absolutely foundational, and that we intuitively know all that it entails as we use it—and if the word self or time or space or cause or other does not actually come in to our consciousness as we go along, then they cannot exist as we have already plumbed the bottom. There is nowhere else to look. We can see it all. And for Rorty this search remains very close to the surface of things, in nothing more than the very words we utter. Does he knock and enter each time he passes a particular notice?

Rorty, in fact, has a very clear notion of the self which goes beyond his articulated characterisation of it as without essence. It entails at least these features: the self, or in its collective setting, the we, is, and is universally, the product of history, and that is the product 'of something relatively local and ethnocentric—the tradition of a particular community, the consensus of a particular culture.... What counts as rational or as fanatical (or good or bad or just anything—I could add) is relative to the group to which we...justify ourselves—to the body of shared belief that determines the defence of the word "we".' And again when he quotes Rawls with approval. 'What justifies a conception of justice is not its being true to an order antecedent to and given to us, but its congruence with our deeper understanding of ourselves and our aspirations, and our realisation that, *given our history and the traditions embedded in our public life*, it is the most reasonable doctrine *for us*' (original emphasis). And to be exceptionally explicit he adds: 'We do not need a categorical distinction between the self and its situation. We can dismiss the distinction between an attribute of the self and a constituent of the self, between the self's accidents and its essence, as "merely" metaphysical.'[39]

[39] *Ibid.*, pp. 259, 265, 267.

This is the self which Rorty sees as foundational: our local history determines us as a 'we', tells us how and what to think and to judge. This is our 'contingent essence', as it were; hardly a chance affair. The self is the impress of its specific local tradition. Its core is a particular, not a universal, and this is universally so. And, he makes abundantly clear, it is our first, last and only justification and benchmark. It determines our totality and presents us with an unassailable brief We do not question ourselves—because we cannot and ought not; we are not equipped to do so.

This is Rorty's pragmatist basis for his utopian liberal democracy. With his rejection of conventional absolutes and rational argumentation, he sincerely believes that we have no other viable option. We can only act, and have trust, in our own self-image. He has found a foundation after all, of an unexpected type—ourselves. The 'we' our history creates, it would seem, serves three related functions: it constitutes us as a community, it separates us from others, and it justifies our actions. The Other is what we are not—different histories have determined that. And we are responsible only to ourselves—simply because, if one were foolish enough to ask why, we are we. No wonder Rorty admits that all this seems 'shockingly ethnocentric'. It does, because to me it is, in an unusually extreme but clever way.

In the sense that, with the best will in the world, we (any 'we') can never entirely step outside our inherited tradition, and that therefore, ultimately, our understanding and our judgement of others will be in part ethnocentrically shaped, seems inevitable. We can never become neutral, detraditionalised; nor can we become the Other as we can never eradicate traces of our 'we' which the Other does not and cannot bear. This ethnocentrism is not shocking. It is not the one Rorty upholds. His is profoundly different. His self lacks any sign of curiosity about itself or the Other. In quite a nonchalant way, it merely says 'this is my self' and is satisfied. It does not wonder why this is so, nor whether it could ever be different let alone whether it could ever be better. What is, apparently, is good enough; or, at least, something totally to be accepted as it is; it is not questioned or worried about or struggled against. In a way, Rorty's utopia redescribes the narcissus myth: the 'we' looks at the 'mirror of culture' and finds itself; immediately falling in love with its own beauty as it has no other benchmark. Transfixed, it stays there, constant, unchanging, immutable, doing nothing other than reproducing its own self-image.

Because he has decided, for very good reasons, that there are no universal truths, has not Rorty resorted to the complete negation of this position as if it were the only viable alternative? He settles with this, once he decides, in his own particular way, to place democracy before philosophy. Because, what that means in this setting, is placing an unthinking 'we' first—and last. The question Rorty asks, and answers sincerely, cleverly, honestly, ruthlessly is, given that the self is the self's only possible benchmark, how do we arrange and defend things for the most efficient betterment of the self. Rorty has achieved, in a powerful manner, a myth of ethnocentrism. The Other remains entirely and permanently outside and irrelevant to the Self; significant only if, for some reason or other, it appears to impinge on the autonomy, wholeness, integrity, purity of the Self: it acquires then its only presence, its only identity—'we' declare it mad, crazy and fanatical because these are the terms we reserve for anything we do not understand—and that means that which is not us.

So, it is ultimately immaterial what constitutes the self or we for Rorty; it may be an individual, a nation, a complex of societies called liberal democracies, it may be the West, its performance and characterisation remain the same: a perfect model of shocking ethnocentrism. And, in this sense, it may serve as a model for an assertive, uncritical and dangerous ethnocentrism anywhere—such as India. Its model citizen has no need to develop the faculties of empathy or sympathy, of self-criticism or of doubt, anxiety and uncertainty, of curiosity of the unknown, of imagination, of excitement at something radically new, of boredom at something seen suddenly as banal and worthless, of wondering who am I and from where do I come. Of course, she may pursue such talents and projects in the safety of one's private world, but not risk communicating it to other, lest it become public and becomes labelled a fanatic. The citizen may learn that the Other not only dwells somewhere beyond the shores, but lurks, albeit latently, within the utopia, even within each individual: she knows, for example, that the Others does not speak an 'untranslatable language' but with 'enough overlap in belief and desire'[40] will always appear a bit like us. An Other might be discovered inside our self, if we dare our self to think. At the same time, the citizen of Rorty's utopia may come to appreciate paradox (having being skilled only in instrumental rationality): and the particular one being that in a

[40] *Ibid.*, p. 281.

utopia which places for its own betterment 'democracy before philosophy' it is odd how everything philosophical becomes political; indeed the simplest of sympathetic sentiments may become political, too political; and that rigid division of public and private corrodes as one finds oneself anxiously looking over one's shoulder.

One could redescribe Rorty's recent writings as defence manuals; as co-ordinated plans for the protection of an ideal liberal democracy, which entail the erection, maintenance and utilisation of Maginot Lines separating the private from the public and ensuring mutual non-interference. The provision and protection of proper places for pure purposes. A few privileged individuals, carrying the requisite identity of ironist liberals, like Rorty himself, have the right to travel back and forth between the demarcated territories. They must, however, comply with the respective ground rules in each. And, by so doing, that author insists, they demonstrate to the rest of us that 'the same person (can be), in alternate moments, Nietzsche and J.S. Mill'.[41]

Rorty's utopia, ultimately, has to be judged an unrealizable failure, yet a dangerous myth, if for no reason other than his particular, mistaken division between the public and the private. He dramatically errs here because, despite metaphor being seen by him as the hub of all things, he fails to treat these two vital terms as metaphors. He handles them as though they were concepts, in the best tradition of metaphysics, as though they represent homogeneous, replete, bounded, mutually exclusive elements of reality. It is only because he does this that he can imagine someone like himself, wishing for the best of both possible worlds, being able to combine being a private self-creator and a public liberal 'in *alternate* moments' (my emphasis). At any one time, apparently, one has to be either one or the other. Rorty cannot entertain the idea that one could be simultaneously both: to think that, he would have had to appreciate the differences and the slippage necessarily involved in the metaphoricity of the two terms. He would then have to appreciate that, at times, being liberal entails also being a self-creator; or that, at times, in the very act of promoting one's self realisation one is engaged, for good or bad, in affecting the public arena, and that one cannot legislate against such practices.

If Rorty 'really' appreciated the significance of metaphor (and not

---

[41] *C.I.S.*, op. cit., p. 85.

just think of it as a new, useful description) he would have had to admit that, for example, an author may find herself in deep political waters neither intended nor desired; and that in such circumstances it is meaningless to try to determine, whether, let us say Salman Rushdie, was acting privately or publicly in writing a particular novel. Rorty would not be able to do this without jettisoning his entire utopian apartheid.

In keeping with his conceptualisation rather than metaphorisation of language, there is a disconcerting, pervasive literalness in all his writings. One senses that he thinks Philosophy comes only in capital letters and is something done by professional philosophers only—that the behaviour of the man in the street is quite untouched by it. Similarly one senses that to Rorty politics is only about things that are 'political'. So I wonder what words he would use to describe his statements which follow:

> Whereas Habermas sees the line of ironist thinking which runs from Hegel through Foucault and Derrida as destructive of social hope, I see this line of thought as largely irrelevant to public life and to political questions. Ironist theorists like Hegel, Nietzsche, Derrida and Foucault seem to me invaluable in our attempt to form a private self-image, but pretty much useless when it comes to politics.[42]

Elsewhere in the book, Rorty tilts it a little more the way of Habermas.

> Abandoning universalisms is my way of doing justice to the claims of the ironists whom Habermas distrusts: Nietzsche, Heidegger, Derrida. Habermas looks at these men from the point of view of public needs. I agree with Habermas that as *public* philosophers they are at best useless and at worst dangerous, but I want to insist on the role they and others like them can play in accommodating the ironist's *private* sense of identity to her liberal hopes. (original emphasis)[43]

And let us remember his criteria for mad, crazy and fanatic. In penning these lines was Rorty being private or public, philosophical or political? I doubt whether he and I would make a similar judgement.

[42] *Ibid.*, p. 83.
[43] *Ibid.*, p. 68.

We should not have been surprised to discover that a common agreement between Feyerabend, Rorty and myself about the lack of universal standards and truths and a common dissatisfaction with that dominant western faith in reason, fail to produce any consensus between us on the consequent implications for handling our partial knowledges and politics. Feyerabend's solution lies in an expansiveness, an unqualified tolerance of diversity, yet constrained by some broadness of vision and a faith in the final wisdom of the people. It is a warm, charitable and catholic vision, marred only by his excessive faith in democracy. Both the voice of the people and its political process no doubt have many virtues, including, not least, a symbolic value of some potency. But, left to itself as the arbiter of our lives and benchmark for our knowledge, the democratic process too easily and too often corrupts a broader vision in the expedient interests of the immediate and the local. I cannot accept Feyerabend's belief or need in a utopian solution. To me there is none, and the task is to suggest how we cope with that reality.

At one and the same time, Rorty appears both more and less realistic than Feyerabend. He insists that we cannot afford playing with high ideals: we do what we do because we are what we are. And yet, in his efforts to ensure the efficient operation of his democracy, he ruthlessly expunges so much as to make the resulting system unworkable, meaningless and vicious. Contrary to his rigid division of labour, private concerns would flow into the political, necessitating the branding of more citizens as fanatic, mad and crazy. Unintentionally, Rorty's utopia ends as a mean-spirited one, which even fails to have the virtue of being practical.

Once alert to the ubiquity of metaphor, we can quickly appreciate the uselessness and danger of Rorty's portrait of the self. Briefly, it is wrong simply because there is no one such thing. There are only selves, which, in our daily lives, we move in and out of without awareness. We are multiple. One may easily confirm this by articulating the sense, one by one, in each use of the word 'I' or 'we' in any day's conversation: our self-identities are many. Added to this are the numerous selves projected and internalised across the world. In all of these we are both singular and plural; in each of these I am unique and typical. We can never determine with any exactitude where the self begins or ends; or what relationship it has with our other selves. And we change. The self is heterogeneous and protean. Any attempt to delineate once and for all one homogeneous self is a metaphysical folly.

The Politics of Irresolution

And a political one. This becomes more evident once we move from this metaphoric-impregnated and enriched notion of self to its associated notion, the Other. Again, it cannot be singular because we are not singular. And it is as protean as we. There is no one big Other, somewhere out there (like The Devil?) which pits its difference as a standard against ours, and against which we must defend ourselves. Our Other is manifold. We can perhaps better comprehend it by conceptualising it in metaphor. It is the difference; it is that which is not similar. It is therefore not something that has been left out or over, the remainder; nor is it restricted to that which we are not, such as our negative self, like our id or basic desires or lack of reason or unconscious. Without necessarily having priority over our selves, it is something out of which we come: we cannot allocate precedence of course to either similarities or differences. The one makes the other, mutually. Accordingly, some others may constitute our oppositional selves—this is the one which receives attention. Some Other may be a synecdochic whole of which a self constitutes a part—like my fellow colleagues or Australians. Some Other may be my metonymic differences—like my childhood. Some Other may be my self's translation—like this manuscript, or my children. Some Other may be my Self's exchange, or may be an isomorphic self. And I need illustrate no further. Relationships between Selves and Others, actually and potentially, are interminable.

But only some are selected for attention, and in certain rather than other ways. Politics could be described as whatever constitutes the current play between certain selves and certain others. Who are the dominant, and the tangential and the quite marginal players; and in what forms of relationships are they; and over what definitions or redefinitions are they struggling to determine? Who is succeeding more in defining its world? In what ways have certain selves and certain others changed in the process? Any perspective on the world, philosophical, sociological or ideological, which posits a single self and its single Other is reductionist and totalistic in its thinking; as analysis it is worthless; as politics dangerous, confrontational and inflexible; and as psychological projection suspicious to paranoid. And we could add: prognosis grim. But there is little need, I am sure, to list here the political arenas in the world which are entirely and sadly characterised by this schema. Personal relations everywhere are undoubtedly being marred by similar dualistic struggles. And, as I have argued earlier, any cultural disposition to think only in terms of 'either-or' will encourage such formations.

But life played out by other than dichotomising intellectuals or by ideological politicos is a more complex phenomenon. One moves in and out of our selves and relates to one and then another Other. Identities, issues and commitments are fluid. Life and politics become complexly interwoven not cumulative, overladen and set, step after step.

What role in politics can someone cognisant with the metaphoricity of social reality play? It is, in all ways, an unrealistic question: the hypothetical person is abstract, identifiable *only* as being cognisant with metaphor. There can never be such a person—but the conception of such a one has been used time and again to show that the writings of people like Derrida and Foucault either have no relevance to political behaviour or that they are oriented to a nihilist or neo-conservative, politics. That conclusion seems nothing other than the product of a misguided, or loaded, question. Let us, nevertheless, now respond.

Being conceptualised as a person abstracted from history makes it meaningless to itemise issues to be given priority: and it is surely a hollow gesture for someone to genuflect, once again, before the altars of Justice, Liberty and Equality. One would, however, have a good nose for cant, be it articulated by the comfortable and bemused establishment, by enemies or by current allies. It is so common to talk in the language of universal and timeless values, to act as if a concept were in fact an accurate mirror of reality, to believe that some insightful perspective on the scene represented some totality of it, to expect any plan to solve, and resolve with finality, a problem, to assume any group to be homogeneous, and thereby characterisable in one image, to believe any value can be equally exchanged for another, to equate words with actions, to assume some conceptual opposition is the only truthful representation of a situation, that each component is mutually exclusive, that one has no option other than to choose one or the other, and that no alternative characterisation is legitimate. There is no need, I am sure, to attempt a fuller recital. The posturings of truth, science, reason, commonsense, language, sincerity, loyalty, faith and dedication are rampant. Once attuned to the necessary metaphoric quality of thought and behaviour, one spots them readily.

This critical function is also constructive; exposing cant can at the same time loosen one's own thoughts; one knows, automatically, that any situation can always be re-seen from a different angle, that some current impasse may merely be the product of the conceptual perspective rather than the situation itself; that a symptom may be a part of more than one whole and, accordingly, respond differently to different stimuli; that something new will frequently appear incongruous even contradictory, but that this strangeness is likely to be a sign of its novelty rather than of its untenability.

Politics entails movement. A static state is one beyond politics: a heaven of consensus or a hell of repression. Radical politics (which I now designate as the politics of the person attuned to metaphoricity) must be oriented even to more change. But let us be clear, this has little in common with the frenzied actions of Modern Man. That is an obsession with action, any action, irrespective of consequences (other than its economic value). That is geared to a mythic new, each movement forward replacing and removing something old. It is engineered by decision-making rather than thought; an ad hocism in the service or progress.

The change of radical politics is of a different order. It is not progressive; indeed, it is not going anywhere in particular—but do not be too alarmed; do we know where progressives are actually going? More significantly, do we know, beyond cliches and slogans, and the occasional apocalyptic note, where going somewhere is (for example, where Rorty is heading)? There may be the odd stagingpost along the way (although like watersheds and turning-points they are mainly symbolic), but there is no end, no solution, no goal. There cannot be until we get there, and once there it will have moved on. And there cannot be without the arrogant imposition of one by theologically-inclined saviours; and theirs is never reached, they only manage to stunt the imagination of others as they themselves presume and proceed to foretell, with some transcendental prescience, the futrue of human society; and, inter alia, condemn others as lacking ethical direction who decline their order of the day. But let us be perfectly clear. Just as debilitating for radical change is the more conventional, hegemonic and complacent doctrine that what we have now is goal/good enough: that western, capitalist democracy as we know it is the terminal point of human evolution, and that all it needs is tinkering at the edges and a continued encouragement of its own inherent mechanism of change—incremental progress.

Radical politics is not going anywhere in these senses. To be of value it must break with all traditional lineal language: it must say, that is, that the idea of directionality is meaningless. Similarly, it must break with traditional dualistic language: it is neither left nor right, conservative or reformist, modern or old-fashioned. These terms were always of limited value; they cast even less light today, not only on the so-called new issues of racism, ecology, feminism and the Third World, but on the old issues as well—poverty, health, education, liberties. Radical politics does not merely have to break with such structured language—as if to begin—it will constantly need to struggle against such ideological, emotive and constraining frames of reference to think and establish its position time after time. Its manifest, from which it will have no respite, is to struggle against formulae; and in politics these symbolically-charged labels have the power to co-opt all issues into its circuit within which all discussion is digitalised. Radicalism must have no one position; on each occasion it must create one—it should be seen as unpredictable.

But (one can hear certain people baying by this stage) how does such a radicalism know where to make its stand time after time? It is all very well to say (one can hear it continue) that it is unpredictable, but it still has to make decisions. Does it toss a coin? The simple answer (which to some will be infuriating) is that it does not know. And this is because there is nothing there for it to know in advance. It creates an answer each time. The radicalism I describe, the politics imbued with an appreciation of the metaphoricity of human reality which I am advocating, can have no method, formula, benchmark. And, just as science maintains itself without the need of any one method (and which, had it one, could have destroyed it), so radicalism will pursue its way, making its way as it goes. This revelation should not be shocking; it is, to some degree, what everyone has always been obliged to do, irrespective of their public veneer: reason, consensus, a community's tradition, a religion, dialogue, a moral stricture or a scientific ideology can never provide its adherents with unequivocal guidelines; it merely restricts their range of responses and, by fiat, labels some illegitimate or mad.

This radicalism refers to individuals and to their separate, idiosyncratic endeavours; it cannot be a collective, a movement. That had to be left to others. And it provides no guarantee. Efforts may be made; success may be thwarted—and these judgements, made in

The Politics of Irresolution

hindsight, can have no more validity, or less, than any other judgement. As we have seen, time and again, there is no benchmark beyond a metaphor's own: but our tradition or scholarship and cultural ideology, not experience, has taught us to ask the wrong questions. And, as we have indicated elsewhere, apparently simple notions like problem or success do not possess the obvious, objective status that is commonly assumed, and in the armoury of scholarly debate, demanded. By asking fresh questions, imagining new associations and creating new metaphors, exchanges, translations, this radical politics is unmappable in our conventional language or directionality: it may restore, reclaim, reprieve, it may recognise, respect. Whatever it does it will regard repetition as an inevitable part of a history, no longer as a compulsive affliction, but as an opportunity to imaginatively link an old with a new.

It will be cautious of the claims to commonsense, habit, certainty and whatever are the currently hallowed authorities. Indeed, not unlike Feyerabend, it will encourage limited respect for the idea of authority. It will be ambivalent towards precedence. It will know that the past is never automatically wrong or irrelevant, yet it will be wary: knowing that two situations, no matter how similar, will always be different as well it cannot assume that what worked in one will be efficacious in the other. Contexts change, so things change. Likewise it will never feel obliged to do what it had done previously. Accusations of inconsistency, self-contradiction (and of course of being illogical and unreasonable) will be expected, and ignored. Readiness to be flexible remains a dominant strategy at all times.

Our radical engaged in politics will neither leap into action nor hasten to seek a consensus. There is no fetish of speed or quick results. No Man of action, or trouble-shooter. He or she will be reflective, thoughtful, alert for the intuitive spark, constantly vigilant and flexible, knowing she is engaged in an endless struggle characterised essentially by irresolutionability. To be radical implies a permanent struggle with and at the boundaries of conventional thought and practice; no matter how trivial the issue may be, the attempt to extend, cut across, breach and transgress will always offend. She will know she will always be unacceptable to and attacked by the many with vested interests in the status quo. Both villainy and stupidity constitute permanent enemies. She will be alienated, in an active and passive sense: both a stranger and an intimate, neither a stranger nor an intimate. I am tempted to disagree, once again, with Rorty.[44] He cannot accept that seeking the sublime and seeking the merely beautiful can be combined: the former he relegates to the intellectual, the artist, the private domain; the latter to politics and public affairs. It seems to me that the radical in politics, attuned to the metaphoricity in all things as she is, attempts such a fusion, and in the process, eliminates the need, perhaps for the first time, to refer to compromise, either as a term of abuse or praise. Here as anywhere, it seems, the quality of the attempt, not some popular notion of a successful result, is the factor of worth. We could rephrase Cocteau: to succeed too easily is to fail.

And, in a way, this problem is crystallised in the radical's appreciation of metaphor, in the realisation that she is engaged in a politics of irresolution, by necessity. No political issue, no matter how simple, can ever be really resolved because certain dualities must remain as permanent paradoxes—to settle them once and for all automatically inscribes some future iniquity. And nothing seems more pervasive and more basic than the public/private dualism. We must not settle that one. No matter how much one attempts to transcend it and to portray it as a false ensnarement, we have to return to its dilemma. Everything is politics—in a way; everything is not politics—in a way. We want both and neither; we seem to have no option, ideally, other than being inconsistent. Neither privacy nor politics deserves to be given a permanent primacy. We may have to admit that society is founded on a contradiction: that its privacy and its politics are necessary prerequisites for each other. No permanent boundary ought ever be erected between them. What we describe and defend as private one day we may need politicize the next. And this is so because we must never uncritically accept or evade our historical contingencies because of some reified standard. The situation is not unlike the basic metaphor of being—it is and it is not.

I give this changingness an ethic. Without foundation or attempt to justify. It is an ethic of search, curiosity, expansion, of enlarging one's human potential. We are not led to do this; it has no clear purpose; it is no means; its rewards are uncertain. It is a certain restlessness, yet not a discontent. It is antipathy to smallness, meanness, narrowness, complacency, pride, certitude. It is a joyous openness to Otherness; an insatiable desire to absorb from others,

[44] *H.L., op. cit.,* pp. 174–5.

to periodically redefine ourselves from the unexpected translations from others. It is not to become the Other, whichever one it may be; and this is, at the same time, a stopping-short of some total responsibility for others. That moral dimension will continue to play its agonising tug-of-war within each self. It is, however, an enlightening and transgressive and challenging effort to overcome one's self.[45] To go beyond. It is a constant search for metaphors which straddle the here and the there, the now and the then, the self and the Other. It may reveal a new auspiciousness of life. At least it's worth a go. Besides, it will remind us how mixed-up we all really are.

---

[45] Rorty's discussion, in the final chapter of *Contingency, Irony and Solidarity*, of 'solidarity' and its extension to wider and wider circles of people perceived to be 'like us' is, of course, quite different from my discussion of the Other here. No matter how charitable and decent the former is, the orientation is the reverse of mine: it gathers in, brings together and makes similar; it gives, paternalistically, to the other to make them like us. I am concerned, perhaps selfishly, but humbly, in learning from others, maintaining differences, and endless curiosity, about oneself and others.

Bibliography

Apollinaire, G. *The Poet Assassinated*, London, Grafton Books, 1985.
Arieti, S. *The Intrapsychic Self*, New York, Basic Books, 1967.
Aristotle. *Poetics*, Chicago, Gateway, 1961.
Arlow, J.J. 'Metaphor and the Psychoanalytic Situation', *Psychoanalytic Quarterly*, 48, 3, 1979.
Ayer, A.J. *The Problem of Knowledge*, London, Penguin, 1964.
Bachelard, Gaston. *The Politics of Space*, Boston, Beacon Press, 1969.
Bateson, Gregory. *Steps to an Ecology of Mind*, St. Albans, Paladin, 1973.
——————. *Mind and Nature: A Necessary Unity*, New York, E.P. Dutton, 1979.
Baudrillard, Jean. *Simulations*, New York, Semiotext(e), 1983.
Benveniste, Émile. *Problems of General Linguistics*, University of Miami Press, 1971.
Black, Max. *Models and Metaphors*, Ithaca, New York, Cornell University Press, 1962.
——————. *The Problem of Knowledge*, London, Penguin, 1964.
Brooks, Peter. 'Freud's Masterplot: Questions of Narrative', *Yale French Studies*, Nos. 55–56, 1977, pp. 280–300.
Bruner, Jerome. *Beyond the Information Given: Studies in the Psychology of Knowing*, London, Allen & Unwin, 1974.
Burke, Kenneth. *Permanence and Change*, Los Altos, Hermes, 1954.
Calvino, Italo. *Six Memos for the Next Millennium*, Cambridge, Harvard University Press, 1988.
Chaudhuri, Nirad. *Hinduism*, London, Chatto & Windus, 1979.
Cirlot, J.E. *A Dictionary of Symbols*, New York, Philosophies Library, 1962.
Clark, C.M.H. *History of Australia*, Vol. 4, Melbourne, Melbourne University Press, 1978.
Cooper, D.E. *Metaphor*, Oxford, B. Blackwell, 1986.
Danto, A. 'Problems in the Philosophy of Science', *Encyclopaedia of Philosophy*, New York, Macmillan & Free Press, 1967, Vol. 6.
Derrida, Jacques. *The Archeology of the Frivolous*, Lincoln, University of Nebraska Press, 1973.

Derrida, Jacques. 'White Mythology: Metaphor in the Text of Philosophy', *New Literary History*, 6,1, Autumn 1974.
―――――. 'The Retrait of Metaphor', *Enclitic*, 2, 2, 1978.
―――――. *Spurs: Nietzsche's Styles*, Chicago, University of Chicago Press, 1978.
―――――. 'My Chances/Mes Chances: A Rendezvous with some Epicurian Stereophonies', *Taking Chances: Derrida, Psychoanalysis and Literature*, J. Smith, W. Kerridan (eds.), Baltimore, Johns Hopkins Press, 1984.
―――――. 'Racism's Last Word', *Critical Inquiry*, 12, Autumn 1985.
Devi, Gayatri. *A Princess Remembers: The Memoirs of the Maharani of Jaipur*, Delhi, Tarang Paperbacks, 1976.
Dodds, E.R. *The Greeks and the Irrational*, Berkeley, University of California Press, 1951.
Eco, Umberto. *Semiotics and the Philosophy of Language*, Bloomington, Indiana University Press, 1986.
Engell, J. *The Creative Imagination: Enlightenment to Romanticism*, Cambridge, Harvard University Press, 1981.
Freud, S. *Leonardo da Vinci: A Study in Psychosexuality*, tr. by A.A. Brill, New York, Vintage, 1947.
―――――. 'Totem and Taboo', *Standard Edition*, Vol. 13, London, Hogarth Press, 1955.
―――――. 'The Unconscious', *Standard Edition*, Vol. 14, London, Hogarth Press, 1955.
―――――. 'The Uncanny', *Standard Edition*, Vol. 17, London, Hogarth Press, 1955.
―――――. 'Remembering, Repeating and Working Through', *Standard Edition*, Vol. 18, London, Hogarth Press, 1955.
―――――. 'Identifjcation', *Standard Edition*, Vol. 18, London, Hogarth Press, 1955.
―――――. 'Dissection of the Personality', *Standard Edition*, Vol. 22, London, Hogarth Press, 1955.
Feyerabend, Paul. *Against Method*, London, New Left Books, 1975.
―――――. *Farewell to Reason*, London, Verso, 1987.
Fish, Stanley. 'With the Compliments of the Author: Reflections on Austin and Derrida', *Critical Inquiry*, 8, 1982.
Foucault, Michel. *Death and the Labyrinth*, New York, Doubleday, 1968.
―――――. *The History of Sexuality*, Vol. 1, London, Allen Lane, 1979.
Gandhi, Ramchandra. *I am Thou: Meditations on the Truth of India*, Pune, Indian Philosophical Quarterly Publication, 1984.
Genette, Gérard. *Figures III*, Paris, Editions au Seuil, 1972.
George, A. *Social Ferment in India*, London, The Athlone Press, 1986.
Goodman, Nelson. 'Metaphor as Moonlighting', *On Metaphor*, S. Sacks (ed.), Chicago, Chicago University Press, 1979.
Gould, N. 'The Structure of Dialectical Reason: A Comparative Study of Freud's and Levi-Strauss' Concept of Unconscious Mind', *Ethos*, 6, 4, 1978.
Gouldner, Alvin. *The Coming Crisis of Western Sociology*, London, Heinemann, 1971.
Habermas, Jurgen. 'Modernity—an Incomplete Project', *Postmodern Culture*, H. Foster (ed.), London, Pluto Press, 1985.
Horton, R., Ginnegan, R. (eds.), *Modes of Thought: Essays on Thinking in Western and Non-Western Societies*, London, Faber & Faber, 1973.
Jakobson, R., Halle, M. (eds.), *Fundamentals of Language*, The Hague, Mouton, 1956.
Jameson, Fred. *The Prison House of Language*, Princeton, Princeton University Press, 1972.

Kakar, Sudhir. 'Psychoanalysis and Religious Healing, Siblings or Strangers?', *Journal of the American Academy of Religion*, LIII, 3, 1985.
———. 'The Cloistered Passion of Radha and Krishna', *Tales of Love, Sex and Danger*, S. Kakar, J. Ross, Delhi, Oxford University Press, 1986.
Kittany, E.D. *Metaphor: Its Cognitive Force and Linguistic Structure*, Oxford, Clarendon Press, 1987.
Kundera, Milan. *The Unbearable Lightness of Being*, London, Faber & Faber, 1984.
Kapur, R.A. *Sikh Separatism: The Politics of Faith*, London, Allen & Unwin, 1986.
Lakoff G. and Turner M. *More than Cool Reason: A Field Guide to Poetic Metaphor*, Chicago, Chicago University Press, 1989.
Lannoy, Richard. *The Speaking Tree*, London, Oxford University Press, 1974.
Levi, Primo. *If This is a Man*, London, Abacus, 1987.
Lévi-Strauss, Claude. *The Elementary Structures of Kinship*, London, Social Science Paperbacks, 1970.
Loewald, H.W. 'Primary Process, Secondary Process and Language', *Psychoanalysis and Language*, J.H. Smith (ed.), Vol. 3 of *Psychiatry and the Humanities*, New Haven, Yale University Press, 1978.
Mahony, P. 'Towards the Understanding of Translation in Psychoanalysis', *American Psychoanalytical Association Journal*, 28, 2, 1980.
Miller, D.F. 'Metaphor, the Writing of History and Manning Clark', *Australia 1888*, 3, 1979.
———. 'Metaphor, Thinking and Thought', pts. 1 & 2, *ETC: A Review of General Semantics*, 39, 2, Summer 1982; 39, 3, Fall 1982.
———. 'Social Policy: An Exercise in Metaphor', *Knowledge*, 7, 2, 1985.
———. 'The Necessity of Euphemism', *Diogenes, International Review of the Human Sciences*, Gallimard, Paris, 134, April–June 1986.
———. 'Six Theses on the Question of Religion and Politics in India Today', *Economic and Political Weekly*, 25 July 1987.
———. '"This Great Organisation of Ours": The Generations of Congress Discourse', *Struggling and Ruling: The Indian National Congress 1885–1985*, J. Masselos (ed.), Delhi, Sterling Publishers, 1987.
———. 'A Maharaga or a Lesson in the West', *Chai: Criticism, Heresy and Interpretation*, 1, 1, 1988.
———. '"I am Thou": Towards a Psychoanalytic Languages of Respect', *Meanjin*, 47, 4, 1988.
———. 'Political Time: the Problem of Timing and Chance', September 1990. Unpublished manuscript.
Mitchell, T. 'Political Acts', *Editions*, 7, 1990.
Nandy, Ashis. *The Intimate Enemy*, Delhi, Oxford University Press, 1983.
———. 'An Anti-Secularist Manifesto', *Seminar*, October, 1985.
———. (ed.) *Science, Hegemony and Violence: A Requiem for Modernity*, Delhi, Oxford University Press, 1988.
Nietzsche, F. 'On Truth and Falsehood in an Extra-Moral Sense', *The Complete Works of F. Nietzsche*, D. Levy (ed.), London, 1909, Vol. 2.
Nisbet, Robert. 'Genealogy, Growth and Other Metaphors', *New Literary History*, 4, 1972–73.
Ortony, A. (ed.). *Metaphor and Thought*, Cambridge, Cambridge University Press, 1979.

Bibliography

O'Flaherty, W.D. *Asceticism and Eroticism in the Mythology of Siva*, Delhi, Oxford University Press, 1973.
Passmore, John. 'Philosophy', *Encyclopaedia of Philosophy*, New York, Macmillan and Free Press, 1967, Vol. 6.
Pandy, G. *The Construction of Communalism in Colonial North India*, Delhi, Oxford University Press, 1990.
Redwood, J. *Reason, Ridicule and Religion: The Age of Enlightenment in England 1660–1750*, London, Thames & Hudson, 1976.
Ricoeur, Paul. *Interpretation Theory: Discourse and the Surplus of Meaning*, Texas, Texas Christian University Press, 1976.
──────. *The Rule of Metaphor*, Toronto, University of Toronto Press, 1977.
Rorty, Richard. *Philosophy and the Mirror of Nature*, Oxford, Blackwell, 1980.
──────. *Consequences of Pragmatism*, Minneapolis, University of Minnesota Press, 1982.
──────. 'Habermas and Lyotard on Postmodernity', *Habermas and Modernity*, R. Bernstein (ed.), Cambridge, Polity Press, 1985.
──────. 'Thugs and Terrorists: A Reply to Bernstein', *Political Theory*, 15, 4, 1987.
──────. 'The Priority of Democracy to Philosophy', *The Virginia Statute for Religious Freedom*, M. Peterson, R. Vaughan (eds.), Cambridge, Cambridge University Press, 1988.
──────. *Contingency, Irony and Solidarity*, Cambridge, Cambridge University Press, 1989.
──────. 'Philosophy as Science as Metaphor, and as Politics', *The Institution of Philosophy: A Discipline in Crisis*, A. Cohen, M. Dascal (eds.), La Salle, Ill., Open Court, 1989.
Rothenberg, A. 'Einstein's Creative Thinking and the General Theory of Relativity', *American Journal of Psychiatry*, 136, 1, 1979.
Rushdie, Salman. Talk, *Kunapipi*, 7, 1, 1985.
──────. *The Satanic Versus*, London, Viking, 1988.
──────. 'In Good Faith', *The Independent on Sunday*, 4 February 1990.
──────. 'Is Nothing Sacred?', The Herbert Read Memorial Lecture, Granta, 1990.
Schafer, R. *A New Language for Psychoanalysis*, New Haven, Yale University Press, 1976.
Schön, D.A. 'Generative Metaphor: A perspective on problem-setting in social policy', in *Metaphor and Thought*, A. Ortony (ed.), Cambridge, Cambridge University Press, 1979.
Sorokin, P. *Social and Cultural Dynamics*, New York, American Book Co., 1942, Vol. 4
Steiner, W. 'Language as Process: Serge Karchevsky's Semiotics of Language', in L. Matejka (ed.), *Sound, Sign and Meaning*, Ann Arbor, University of Michigan Press, 1976.
Thapar, Romila. 'Syndicated Moksha', *Seminar*, 313, 1985.
Toulmin, S. *Philosophy of Science*, London, Hutchinson University Library, 1958.
──────. *The Return to Cosmology: Post-Modern Science and the Theology of Nature*, Berkeley, University of California Press, 1982.

Visvanathan, S. 'On the Annals of the Laboratory State', *Science, Hegemony and Violence: A Requiem for Modernity*, A. Nandy (ed.), Delhi, Oxford University Press, 1988.

Vygotsky, L.S. *Thought and Language*, Cambridge, M.I.T. Press, 1962.

Wellek, R. and Warren, A., *Theory of Literature*, Middlesex, Penguin, 1973.

Whyte, L.L. *The Unconscious Before Freud*, London, Julian Freedman Publication, 1979.

Wolf, E.S. *Treating the Self*, New York, Guilford Press, 1988.

Wood, D. and Bernasconi, R. *Derrida and Differance*, Coventry, Parousia Press, 1985.

Index

The index needs to be used with caution. Readers ought to think of each entry as if within quotation marks so as to be reminded of its diverse metaphoric properties. There is no separate entry named 'metaphor'. What follows is a classification which supplements that of the chapter titles. Each is merely a loose guide to reading.

Action, 24, 27–29, 30, 60–63, 108–13, 135–37, 232–33, 241–44, 257–59
Analogy, 45, 59–60, 78
Apartheid, 25–26, 251
Apollinaire, G., 47
Arieti, S., 94
Aristotle, 32, 36, 40, 57–58, 69, 72, 75, 82, 90, 118
Auspicious, 21–22, 24, 219–22, 259
Ayer, A.J., 66

Bachelard, Gaston, 123–24
Bateson, Gregory, 23, 60–61, 89–91, 133–34
Baudrillard, Jean, 135
Benveniste, Emile, 21–23
Black, Max, 57
Boundary (and its transgressions), 32–35, 39–40, 48–54, 90–93, 143–47, 159–62, 173–76, 185–203
Breton, Andre, 46
Bricoleur (see also Change (Uneven), Multiplicity, Irresolution), 128

Brooks, Peter, 121
Burke, Kenneth, 36, 40, 128

Calvino, Italo, 5, 129–30
Caricature, 64
Causality (see also Metonymy), 66, 116–17
Chance, 37, 159–61, 244–46
Change, 25–30, 74, 116–17, 149–50, 167–71, 255–59; Uneven change, 126–28
Chaudhuri, Nirad, 164
Clark, C.M.H., 140–41
Cocteau, Jean, 258
Commonsense, 32, 41, 42, 69, 235, 247, 257
Communication, 60, 70–73, 85–86, 132–34, 222
Conscious (intention, awareness), 32, 41, 43–46, 93–94, 99–100, 166–71
Context (see also Repetition), 31–33, 153–54, 169, 257–59
Contradiction (binary opposites, paradox, negation), 21–23, 33, 39,

43–46, 56, 63–65, 101–2, 126–27, 143–45, 159–61, 168–70, 177–78, 185–200, 205–8, 210–19, 235–51, 258

Danto, Arthur, 48–49
Derrida, Jacques, 5, 25–26, 73, 136, 160–61, 187, 222, 251, 254
Detour, 130–31
Devi, Gayatri, 204
Dewey, John, 234–35
Difference, 23, 30, 57, 92, 171
Disenchantment, 146, 236–38
Double-bind, 29, 134, 177
Duchamp, Marcel, 181, 185
Dumont, Louis, 171

Eco, Umberto, 55
Economics, 136–37
Education, 118, 227
Einstein, Albert, 78
Eliade, Mircea, 134
Engell, J., 38–39
Enthusiasm, 143, 173–75
Ethnocentrism, 59–60, 165–66, 169, 179–80, 234–38, 246–50
Euphemism, 21–30
Exchange, 61–63, 78, 110–14

Feminism, 37, 64–65, 73–76, 241
Feyerabend, Paul, 114, 226–33, 252, 257
Fish, Stanley, 133
Foucault, Michel, 23, 116, 124, 167–68, 190–91, 251, 254
Freud, Sigmund, 26, 33, 37, 43–46, 48, 58, 61, 67, 84, 94, 120–24, 151, 154–55, 159–61, 180–203, 245
Frost, Robert, 38

Gandhi, Ramchandra, 195–97
Genette, Gerard, 58, 65
Godard, Jean-Luc, 124
Goodman, Nelson, 47
Gouldner, Alvin, 127–29

Habermas, Jurgen, 120, 135, 251
Havel, Vaclav, 154

Heidegger, Martin, 26, 41, 52, 73, 234, 250
Hinduism, 163–66, 170–73, 210–22
Homogeneity (see also Proper, Literalism, Multiplicity, Impurity), 77, 86–88, 163–66

Imagination, 38–40
Impurity, 144–45, 150–51, 197–200
Incongruity, 17, 25, 36–37, 40, 65
India (Indian), 17, 162–80, 192–96, 204–22; Indian nationalist leaders, 174–76; Indian communalism, 166–73, 176
Innovative (creative), (see also Newness, Modern Man, Repetition), 35–40, 143–44, 148–50
Irresolution (see also Multiplicity), 232–33, 253–59

Jakobson, Roman, 58, 64, 65, 67
Janus-Face, 87
Judgement, 114–16, 178–79, 226–27, 230–34, 251–59

Kakar, Sudhir, 159, 161, 162, 169, 192–94
Kitsch, 134
Klein, Melanie, 77
Kundera, Milan, 134

Lacan, Jacques, 58, 83
Language, 21–30, 31, 44–48, 69–94, 144–48, 152–55, 196–200, 213, 222, 239
Lannoy, Richard, 171
Leonardo da Vinci, 180–92, 197–203
Levi, Primo, 132
Levi-Strauss, Claude, 56, 58, 62–63, 67, 111
Literalism, 28–29, 41, 45, 89–93, 145, 177, 197–99, 207–8, 250–51
Literature, 142–55
Loewald, H., 48

Magritte, Rene, 28, 60, 84, 132–33
Means/ends, 22–23, 211–16, 234

Metonymy (contiguity), (see also Causality), 42, 65–67, 78, 94, 107, 116, 126
Modern Man (see also Modernity), 124, 136–39, 213, 218–19, 255
Modernity (see also Modern Man), 119–41
Montaine, 43
Multiplicity (and Ambivalence), (see also Irresolution), 128–30, 178–80, 253–59

Nandy, Ashis, 75, 88, 170
Newness (see also Modern Man, Modernity, Repetition, Innovative), 125–27, 152–53
Nietzsche, F., 42, 120, 237, 239, 250–51
Nisbet, Robert, 38

Obvious (see also Commonsense), 102–3
O'Flaherty, Wendy, 165
Omnipotence, 151–55
Opportunity (see also Chance), 219–23
Orwell, George, 27, 29, 243–44
Other, 248–59

Pandey, Gyan, 168
Passmore, John, 50–54
Perspective (see also Multiplicity), 29, 97, 128–29
Poincare, Henri, 37, 78
Politics (see also India, Public/Private, Rorty, State), 24, 37, 55, 59–68, 88, 138–39, 142, 145–46, 148–54, 165, 170–80, 225–59
Present (the), 211–15; Presentcentrism, 242
Problem-setting, 97–99, 115, 176–77, 185–87
Progress (and Development), 116–18, 125–27, 254–58
Proper (purity, place), 29–55, 88, 143–45, 149–51, 185–88, 198–200, 205–10, 216–22, 235–59

Public/Private (see also India, Politics, Rorty, State), 173–80, 200, 205–9, 235–51, 258

Quotation (see also Repetition), 139–41, 142

Rationality (philosophy), 32, 38–39, 44–46, 48–54, 70, 93–94, 104–8, 116–18, 127, 200–3, 234–38
Redwood, J., 5, 175
Religion, 49–50, 143–50, 159–80, 202–3, 236–39
Repetition (and similarity), (see also Quotation), 119–24, 132–34, 139–41, 257
Respect, 198–200
Ricoeur, Paul, 36, 40, 42, 57
Rorty, Richard, 114–15, 143, 234–52, 255, 259
Rushdie, Salman, 119, 131, 135, 142–55, 251

Sacred, 134, 145–48, 151–154
Sacrilege, 165–66, 178–80
Schafer, R., 33–34
Schon, Donald, 97–118
Science, 32, 34–35, 67, 116–18, 125–26, 159–61, 174–75, 182, 185–89, 199–203, 227, 229–32
Secularism, 143–51, 165, 173–80, 236, 239
Shout (beyond language), 21–23, 29
Silence (beyond language), 21–24, 28–29, 159, 195, 200
Simulacra, 138–41
Social Policy, 90–93, 97–118, 234–36, 239–46
Sorokin, P., 128
State (see also India, Politics, Public/Private), 173–79
Surrealism, 46–47
Symbolism (see also Synecdoche), 30, 129–35
Sympathy, 35
Synecdoche (see also Symbolism), 64–65, 94, 103–4, 181–92

Terrorism, 26
Thapar, Romila, 163, 165
Tolerance, 168, 171–73, 227–29, 234–52
Toulmin, Stephen, 35, 49–50
Translation, 60–61, 70–72, 74, 82–93, 108–10, 132–34, 138–41, 176, 183, 187–91, 204–22
Triage, 125–26

Uncanny, 154–55
Unconscious (see also Conscious), 26, 41, 43–46, 48–49, 75, 93–94, 120–24, 178–80, 244–49

Universal, 69–73, 80–82, 88–89, 92, 162, 209–11, 227–28

Value, 33, 61–63, 110–14, 136–37, 178–79, 204–22, 225–59
Vygotsky, L., 79–86

Wellek, Rene, 34
Western thought, 56–57, 69, 75, 116–18, 120, 136–37, 153, 165–66, 168–70, 198–200, 204–22
Whyte, L.L., 41
Wolf, E., 142